The Western Perception of Islam between the Middle Ages and the Renaissance

The **Western Perception** of **Islam** between the **Middle Ages** and the **Renaissance**

The Work of Nicholas of Cusa

Marica Costigliolo

FOREWORD BY
Cary J. Nederman

◆PICKWICK *Publications* • Eugene, Oregon

THE WESTERN PERCEPTION OF ISLAM BETWEEN
THE MIDDLE AGES AND THE RENAISSANCE
The Work of Nicholas of Cusa

Copyright © 2017 Marica Costigliolo. All rights reserved. Except for brief quotations in critical publications or reviews, no part of this book may be reproduced in any manner without prior written permission from the publisher. Write: Permissions, Wipf and Stock Publishers, 199 W. 8th Ave., Suite 3, Eugene, OR 97401.

Originally published in Italian by De Ferrari Editore.

Pickwick Publications
An Imprint of Wipf and Stock Publishers
199 W. 8th Ave., Suite 3
Eugene, OR 97401

www.wipfandstock.com

PAPERBACK ISBN: 978-1-4982-0819-2
HARDCOVER ISBN: 978-1-4982-0821-5
EBOOK ISBN: 978-1-4982-0820-8

Cataloguing-in-Publication data:

Names: Costigliolo, Marica. | Nederman, Cary J. (Foreword)

Title: The Western perception of Islam between the Middle Ages and the Renaissance : the work of Nicholas of Cusa / Marica Costigliolo.

Description: Eugene, OR: Pickwick Publications, 2017 | Includes bibliographical references.

Identifiers: ISBN 978-1-4982-0819-2 (paperback) | ISBN 978-1-4982-0821-5 (hardcover) | ISBN 978-1-4982-0820-8 (ebook)

Subjects: LCSH: Nicholas, of Cusa, Cardinal, 1401–1464 | Islam—Relations—Christianity | Christianity and other religions—Islam | Islam—Relations—Christianity—Early works to 1800

Classification: BX4705.N58 C677 2017 (print) | BX4705.N58 (ebook)

Manufactured in the U.S.A. 10/25/17

To Giuliano

Contents

Foreword by Cary J. Nederman | xi
Acknowledgments | xv

Chapter 1: Method and Theories | 1

    1 Introduction | 1
    2 Notes on Dialogue as a Genre in the Middle Ages | 1
    3 Methodology | 4
    4 The Theory of Jan Assmann | 6
    5 Comparative Political Theory | 7
    6 The Metaphor | 9
    7 Division of the Book | 11

Chapter 2: *De concordantia catholica*, Metaphor of Body | 16

    1 Introduction | 16
    2 Context | 16
    3 Hierarchy | 19
    4 Church as Corpus Mysticum | 23
    5 Defense of Body | 24
    6 Relations between King and Emperor | 25
    7 Relations between Emperor and Pope | 25
    8 Emperor as Physician | 27
    9 Conclusions | 28

CONTENTS

Chapter 3: *De docta ignorantia*, Identity and Difference | 30

1 Introduction | 30
2 The Model of *De docta ignorantia* | 31
3 Identity (Sameness), Difference and Diversity | 34
4 The Metaphor of the Sphere: The Perspective | 38
5 Interreligious Dialogue in *De docta ignorantia* | 40
6 Conclusions | 42

Chapter 4: *De pace fidei* and the Interreligious Dialogue | 43

1 Introduction | 43
2 Sources of *De pace fidei* | 44
3 Difference and Diversity | 54
4 Wisdom | 57
5 Equality and Unity | 59
6 The Metaphor of the King | 62
7 The Psychological Foundations of Faith | 64
8 Rituality: The Different and the Ridiculous | 66
9 Tolerance | 70
10 Peace | 73
11 Identity, Difference, Unity | 76
12 Freedom | 80
13 Conclusions | 82

Chapter 5: *Cribratio Alkorani*, The Change of the Perception of Islam | 84

1 Introduction | 84
2 Sources of the *Cribratio Alkorani* | 85
3 Structure of *Cribratio Alkorani* | 91
4 *Manuductio* and *pia interpretatio* | 93
5 The Metaphor of Glass | 94
6 The Nestorian Heresy | 96
7 Textual Differences: The Qur'an and the Gospel | 99
8 Unity, Difference, and Equality | 103

CONTENTS

9   Sin | 106
10 Heaven | 108
11 Difference and Diversity | 110
12 Method of Cusanus | 111
13 Kalam | 113
14 Happiness | 115
15 Muhammad's Persecution of Christians | 116
16 The Theme of War | 117
17 The Speech to Muhammad II | 121
18 Conclusions | 124

Chapter 6: Cusanus and others: the Western Perception of Islam | 125

1 Introduction | 125
2 The *Contra Legem Sarracenorum* | 126
3 Fazio degli Uberti | 127
4 Byzantine Authors: Demetrius Kydones and George Trebizond | 129
5 Use of *Praesuppositio*: Marsilio Ficino | 135
6 Enea Silvio Piccolomini | 137
7 Conclusions | 141

Chapter 7: General Conclusions | 143

Bibliography | 151

Foreword

Nicholas of Cusa was among the most prolific and multifaceted, as well as challenging and astonishing, intellectual figures of the fifteenth century. In particular, his career and thought embrace a series of antinomies (or sometimes just downright contradictions). A man of humble origins, Cusa achieved high office in the Roman Church. A scholar with splendid humanist credentials, he clung to many of the ideas and ideals of the Middle Ages. A devotee of the mystical elements of neo-Platonism, Cusa was also an ardent rationalist. An early and vocal advocate of the supremacy of the General Council of the Church during the Great Schism, he became an outspoken supporter of absolute papal power. An orthodox churchman, he demonstrated a pronounced interest in promoting nonviolent interreligious understanding and mutual respect. These contrasts could be multiplied many times over.

Arguably the most enigmatic of Cusa's writings was a little treatise, composed in 1453, entitled *De pace fidei* (*On the Peace of the Faith*), in which he endorses toleration of a diversity of religious practices and forms of worship. The immediate stimulus for the composition of *De pace fidei* was initial word of the fall of Constantinople together with stories of Turkish atrocities that soon spread throughout Europe. Nicholas had earlier served on a diplomatic mission to Constantinople and was clearly shocked by reports (for the most part exaggerated) of the destruction of the ancient city and its Christian inhabitants. *De pace fidei* laments and condemns persecutions stemming from religious diversity and calls for a peaceful harmonization of discordant faiths, motivated by a sincere desire to see all of the world's peoples reconciled in amiable coexistence. But Nicholas's passion for harmony does not blind him to (indeed, it encourages him to speculate upon) the causes of conflict and discord. In doing so, he admits the intractability of political and cultural divisions; yet he proposes that this is a strength rather than a weakness of humanity, even suggesting that "national" diversity may in fact serve to strengthen reverence for God. Ultimately, Nicholas adopts the view that, given the ineliminable character of social differences, religious concord can only be achieved in a partial and muted fashion—"one religion in a variety of rites," to use his now famous phrase.

Many, many questions have been raised about *De pace fidei*. Is it a forward-looking defense of universal human dignity? Or a reflection of Cusa's troubled times? Does it afford true respect to the world's religions? Or is it merely a clever form of Christian apologetics? Does it reflect broader trends of Cusa's political, moral, and theological perspective? Or is it an occasional piece that should be treated in isolation from the rest of his oeuvre? Marica Costigliolo's study of Nicholas of Cusa attempts with remarkable clarity to resolve the many tensions characterized by his writings. She challenges, in particular, the conventional interpretation of *De pace fidei*, pioneered by Ernst Cassirer, that Nicholas belongs within a wholly original movement of Christian humanism that broke with the medieval past and promoted "truly grand tolerance," presaging more modern proponents of toleration such as Jean Bodin. In a similar vein, John Patrick Dolan proclaims *De pace fidei* "to be one of the finest and most practical treatises on the question of religious tolerance, . . . free from the typical Scholastic provincialism and lack of toleration." The premise of such readings of *De pace fidei*, demolished by Costigliolo, is that it must be a work "before its time" because the beliefs typical of the Latin Middle Ages were entirely incompatible with tolerant attitudes and doctrines.

Costigliolo resists the "modernizing" interpretation of *De pace fidei* on a number of counts. For instance, she examines the numerous medieval precedents for interreligious dialogue, such as Peter Abelard and Raymond Lull. (Nicholas seems to have known the works of the latter.) Moreover, she demonstrates how "modernizers" dismiss at great peril his dedication to neo-Platonic philosophy. In place of the view that Nicholas was an early advocate of a modern idea of religious toleration, Costigliolo emphasizes how the teachings of *De pace fidei* extend and elaborate his philosophy and theology as well as his ecclesiology. In particular, she directs our attention to the substance of Nicholas's case for a "single easy harmony" between apparently disparate faiths. On her account, *De pace fidei* applies the Cusan methods of "concordance" and *coincidentia oppositorum* to the issue of religious conviction, yielding a unity of belief in matters of salvation. Nicholas is thereby shown to retain a concerted universalism in his attitude to religion, even while the primary tenets of Christianity are vindicated over the course of the dialogue, and proponents of divergent faiths (including polytheism, Judaism, Islam, and Hinduism) are induced to admit the superior wisdom of Christian theology.

Costigliolo's examination of Cusa's thought teaches us that what distinguishes *De pace fidei*'s idea of religious pluralism is its irenicism; violent persecution and coerced conversion must be replaced with rational debate and proof as the means for realizing the universal truth of Christian doctrine. Costigliolo's recognition of the debt owed by *De pace fidei* to central elements of Nicholas's philosophy, theology, and ecclesiology certainly provides a vital corrective to previous, excessively modernizing interpretations of the work. But as a consequence, Costigliolo's interpretation confronts those reluctant to speak of the relevance of *De pace fidei* to the history of toleration. Presumably, they accept the same premise as their predecessors, namely, that a defense of tolerance can only be constructed on certain distinctively modern grounds. To the extent that this assumption is flawed, it becomes possible to view *De pace fidei* as a work issuing from characteristically medieval forms of discourse and simultaneously as a contribution to the development of tolerant principles in European thought.

At the same time, Costigliolo's book brings Cusa's theme of "harmony" into fruitful tension with his treatment of "difference" and "otherness" in the *Cribratio Alkorani*, probably written in 1461. Indeed, she insists that the works are really two parts of a single Cusan worldview constituted by a dialectic of "identity" and "difference." In the *Cribratio Alkorani*, Nicholas produces a commentary on the Qu'ran that extends the work of *De pace fidei* by examining harmonies between Islam and Christianity while also illuminating their intractable conflicts. The *Cribratio Alkorani* has sometimes been read as merely and solely an *apologia* of Christian belief and a refutation of Islam, but Costigliolo reveals to us how Cusa is engaged in a far more complicated and important project that builds upon his previous writings. In developing this case, she carefully reconstructs the sources of the *Cribratio Alkorani* in order to demonstrate how Cusa's method leads him to find resources for constructing forms of genuine interreligious understanding that nevertheless admit the real and deep differences between Christianity and Islam. Thus, in the *Cribratio Alkorani* no less than in *De pace fidei*, Nicholas is primarily concerned with the premises that give rise to intolerant actions and attitudes, such as were in evidence in the purported bloodshed and repression at Constantinople. He therefore sought to explain how divergences in matters of religious belief need not result in violence and persecution, but should be accorded tolerance.

Cary J. Nederman,
Texas A&M University

Acknowledgments

In 2006, during my first year in the PhD program at the University of Genoa, I started working on Nicholas of Cusa. A year later I began to focus on Cusanus' approach to Islam and the wider issue of Western perceptions of Islam in the course of history.

In Italy these themes seemed unusual at the time. But today things are changing, and more and more Italian scholars dedicate their studies to the relationship between Christianity and Islam.

In the course of my research I met people who have encouraged me, and I wish to thank them. Donald Duclow helped in revising the text, and offered me the opportunity to speak at the American Cusanus Society's Gettysburg conference in 2012. I thank other members of the Society, especially Gerald Christianson and Thomas Izbicki. I would like to thank Cary Nederman for writing the preface to this book. I also thank Vasileios Syros for his helpful comments.

I would thank Claudio Risso, Sandro Segre, Gergely Bakos, Anna Maria Lazzarino and the editors Fabrizio De Ferrari and Matthew Weimer.

This book is partly based on my monograph *Islam e Cristianesimo: mondi di differenze nel medioevo: il dialogo con l'Islam nell'opera di Nicola da Cusa* (Genova: Genova University Press, 2012). Special thanks go to Nora Stern who translated the book and to Juleen Eichinger for editing it.

I wish to remember Morimichi Watanabe who, in 2009, invited me to read my first paper on Cusanus and Islam at the International Congress on Medieval Studies in Kalamazoo and Olivia Remie Constable for choosing my research project on Ficino for a post-doctoral fellowship at the University of Notre Dame. I would also mention Father Paolo Dall'Oglio, whom I met at an international meeting on interfaith dialogue at the center of Mar Musa.

― 1 ―

Method and Theories

1. Introduction

HERE I INTEND TO illustrate my method, which is grounded on the following issues:

1. An approach to medieval dialogue as a dialectic creation in which the problem of conflict is thematized. In this regard, I shall consider studies by Thomas Burman on the transmission of knowledge of the Islamic world and culture in the Muslim tradition, and studies by Nancy Bisaha on the relations between Christianity and Islam in the Renaissance.
2. An exegesis of Cusanus' text through an analysis of the theme of difference.

Following the model developed by Jan Assmann, I try to understand the changes undergone by the theme of difference in the light of what Assmann defines as "textual coherence" and according to the definition he provides of the term "canon," identified in Cusanus' works in the problem of difference. Therefore, I shall analyze the metaphors, the figures of speech, and the textual references included in Nicholas of Cusa's works. Finally, I shall partly follow Cary Nederman's idea of an interpretation of the history of medieval dialogue in its approach to the theme of difference.

2. Notes on Dialogue as a Genre in the Middle Ages

Conflict is a condition that needs to be resolved and reveals a pre-existing state of inadequacy, because lack of understanding or lack of awareness mean inability to reach truth.[1]

---

1. Reiss, "Conflict and Its Resolution in Medieval Dialogues," 863. See also *La*

Medieval authors and scholars made use of the metaphor of conflict as a starting point for creating a positive ground for discussion and debate: they aimed at making their public accustomed to the need to find a solution to the apparent tensions set forth in order to get closer to the truth.

As conflict, according to Augustine, originated from human inadequacy, there was no actual reality of evil, and a large part of medieval literature "is properly seen as a catalyst for the action to follow."[2]

Thus, the form of dialogue represented the structure within which the problem of conflict could be thematized. Medieval literature includes several forms of dialogue: *altercatio, disputatio, disceptatio, certamen* or *conflictus*, as well as the so-called *Streitdialog* (conflict-dialogue) a term coined by Hans Walther.[3]

The *Streitdialog* was a teaching model:[4] in this kind of dialogue, conflict was used as a device for comparing different ideas outside the classical didactic model. We find examples of these "conflict-dialogues"[5] in many works focused on a confrontation between Christians and non-Christians. One of these works, Minucius Felix' dialogue *Octavius*, written in late second century A.D., introduces a debate between a heathen and a Christian: Octavius, the Christian, defends his faith in reply to Cecilius' attacks. At the end of his arguments, he declares his firm belief that Christianity is destined to become far more widespread than any other religion.

"Conflict-dialogues" may have different solutions. As Reiss argues, "In some cases the conflict is resolved when a true statement is finally distinguished from a false one, or a better utterance form a less good one: and when with this recognition there comes an acceptance."[6]

---

propaganda politica nel basso Medioevo: atti del XXXVIII Convegno storico internazionale.

2. Reiss, "Conflict and Its Resolution in Medieval Dialogues," 863: "This action may be of various kinds: it may occasionally take the form of a destruction resulting from the inadequacy and flaws of the characters, but it is more apt to be something like a journey to understanding that the characters take, a soliloquy involving self-analysis and re-evaluation, or even a dialogue leading ultimately to awareness and truth. It is this last use of conflict that I want to examine here, specifically to understand how dialogue functions as a rhetorical and dialectic tool in medieval literature and to see some of the ways its conflict are resolved."

3. Walther, "Das Streitgedicht in der lateinischen Literatur des Mittelalters."
4. Reiss, "Conflict and Its Resolution in Medieval Dialogues," 864.
5. Ibid., 863.
6. Ibid., 865.

In particular, we find in *Octavius* two *quaestiones*, which seem derived from previous dialogues, and in their way could be considered a sort of *Streitdialog*.[7] In the anonymous *De recta in Deum fide*, written in Greek at the beginning of the fourth century and later translated into Latin by Rufinus (345–410/11 A.D.), the representatives of different heresies meet a representative of Christianity: each participant defends his point of view, and at the end, the conflict is resolved through the decisions of a heathen arbitrator, who agrees with the arguments supported by the Christian and declares him the winner of the dispute.

The most famous patristic text of this kind is Jerome's (354–420) *Dialogus adversus Pelagianos*, in which the Christian Atticus guides the heretic Critobulus to the discovery of his errors. According to Reiss, "it is easy to see how the debate form can lead finally to a monologue in which the speaker of the accepted truth delivers an apologia of his cause."[8] In the *Disputatio Iudei et Christiani* by Gilbert Crispin,[9] the author and a Jew politely discuss Christian theology using complex and profound arguments. The peculiarity and originality of this work consists in that it ends without singing praises of the victory of Christianity over the other religions.

The debate between Christians and Jews was a common formula over the Middle Ages. Some outstanding examples are the second-century *Dialogue with Trypho*, written by Justin Martyr,[10] the Pseudo-Augustine's *Altercatio ecclesiae et synagogae*, written in fifth century, and later, in eleventh- and twelfth-century the works of Pier Damiani (1006–72), Rupert of Deutz (1076–1129), William of Châtillon (1135–?), Pedro Alfonso, as well as Abelard's three dialogues among heathens, Jews, and Christians.[11]

All these texts do not always take a definite stance, since in some cases the author's arguing does not rely on the tenets of orthodoxy, and problems are discussed depending on the sources the author has available. Sometimes this method may even lead the authors to make theological mistakes, but quite frequently a rational process emerges in these works, which leads to a truth that is not only the revealed truth to be administered to the readers,

---

7. Ibid., 866.

8. Ibid.

9. Reiss defines this dialogue as "another work that seems to be the record of an actual conversation."

10. The Italian edition of this dialogue is in Visonàtore, *Dialogo con Trifone, Letture cristiane del primo millennio*.

11. Reiss, "Conflict and Its Resolution in Medieval Dialogues," 869.

but also it is not chance that some of these dialogues are addressed against the teachings of particular circles or persons.

A twelfth-century anonymous work, *Dialogus de conflictu Amoris dei et Linguae Dolosae,* chastens some Benedictine monks for having told lies and for not having charitably acted. A quite similar tone can be found in Rupert of Deutz' *Altercatio monachi et clerici,* in which the author argues that monks should have the permission to preach.

Streitdialogen flourished particularly in twelfth century, after Peter Abelard's composition of *Sic et non.*[12] As conflict, according to Augustine, originated from human inadequacy, there was no actual reality of evil, and a large part of medieval literature is therefore devoted to the collection of suggestions on the way in which men must behave and act in order not to fall into error.[13]

It is important to stress that, according to Reiss, dialogue was conceived as the most suitable structure and form in which the problem of conflict could be thematized. Cusanus' work perfectly enters this tradition. Religious conflict is the central theme of *De pace fidei,* and all the efforts of the author are addressed to find peaceful solutions. The *Cribratio Alkorani* pursues the same goal, despite its profound difference from the point of view of style and contents.

3. Methodology

The question we should ask ourselves is in what way we want and can proceed in the analysis of interreligious dialogue. Can a fifteenth-century

---

12. Reiss argues that "while this work is probably not the source or even the starting point for those alter works favouring irresolution, it still may be seen as a landmark at the beginning of a new trend: the *Sic et non* is a real attempt to find the truth that now elevates the dialogue form, and makes it, in many instances at least, much more than a literary device or a piece of rhetorical ornamentation. It may even be said by way of generalization that by the thirteenth century the dialogue form becomes properly the possession of literature while the dialogue spirit, the search for truth, becomes the norm of philosophy." Reiss, "Conflict and Its Resolution in Medieval Dialogues," 870.

13. Ibid., 863: "This action may be of various kinds: it may occasionally take the form of a destruction resulting from the inadequacy and flaws of the characters, but it is more apt to be something like a journey to understanding that the characters take, a soliloquy involving self-analysis and re-evaluation, or even a dialogue leading ultimately to awareness and truth. It is this last use of conflict that I want to examine here, specifically to understand how dialogue functions as a rhetorical and dialectic tool in medieval literature and to see some of the ways its conflict are resolved."

author like Nicholas of Cusa make a contribution to this debate?[14] According to Ridenauer, to understand Cusanus' approach to interreligious dialogue, it is necessary to start from the question with which he opens his reasoning: which word is capable to express every concept of God?[15]

Nicholas explicitly declares that truth is always present only in difference and not in coincidence with unity.[16] The awareness of difference in the cognitive and critical process takes for Cusanus the value of truth,[17] but the process of reason is not sufficient in itself to make us understand. Thus, Cusanus thematizes the difference between reason and intellect, the latter being defined by him as vision or intuition. In this way, Cusanus puts a sort of metaphysical causality principle in connection with a radical thought of infinity.[18]

As truth can only be known in relation to difference, the "other" is, in its difference, related to desire, since we long for what we do not have or do not fully know. The awareness of difference, in its critical-cognitive significance means for him knowledge, as he writes also in his *Deo abscondito*.[19]

An analysis of the problem of interreligious dialogue leads us unavoidably to wonder about the nature of discrimination of the other on grounds of religious difference.

This is, in my opinion, a key issue we must always bear in mind and stress when we talk about interreligious dialogue, as we should first of all wonder whether a genuinely philosophical, Platonic dialogue is possible when we start from different religious positions.

Determining to what extent linguistics and discourse order are implied in this discussion seems evident in itself: the organization of thought, its elaboration, the use of figures, are all elements that cannot be disregarded both for understanding a text, and consequently an idea, and for trying to deconstruct an idea.

I have tried to analyze the method I followed to identify some topics and communication mechanisms in Nicholas of Cusa's thought, focusing

---

14. See Lutz-Bachmann and Fidora, *Juden, Christen und Muslime, Religionsdialoge in Mittelalter*.

15. Riedenauer, "Logik, Rationalität und religiöse Rede nach Nikolaus Cusanus," 192–220.

16. *De Deo Abscondito*, H. IV n. 1, Z. 4–12, S. 3

17. *Apolog*. N. 18 II.

18. Riedenauer, "Logik, Rationalität und religiöse Rede nach Nikolaus Cusanus," 199.

19. *De Deo Abscondito* IV n. 8, but also in *Apolog.*, II 12.

on the dialogic form of his communication related to interreligious dialogue, and in particular on the three pivotal themes of unity, equality, and connection (multiplicity), which characterize the most representative work of Nicholas' political thought, *De concordantia catholica*.

4. The Theory of Jan Assmann

Following the model outlined by Jan Assmann,[20] I have tried to understand how these three themes change in the light of what Assmann defines as "textual coherence" and "canon," which is identified, in Cusanus' works, in the problem of difference.

Concerning the concept of canon, Assmann argues that in laws and holy texts there is a binding aspect, which "forms the ways of life." In fact, the relation between history and politics concerns the creation of linguistic codes and their transmission within the social context, as well as the relations between religion and society, between sacred and political, are problems concerning the dynamics of power and the communication of power in history, both in cultural and in existential practices.

But how does a canon form?

> Endocultural scismatic polarizations give the canon a shape.... The semantic potential has focused on this point in a manner particularly pregnant with consequences. As a matter of fact, we can and must highlight a historical line which, from the separation between the canonical and the apocryphal (which at the beginning is merely a different value accentuation between essential and non-essential), has led to a division between orthodoxy and heresy—thus not only between what is one's own and what is extraneous, but also between friend and enemy. By no longer applying the canon rule to objects and facts, but instead to men, all decisions have always fallen on being and not being, on life and death.[21]

In particular, the canon-fixing process takes place through repetition. In conjunction with the fixing in writing of traditions, a gradual transition is made from the predominance of repetition to the predominance of making topical, from ritual coherence to textual coherence. In this transition, the emerging forces which connect the structure are exegesis and memory.

---

20. Assmann, *Erinnerungsräume: Formen und Wandlungen des kulturellen Gedächtnisses*.
21. Ibid., 95.

According to Assmann, there are two elements of the culture of writing: ritual coherence and textual coherence. The latter is characterized by the canon-"fixing" an object of speech/study through its repetition. In Cusanus' writings, for example, the reproposal in various forms of the theme of "difference" is evident. Nicholas poses this problem by analyzing it in depth, especially in his attempt to reconcile religions in a peaceful and rational way, thus revealing that "fixing" the canon of difference becomes essential to reach a common solution.

5. Comparative Political Theory

If, on the one hand, I availed myself of Assmann's theory to achieve a deeper exegetical approach to the text, on the other, as regards the comprehension of interreligious dialogue, I followed both Reiss' and Friedlein's studies on medieval dialogue, as well as some elements of the rising discipline of comparative political thought, especially the research guidelines proposed by Cary J. Nederman. According to this scholar, medieval dialogues can be divided into five major forms: dialogues based on rational demonstrations, dialogues based on mutual constructive positions, dialogues based on mutual incomprehension, dialogues based on self-criticism, dialogues aimed at attaining a common solution. According to Nedermann, comparative political theory (CPT) should help developing methodological principles capable to make us understand the historical process and the contents of dialogues, rather than aim at reaching a "fusion of horizons" according to Gadamer's perspective.[22] Furthermore, in his *Worlds of Difference*, Nederman proposes to understand the approach to alterity/otherness of the medieval texts starting from an analysis of the theme of difference.[23]

In her contribution "Für eine Dialog der Kulturen," Helga Zepp-La Rouche examines the problem of intercultural dialogue starting from a critical remark to Huntington's theory of the "clash of civilizations." According to Samuel Hungtington,[24] there are irreconcilable differences among the different religions (Hinduism, Confucianism, Islam, and Christianity).[25] In her analysis of another book of Huntigton, *The Soldier and the State*,

---

22. Ibid., 59.
23. See Nederman, *Worlds of Difference*.
24. In particular see Huntington, *The Clash of Civilizations and the Remaking of World Order*.
25. Zepp-La Rouche, "Für einen Dialog der Kulturen," 2.

Zepp-La Rouche identifies a key theme developed in the text, and pointed out by the author for the purpose of continuing the discussion on the possibilities of intercultural dialogue, consisting in the extreme easiness with which human beings can be manipulated, once a creed is instilled in them.

Nicholas of Cusa undertook the difficult attempt to find intellectually valid and effective ways to resolve this conflict through his work *De pace fidei*, which as underlined by Zepp-La Rouche, aimed at establishing dialogue and reconciling different points of view. The most surprising thing for a modern reader is that this dialogue was written in a moment of extreme tension in Europe, just after the fall of Constantinople under the Turks' domination. Nicholas' firm belief that all religions can find a common ground in a shared, universal truth becomes the central issue of this dialogue. Through different theologies we can find a possibility of dialogue and the resolution of religious conflicts.

The author examines the Hindu cosmology to show the affinities existing among the holy books of different religions. She identifies in the *Rigveda* several analogies with the Old Testament, and in the *Upanishad* quite a few similarities with the New Testament. In particular, two concepts in the works of the Hinduist tradition have to be pointed out: *Saguna Brahman* and *Nirguna Brahman*. These terms express the highest form of a being, however without any specific attribute. According to Zepp-La Rouche these concepts show close analogies with the *non aliud* concept formulated by Cusanus: it is not possible to attribute a positive name to God because the divine being can be only indicated through the formula "the non-other is nothing but the non-other."

Fred Dallmayr,[26] too, makes an interesting comparison between *De pace fidei* and the Hindu and Buddhist philosophies. According to this author, the themes of learned ignorance and coincidence of the opposites tackled by Cusanus show close affinities with the Buddhist teachings, and especially with those of the philosopher Mahayana Nagarjuna and his outline of a middle way between opposites. Furthermore, Cusanus' thesis concerning the "non-other" (*non aliud*) nature of the divine shows many similarities with the Hindu Brahman concept developed by Veda philosophy.

These studies show how many relations is possible to recognize among different religions, and the richness of significance of Cusanus' work.

---

26. Dallmayr, "Nicola Cusano, L'infinito e la pace," 64–66.

6. The Metaphor

Metaphor is a generalization of conceptual orientation as Assmann writes: "Metaphors are not only descriptions but also mediators and instruments of a memory therapy. . . . Words and metaphors have the power to tame spectres."[27]

The problem of memory pours into metaphors and

> we should consider them "figures of thought," since they always tend to shed light on new aspects of this extremely complex phenomenon. A new metaphor does not necessarily involve a new theoretical model: for example, along with the Platonic metaphor of the wax tablet, which represents the anamnesis or the reproduction of a original imprint, the Arabs introduced in the Middle Ages the image of the mirror, which reveals the active side of the process of bringing memory up-to-date, because its metal surface must be continuously polished to avoid the risk that it become opaque. As a consequence, a new image does not necessarily bring a new model of thought with itself.[28]

We owe to Rabanus Maurus (tenth century) the theorization of the four ways in which the Holy Scriptures can be interpreted, based on a literal, allegorical, moral or anthropologic, and an anagogic sense. The fathers of the church and Augustine start typological exegesis as a philosophical principle of allegory.

The Middle Ages resume and develop figurative interpretation by distinguishing allegory *in verbis* from allegory *in factis*, and consider the metaphor similar to allegory and symbol.

Differently from allegory, metaphor does not have a cognitive value: in the Middle Ages the one who, speaking through real metaphors, can teach us something is God, and man just has to discover the metaphoric language of creation, and if man speaks of God, then no metaphor is effective, and literal language does not succeed in accounting God's unfathomable nature.

27. Assmann, *Das kulturelle Gedächtnis*, 392. "The archive as memory of power develops before the archive as historical memory. The former consists in the documental heritage and in the historical sources which legitimize any claim for power, property and descent. In the Middle Ages, the archives of princes, convents, churches and towns kept any document useful for legitimizing institutions and groups.

28. Ibid., 196: "Fixing a text in writing does not only mediate eternity, but is also a support to memorization. Writing and carving are the most ancient metaphors for memory, and still today, the most topical throughout the whole history of mediators."

The metaphor had to be codified according to the scriptural tradition, and therefore it was absurd to use metaphoric figures that were not immediately understandable. Furthermore, some medieval authors made no clear distinction between metaphor and allegory, as for example the Pseudo-Dionysius, one of the sources of Nicholas of Cusa. To what extent a metaphor (and in general any figure of speech) that we encounter in medieval texts, and specifically in the works of Nicholas of Cusa, can be analyzed as a political metaphor is a problem that should be placed within specific parameters.

According to Trupia,[29] political discourse is the place in which the categories of politics are expressed for the purpose of persuasion, dialogue, mobilization, etc. However, this does not directly concern our case, because Nicholas' texts do not only have political content, but also theological, philosophical, and a mathematical content, and quite often these areas cannot be divided from each other, and even less frequently they are treated separately. We need therefore to start from the communication structure of political discourse, wondering about the discursive strategies that have been created and used, and about the relations these strategies keep with earlier ones. The problem consists in the transmission of a code, or a set of codes, and in understanding how much the transmission system may have weighted on social and political conditions, on institutions, or on the social system.[30] If, for example, the circulation of the medieval metaphor was grounded on the reference to known identities, the author who made use of this figure must have assumed that it were properly understood and shared in a particular sphere of knowledge.

---

29. See Trupia, *Logica e linguaggio della politica*.

30. Assmann examines the relation between canon (which, in my opinion, is in this case a more appropriate conceptual definition than "code") and identity. Talking about disruptive contexts marked by conflicts, he affirms that "canon embodies the claim to represent the best tradition, the only genuine one. Those who adhere to it convert and at the same time profess a normative self-definition, an identity in harmony with the precepts of reason or revelation. Canon and conversion are two phenomena which match each other." Assmann, *Das kulturelle Gedächtnis. Schrift, Erinnerung und politische Identität in frühen Hochkulturen*, 95. Canon, as a both cultural and existential orientation model, is the representation of a common normative heritage, it strengthens one's sense of belonging, and consolidates collective identity. If a particular tradition is acknowledged as a normative reference of a community, the community itself will be acknowledged as bearer of the significance and value of that particular tradition.

In nuce, we intend in this case the communication of political discourse as the relation between knowledge and power, all the more considering that metaphor and metonymy are figures of speech which need to be interpreted.

7. Division of the Book

This book is based on an analysis of some of the most important works written by Nicholas of Cusa and is aimed at identifying the problems and concepts connected with the theme of interreligious dialogue summarized in *De pace fidei*.

The second chapter is dedicated to *De concordantia catholica*. Through complex theological arguments, Nicholas of Cusa intends to stress the possibility to harmonize any difference within the church with a view to universal concordance. To carry out this ambitious project, Cusanus deems it necessary to make a careful and accurate description of the empire and the emperor's role, going as far as claiming the falseness of the *Donatio Costantinii*. Cusanus is interested in laying the foundations for putting an end to the conflicts and the state of decadence that affect fifteenth-century Europe. To achieve this purpose, he thinks it is imperative to draw on the truth contained in the sources of our cultural tradition.

A state-body and church-soul organic metaphor goes across this writing: in the works of Nicholas of Cusa there is an endless number of figures of speech, including metaphors. As Jan Assmann argued, the problem of memory is implicit in the use of metaphors, which should therefore be considered real figures of thought, since they tend to highlight ever-new aspects of this complicated phenomenon.

To what extent metaphors, and in general each figure of speech we encounter in medieval texts, may be rightfully analyzed as political metaphors is a question that concerns the transfer and circulation of knowledge, the access to sources and the interaction between different religious traditions during the Middle Ages.

The third chapter examines the *De docta ignorantia*. This writing shares the recurrence of some fundamental concepts, as identity and diversity, equality and unity. In *De docta ignorantia* the Author formulates his philosophical position: man's awareness of his inability to completely understand truth is the starting point for undertaking the way to knowledge. In this work, Cusanus' dialectic succeeds in perfectly grasping the problem of the relation between unity and difference: unity and identity are thought through the concept of absolute identity as the limit of all coincidences (theory of *coincidentia oppositorum*, or coincidence of the opposites).

In examining *De pace fidei* (chapter 4) I made an analysis of the sources on Islam, as in the period he wrote this work, Nicholas of Cusa was already considerably acquainted with the Islamic doctrine he further developed some years later in his *Cribratio Alkorani*.

The analysis of *De pace fidei* continues by stressing the concept of difference and diversity developed by the author in its different meanings. Nicholas of Cusa not only tackles the issue of difference and diversity from a theological or a philosophical point of view, but goes as far as giving it a sociological motivation. The difference in rituals becomes the key issue of *De pace fidei*, and leads unavoidably to the problem of tolerance: difference is necessary, as in the political community functional differences within the different groups are necessary, as well as the external differentiations with other communities. A plurality of confessions and rituals becomes therefore unavoidable, but it does not mean that peace cannot be sought and achieved through a rational understanding of the different positions. The problem of the diversity of the parties that harmonize with each other to achieve collective stability (peace) is then resumed and applied to the difference in rituals, as in this way, each religious representative must reach a position of tolerance through dialogue.

A sounding of some dialogic works reveals, in fact, that the term "dialogue" has sometimes a different meaning from the one we attribute to this word today, and this seems particularly relevant, since some scholars have debated the irenic value of *De pace fidei*. Roger Friedlein argues that medieval dialogue should not be mistaken for the Platonic dialectic process.

The medieval concept of dialogue includes commentary, paraphrase, interpretation, and not only an intellectual exchange between two or more interlocutors. The latter concerns instead the complexity of dialogue between different religions, as this complexity unwinds itself through many concepts and problems, such as identity, diversity, and equality, which represent some of the conceptual bases of multi-religious and multi-cultural dialogue.

The fifth chapter deals with the work *Cribratio Alkorani*. One of the most fascinating questions a reader comes across with concerns the sources used by Nicholas. He explicitly mentions, among his sources, *De rationibus fidei contra Saracenos, Grecos et Armenos, ad Cantorem Antiochiae (On the*

Reasons of the Faith against the Saracens, Greeks, and Armenians, to the Cantor of Antioch) by Thomas Aquinas, and *Contra legem Sarracenorum* by Riccoldo da Montecroce. The latter, in particular, is the "model" Cusanus continuously refers to in his argumentation on Islam. Nicholas' notions about the Muslim tradition and culture are drawn from Riccoldo's work, and this gives origin to a few and non-negligible textual and theoretical misinterpretations in the *Cribratio*.

I have also tried to highlight some themes that had emerged in Cusanus' previous works and are also included in *Cribratio Alkorani*: for example, difference/diversity, in this work, is both textual (between the Qur'an and the Gospel), theological (Trinity as unity, diversity, and equality), and "anthropological" (differences between Muslims and Christians).

The last chapter will investigate the diversities and the commonalities between the medieval and the Renaissance approaches to Islam by analyzing Christian authors' perceptions of Islam from the thirteenth to the fifteenth centuries, tracing the way in which Latin and Byzantine thinkers defined their own civilization over against Islam as its "other."

I will analyze the work of Fazio degli Uberti, Demetrius Kydones, George of Trebizond, Marsilio Ficino, and Enea Silvio Piccolomini, comparing to the work of Riccoldo da Montecroce, one of the main sources of Nicholas of Cusa about Islam. I will show how the Western perception of Islam is changed in the course of the fifteenth and sixteenth centuries, according to the thesis of Nancy Bisaha in her *Creating East and West*.

This change process is evident in the work by Nicholas of Cusa, *Cribratio Alkorani*, which belongs to his late maturity: it raises three kinds of questions, the first concerning Cusanus' position towards Islam, which seems to have radically changed compared to *De pace fidei*. Another question concerns the communication form of Cusanus' political project: while he chose a dialogic form in writing *De pace fidei*, *Cribratio* is instead a commentary of the Qur'anic text showing a strong apologetic *intentio*; though it is not a dialogue, the key problem consists however in the relations between the two religions—the Christian faith and Islam. Furthermore, in *Cribratio*, the argumentation on Islam is more extensive than in *De pace fidei*, and Nicholas shows that he knows the Qur'an and Muhammad's biography, as well as some works of Avicenna and Al-Ghazali. According to Thomas Burman's thesis, which in many respects coincides with that expounded by Roger Friedlein,[31] even the strong critical and polemic purpose of the

---

31. See Friedlein, *Der Dialog bei Ramon Lull*.

writings on Islam and on other religions different from the Christian faith, is an integral part and evidence of the deep interest shown by the thinkers of the Western world to the Islamic religion and culture. These scholars, indeed, had to solve a number of grammar, lexical, exegetical, and interpretative problems depending above all on the linguistic differences between Arabic and Latin. In addition, quite frequent was the use of excerpts translated from the Qur'an into the manuscripts of the Bible or in other Christian texts. The relationship between these two worlds began to be established just in this way: starting from an apologetic *intentio*, this complex relationship—on which scholars continue to focus still nowadays—began gradually and almost "unintentionally" to develop. Cusanus is fully part of this process, as starting in his *Cribratio* from a very marked *vis polemica*, he comes to a systematic study of the Islamic doctrine availing himself of the translation of the Qur'an into Latin by Robert of Ketton.

A comparison between *Cribratio* and the letter addressed by Enea Silvio Piccolomini to Mehmed II (chapter 6) has further strengthened my thesis on the strong dialogical purpose of *Cribratio*: in the epistle, the Pope's attitude is extremely concrete, deeply rooted in the social and political events of his age, whereas Nicholas of Cusa does not deal at all with the commercial or strategic relations between the Sultan and the Pope, but focuses, instead, exclusively on theoretical motivations aimed at attaining a form of pacification making use of reason and speculative discourse. At the same time, the letter of Piccolomini shows the change of perception of Islam, as I also show in chapter 6.

My work intends to investigate the use of metaphors, sources, and text comparison in order to ascertain the way in which Nicholas' positions on interreligious dialogue were constructed. It aims therefore at giving a double contribution to research: first, to succeed in understanding the genealogy of the concept of interreligious dialogue in the major works written by Cusanus by analyzing its continuity and repetition within each writing. When I began studying Nicholas of Cusa's work, I immediately met with the problem of whether this theologian belonged to the Middle Ages or to the modern age. This *querelle* concerns many texts I consulted, and seems difficult to solve, also because their dating is still an open question. The most recent criticism has forsaken this debate and is mostly focusing on an analysis of his works aimed at evaluating their conceptual and thematic continuity. A continuity between *De pace fidei* and *Cribratio* can emerge on condition the methodological assumption is not that of considering these two works an *ante litteram* model of interreligious dialogue, but instead of considering the genre of dialogue from a historical point of view, and consequently, examining its potential originality within a historical-philosophical discourse.

If the problems I have outlined up to now concern specifically Cusanus' doctrine, another question is emerging from an analysis of his work: how, and to what extent does interreligious dialogue weigh in the history of political thought? Therefore, the second contribution this study intends to provide is a reflection on how dialogue between different confessions can be interpreted, whether it is possible or not, and which are the primary conceptual consideration it is based on. Furthermore, is there a non-theological and not exclusively philosophical—but instead a historical-cultural—way to approach this issue so as to fully understand its political value?

Another problem consists in determining the area of study this work belongs to, as its thesis includes a number of theological subjects. This kind of approach proved essential to understand Cusanus' works, as he is neither a philosopher, nor a statesman, nor a diplomat. In other words, Nicholas of Cusa holds all these characteristics in himself, but the predominance of a theological interest is self-evident and clearly emerges from a reading of the text not conditioned by forcing or *a priori* paradigms. Therefore, my intention was to develop the theological themes strictly connected to the central theme of my work—Western perception of alterity in the interreligious dialogue—finding however the marks of a thematic continuity on which this theologian constructs his position on religious dialogue matters. Consequently, the problems of unity, identity, and diversity become essential.

How can these problems be tackled? The key can be found in his works: the theologian Nicholas of Cusa lists these themes endlessly and deals with them in the most diverse ways, through the Bible, through philosophy, by resorting to analyses and personal remarks. In summary, in order to show the change of the Western perception of Islam, the process I adopt, is divided into the following steps: analysis of Cusanus' texts, genealogy of the concept of dialogue constructed on the themes of difference/diversity and identity/unity, comparison to other texts of the Middle Ages and Renaissance.

— 2 —

De concordantia catholica, Metaphor of Body

1. Introduction

THIS CHAPTER HIGHLIGHTS THE organic metaphors in *De concordantia catholica* of Nicholas of Cusa.[1] Using these metaphors, he describes the functions of power, as well as the relations between pope and emperor and the relations between king and emperor; furthermore he wants to illustrate the crucial role of the concepts of "hierarchy" and "unity" inside the church. In *De concordantia catholica* are found important examples of the transposition of the metaphor of *corpus mysticum* from the church to the empire. Indeed, according to the theory of Ernst Kantorowicz, this metaphor expresses a deeply rooted vision of political theology and the passage from the ecclesiastical world to secular world.

2. Context

The Council of Basel (1431–38) is considered the highest expression of conciliarism. It represents the beginning of the modern era in relations between temporal and spiritual power.[2] The conciliarism of Basel is founded on the interpretation of the decree "Haec Sancta," formulated in 1417 at Constance,[3] which affirmed that the council should convene periodically and proclaimed the superiority of the council over the pope in case of schism or heresy. The Council of Basel took the decree of Constance to

---

1. This chapter adapts my article "Organic Metaphor in *De Concordantia catholica* of Nicholas of Cusa," (*Viator* 2013), I thank *Viator*'s editor for permission to use the article here.

2. See Jedin, *A History of the Council of Trent*, 21.

3. See Stump, *The Reforms of the Council of Constance 1414–1418*. Decaluwé, "Three Ways to Read the Constance Decree *Haec sancta* (1415)."

the extreme by establishing the perpetual superiority of the council. Basel furthermore elaborated some fundamental principles in the ecclesiological and canonical fields: the infallibilità of the council, the full powers of the conciliar assembly in ecclesiastical legislation, and the designation of the council as the supreme court of the church.[4] In this way, the idea of an absolute sovereignty over the entire community of the church was affirmed. The idea of community in the medieval mentality is related to the problem of the corporate principle, which posits *universitas* as the whole powerful church guiding every single member. The community, according to this principle, is organically organized and is governed by law.

Nicholas of Cusa wrote the treatise *De concordantia catholica* during the Council of Basel (1433)[5] with the aim of illustrating some ideas and proposals for reconstructing the lost harmony within the church.[6] To achieve this aim, Nicholas divides his works into three books, in which he first analyzes the historical context, then elaborates some possible solutions. The concept of universal concordance is constantly repeated to express the idea of the unity of the church and its goal of seeing the "harmonic" peace, which derives from Christ and from heaven, in everything. Previous scholarship has focused on various themes in *De concordantia catholica*. Paul E. Sigmund focuses his analysis on the political themes.[7] He asserts that *De concordantia* has a dual structure, with the two fundamental concepts being hierarchy and equality. According to Claudia D'Amico, *De concordantia catholica* is a deeply theological work that is founded on canonical arguments.[8] The expressions "unitas fidelium" or "congregatio fidelium" include the whole of Christianity, she argues; Christian society must overcome the power struggles between the papal party and conciliarism, between Western and Oriental Christians, and between spiritual and temporal power. Although the work presents the project of an ecclesiastical reformation, Nicholas is aware that reformation is possible only through a renewal of temporal power and of relations between temporal and spiritual power.[9] Both emperor and priesthood are considered "holy," since both

---

4. Black, *Council and Commune*, 113.
5. Alberigo, *Chiesa Conciliare, Identità e significato del conciliarismo*, 31.
6. *De concordantia catholica*; I.IV.1–6 in Nicolai de Cusa, *Opera omnia*.
7. See Sigmund, *Nicholas of Cusa and Medieval Political Thought*.
8. D'Amico, Machetta, *El problema del conocimiento en Nicolás de Cusa*.
9. According to Giuseppe Alberigo, the peculiarity of this text is related to the historical events through which Nicholas lived (*Chiesa Conciliare*, 243).

proceed from God, the unique source of power, and both have peace as the main objective. The emperor desires to establish peace in the earthly city; the church is a guide to eternal salvation. The three books of *De concordantia catholica* focus respectively on the unity of the church (book one), spiritual power (book two), and temporal power (book three). Throughout the work, Nicholas stresses the theme of hierarchy as essential to achieving harmony and unity in the church. However, he also consistently draws parallels between the unity of the church and the unity of the soul and body in human beings. I will focus on the organic metaphors that Nicholas uses in his argument.

Nicholasus Krebs (Chrypffs) was born in 1401 in Cues, a small village on the Mosel, in the diocese of Trier, the oldest Christian city of Germany. When Nicholas was sixteen, he was matriculated at the University of Heidelberg.[10] In Heidelberg, he worked towards a philosophy far from Aristotelian scholasticism.[11] In October 1417 he went to the University of Padua, where he received the degree of doctor of canon law in 1423. In those years Cusanus met the canonist Prosdocimus de Comitibus (d. 1438) and other prominent canonists who kept conciliarism alive at Padua, such as Francis Zabarella (1360–1417).[12] In 1425 Nicholas went to Rome, before the end of the jubilee announced by Pope Martin V after the death of the anti-pope Benedict XIII (Pedro Martínez de Luna y Pérez de Gotor). That same year

---

10. On the historical context of the German territories in the twelfth through fifteenth centuries: see Tabacco, *Profilo di storia del medioevo latino germanico*, 14: Cf. also Bosl, Weis, *Die Gesellschaft in Deutschland, Statuti città territori in Italia e Germania tra medioevo ed età moderna*; Althoff, *Medieval Concepts of the Past*.

11. See Meuthen, *Nicholas of Cusa*, 15.

12. Cf. Federici Vescovini, "Cusanus und das wissenschaftliche Studium in Padua zu Beginn des 15. Jahrhunderts," 93–114. Morimichi Watanabe highlights the importance of the Paduan period for Nicholas: cf. Watanabe, *The Political Thought of Nicholas of Cusa*, 13; "At that time Padua was one of the most famous universities in Italy, not only for its canonists, but for its scientists, mathematicians, and humanists. It was in Padua that Nicholas met several professors whose influence left a permanent mark upon him. Prosdocimo de' Beldomandi, the mathematician and astrologer, and Paolo del Pozzo Toscanelli, the famous natural philosopher of Florence, must have introduced him to Pythagorean doctrines. His interest in Islam and his respect for Avicenna may have been aroused by Ugo Benzi, the famous Hellenist of Siena. Thus at Padua Nicholas studied astrology, mathematics, dynamics, and cartography"; Kristeller, *Studies in Renaissance: Thought and Letters*; Vasoli, "Cusano e la cultura umanistica fiorentina"; Thurner, *Nikolaus zwischen*, 77. Cf. Schnarr, "Fruhe Beziehungen des Nikolaus von Kues zu italienischen Humanisten"; Thurner, *Nikolaus zwischen*, 78. Cf. Monfasani, "Nicholas of Cusa, the Byzantines, and the Greek Language," 215–52.

Nicholas moved to Cologne, where he stayed for one year. During this time he met Cardinal Giordano Orsini, apostolic legate in Germany, who designated him as secretary.[13]

Nicholas participated in the Council of Basel[14] as *nuncius et orator* of the count Ulrich of Manderscheid. Indeed, the count wanted to assign to him the archbishopric of Trier, which ultimately was given to Jacob von Sierck in 1439.[15] For Nicholas, his juridical mission at the council was less important than his desire to participate in the debate among the fathers of Basel. After two years, he presented *De concordantia catholica*[16] (1433) as a proposal to help solve the church's crisis. A compromise was reached on 15 December 1433, thorough a papal decree of Eugenius IV that recognized the council. Eugenius withdrew his bull to dissolve the council, because, he said, it should have to deal with many crucial problems, such as heresies, peace inside Christianity, and reformation of the church.

3. Hierarchy

De concordantia catholica touches on many themes. Above all, reformation stands out as a crucial theme and as the general aim of the entire treatise. One recurrent topic is the idea that hierarchy is related to the idea of unity.[17] Nicholas describes the organic and hierarchical structure of the church, developing his discourse through the ideas of consent, unity, and hierarchy. The principle of hierarchical unity is reflected in the concept of the supremacy of the Roman diocese. Supremacy is related to the following question: who has the authority in case of disagreement between the pope and the council?[18] In the Middle Ages, the councils were attended by cardinals, abbots, bishops, and canonists, and the emperor had an important role; as a consequence of its representative form, the council had decision-

---

13. Kapr, "Gab es Beziehungen zwischen Johannes Gutenberg und Nikolaus von Kues?" 32–40.

14. Black, *Council and Commune*.

15. See Rotta, *Il cardinale Niccolò da Cusa*, 44.

16. *De concordantia catholica*; II; I

17. Watanabe, *The Political Thought*, 69 and 75: "for the preservation of *pax* and *ordo* within the church, the Roman church could exercise a great deal of power. As we shall see later, this pro-papal, 'undemocratic' side of Nicholas's thinking grew stronger as the years went by. We must always bear in mind that the origins of Nicholas's later development can already be found in *De concordantia catholica*."

18. Ibid., 80.

making power. Conciliarism asserted that only through the decision of an ecumenical council could the crisis of the church be solved. According to the ecumenical council, a true reformation of the church can be achieved only if papal power is limited.[19] Supreme spiritual authority rests not with the pope but with the universal church, which, through the ecumenical council, can exert authority even over the pope.

In the first lines of *De concordantia catholica*, Nicholas states his main objective, clarifying that he wants to explain the principle of divine harmony of the church.[20] According to Nicholas, man has a predisposition toward this harmonic peace, and one expression of this is man's capability to accept Christ. This predisposition, according to Nicholas, is expressed in Genesis, where it is written that man will leave his own native family to start a family with his wife. Just as the union of Adam and Eve was a sacrament in Christ and in the church, and just as Eve was bone of the bones of man and flesh of his flesh, in the same way the church is composed of the limbs of Christ.[21] Nicholas asserts that man will reunite with God, but it is necessary to have faith. Members of the church, indeed, participate in the unique body of the congregation to create one divine house.[22] In this way a great organism is created that is related to Christ in a harmony of functions and strengths. Nicholas asserts that in divine essence, where life and being are perfectly identified, concordance is infinite and absolute. It is true, therefore, that concordance is absolute where difference is slightest, and it is eternal where there is no conflict. This is demonstrated in the Trinity and in the unity of God, since God the Father and the Spirit are united in the same essence. Therefore the church can regenerate man and realize the unity of Spirit.[23] All creatures are divided into spiritual, corporeal, and mixed, and already in this classification is reflected the image of the Trinity. Angelic spirits belong to the category of spiritual beings, which is divided into three orders, with each order further divided into three choirs;[24] all together they reflect the unity of Trinity.

19. Jedin, *A History of the Council of Trent*.
20. *De concordantia catholica*, I, 29. "Enim est id, ratione cuius ecclesia catholica in uno et in pluribus concordat, in uno domino et pluribus subditis. Et ab uno infinitae concordantiae rege pacifico fluit illa dulcis concordantialis harmonia spiritualis gradatim et seriam in cuncta membra subiecta et unita, ut sit unus deus omnia in omnibus."
21. *De concordantia catholica* I; cf. Ef., I, 5.
22. *De concordantia catholica*, I, 31.
23. *De concordantia catholica*, I, 33.
24. Pseudo-Dyonisus, *De eccl. hier.*, c. I, 3.

Nicholas of Cusa stresses that his view contemplates all creatures, and he attempts to explain that everything starting from the *Principium*. Indeed, inquiring on wonderful and different concordances of the universe, the sages achieve knowledge of the infinite combinations of beings. All creatures share a similarity with the *Principium* and are united to it through a intrinsic concordance to survive. Thus, the rational spirits are united to the church in different grades. He searches for traces of the Trinity in the church, and he affirms that the church is articulated in triumphant, sleeping, and militant orders. Every order has three choirs, and each choir has many other tripartite divisions. To illustrate this concept, Nicholas quotes Leo IX, who wrote that the church is the body of Christ, and whosoever participates in the church participates also in the body of Christ: "If a member is glorified, all the members are glorified."[25] The body, derived from Adam, became spiritual through regeneration in Christ: indeed, this body is dead and, through Christ, is resurrected as a new and spiritual man. Obviously, Nicholas considers the body of the church to be comprised of only men who are predestined to salvation, because only the predestined can have the divine legacy.

The church, Nicholas asserts, can be considered as a faithful spouse who obeys the highest part of herself to remain faithful to her bridegroom. Therefore, the believer is he who subjects his own intellect to believe the Trinity. Man submits to Christ through his intellectual spirit, and in this way he enters into the church. Nevertheless, this is not sufficient; in order for man to become the image of divine trinity, it is necessary "ad percipiendam illam vitalem concordantiam,"[26] through faith, hope, and charity. The soul should be perfect to have success in understanding the Spirit of God, and finally, through the resurrection, the body also will revert back to its own spiritual essence. Nicholas likens the militant church to an army that recognizes Christ as its emperor. And even if someone does not do good works, if faith remains, it is possible to unite to the church. When the faith is there, Nicholas affirms, the church has the image of a spouse even if there are some sinners in it.[27] From this it is possible to deduce that the promise of the marriage of Christ with the militant church is similar to the promise of the emperor to marry the queen of France with the condition that she offer her kingdom to her spouse. Therefore, even if the queen re-

---

25. Leo ix, *Ad Michaelem patriarcham Constatinopolitanum* (PL 143, 767 ff.).
26. *De concordantia catholica*, I, 46.
27. Cf. Augustin, *De correctione Donatistarum*, 7 (PL 33, 806).

mains faithful to her spouse but does not repress her kingdom's revolts, the marriage could be annulled. In this case, indeed, the spouse did not request impossible things, only difficult ones.[28]

After treating the sacraments, Nicholas considers the order of the priesthood, which has been assigned the task of assuring the continuity of the church by handling every challenge. The priesthood has a hierarchical order,[29] with different functions for its various members. To explain this concept, Nicholas quotes a text of Cyprianus: "all the apostles had the same dignity of Peter and they had the same power."[30] Nevertheless, Peter represents *unitas in concordantia*,[31] and this eliminates the possibility of schisms and keeps the peace among believers. For these reasons, the head (cathedra) must be a hierarchical disposition, similar as to the position of a temporal king. Indeed, Nicholas asserts, quoting Jerome, a bishop is elected head in the same way as a military captain, who is elected with the consent of all his soldiers. Therefore, as the *res publica* is a collective institution and is related to the "nation," that "est hominum multitudo in quodlibet vinculum concordiae redacta."[32] In the same way, inside the government of the church, the bishop has the same function of the emperor. Therefore, the subjects of the emperor are united to the chair, as body is united to soul. It is fundamental, Nicholas concludes, to remember that the church is in the bishop and in its union with him.[33] Leo IX also wrote that the episcopate has a hierarchical disposition.[34] Indeed, some bishops are superior because they govern famous and important cities. This comparison is important, Nicholas explains, since it shows that spiritual power supersedes temporal power as the soul does the body. But Nicholas points out that throughout the hierarchy, harmony connects the different hierarchies.[35] The priesthood functions as intercessor between God and the community.[36] And the body of believers is ruled by several earthly principates, whose head is the Holy Roman Empire. Peter, like his successors, was nominated as head through

28. *De concordantia catholica*, I, 47.
29. *De concordantia catholica*, I, 54–55.
30. Cyprian, *De unitate ecclesiae*, 5, e 4 (PL 4, 515 e ff)
31. *De concordantia catholica*, I.VI, 56.
32. *De concordantia catholica*, I.VI, 57; Augustin, *Ad Marcellium* (PL 33, 529).
33. *De concordantia catholica*, I, 58.
34. Leo ix, *Ad Petrum et Joannem episcopos* (PL 143, 730).
35. *De concordantia catholica*, I, 60.
36. *De concordantia catholica*, I, 66.

a divine decision. Peter was prince of bishops, and in the same way the Roman pope is prince of bishops. Therefore, all men of faith, Nicholas explains, should submit to the primate of the church, as his position is granted by their faith.[37] This transcendent origin of power is the main difference between the theories of Nicholas and those of Marsilius of Padua, who thinks that the concept of sovereignty is related to the immanent sphere.[38]

4. Church as *Corpus mysticum*

The pope's power is derived from the consent of the church. The council as *congregatio fidelium* and *corpus mysticum* expresses this consent.[39] Nicholas of Cusa drew the concept of *corpus mysticum* from Paul in order to stress that the church is a whole,[40] which is superior to any single member. Inside the church, the pope is a member, although he is higher than all others ("licet altior"). The church, as a *corpus mysticum*, is an organic unity or *concordantia* and exercises its powers through a representative organism, which is an expression of common consent. This organism is the council, which represents the church in its unity. According to Nicholas, the council and the church have the same infallibility: the sacerdotal body is fallible in each member, but is not fallible in its whole, as long as the majority remains inside faith and law of Christ.[41]

Body as Council

Nicholas hopes that the church can reach harmony between the conciliarist party and the papal party. He believes that an external harmony is possible between the church and the emperor. To reach the *concordantia*, however, it is necessary to accept the different traditions and cultures. The council is like a body, and the bishops and cardinals are its main members. The parts of the church should be constituted through consent, Nicholas

---

37. *De concordantia catholica*, I.XV, 81.

38. Cf. Syros, *Die Rezeption der aristotelischen politischen Philosophie bei Marsilius von Padua, Eine Untersuchung zur ersten Diktion des Defensor pacis.*

39. *De concordantia catholica*, I, 34.

40. Cf. on the idea of *Corpus mysticum* cf. De Lubac, *Corpus Mysticum. L'Eucaristia e la Chiesa nel medioevo* and Bagliani, *Il corpo del Papa*.

41. *De concordantia catholica*, I, 8.

believes, according to the divine and natural law.[42] Indeed, from God the divine power descends on him who represents the totality of the church—the pope. Through consensual election of the pope, it is possible to reach a *concordantia* among all the different participants in the council, in the same way that the soul receives the rational part as a divine gift.

5. Defense of Body

In the third part of *De concordantia catholica*, Nicholas argues on the necessity to follow the principles of the philosophers about the foundation of the political community.[43] Each creature has the right to defend its body and its life, and each person is different from all others, according to individual immanent principles (instinct, appetite, reason). Because of innate reason and instinct, men understood the necessity to unite themselves in a political community, to build villages and cities.[44] They also understood the need to choose some of their number as guardians of the law, to keep the common good through law.

Nicholas of Cusa asserts that man received from God the impulse to socialize, and it allows man to grasp the importance of the political community to achieve the common good. The common good can be achieved through the law as an expression of everyone, or at least of the sages elected by the consent of the people. Man, Nicholas affirms, is a political animal, and he tends to live in a political community. Therefore, as Aristotle wrote, the strongest part of the people must be well disposed to preservation of the law if they are to keep peace inside the political community.[45] Furthermore, God gave fools a natural inclination to be servants; they are faithful to the rulers, following law and helping to preserve the society.

---

42. Cf. Merlo, *Vinculum concordiae. Il problema della rappresentanza nel pensiero di Nicolò Cusano*.

43. *De concordantia catholica*, III; Proemium, 313. "Naturalia quidam iura cunctas humanas considerationes et antecedunt et ad omnia illa principia."

44. *De concordantia catholica*, III, Proemium, 314. "Et nisi homo pacis servandae ob corruptum multorum affectum regular invenisset, parum unio saluti contulisset."

45. *Polit.*, I, 2, 1253 a 29; MA I, 13, §. 2 (70, 11–28). Cf. on this point also the Cicero's philosophy and his influence on the medieval thought in Nederman, "Nature, Sin, and the Origins of Society," 3–26.

6. Relations between King and Emperor

According to Nicholas, the emperor is the supreme head of everyone, and he has power over all kings of the empire. Kings and princes must join with the emperor like members join to their head. These various members are bodies and magisters of great social bodies, for example senate members. They are divided into three grades: 1) *illustres*, who stay near the emperor; 2) *exspectabiles*; and 3) *carissimi*. It is necessary to consult the *Digestum* to know the duties of each grade.[46] Likewise, participants in the diets were divided in three orders: 1) king, principals of empire; 2) dukes, bishops, and the like; and 3) counts and other nobles.[47]

Nicholas recalls that several ancient sources testify how the Roman pope used to honor the emperors.[48] According to the emperor, the pope should be satisfied that bishops must obey the pope's command. He should remember all the magnificent gifts and the protection and defense he received from Roman Empire during the period of crisis of the church. According to Nicholas, the pope should have a supremacy similar to that which the sun has over the moon and the soul has over the body,[49] without affirming that imperial power derives from papal power.

7. Relations between Emperor and Pope[50]

Nicholas asserts that in any period of crisis, the pope should have the capacity to submit the church to the emperor.[51] Nicholas cites the case of Leo VII, who gave back to Otto I and his successors all assets the church had received in donation. The pope should be satisfied that the empire is ready

---

46. Cf. Di. I, 9–19.
47. *De concordantia catholica*, III, 422.
48. Cf., *De concordantia catholica*, I.II.
49. Cf. Tierney, *Crisis of Church and State 1050–1300*.
50. On the metaphor of Body: Cf. Kantorowicz, *The King's Two Bodies*; Canning, *A History of Medieval Political Thought, 300–1450*; Ullmann, *Medieval Papalism*.
On the Rhetoric and Medieval Rhetoric: cf. *La predicazione dei frati dalla metà del '200 alla fine del '300, Centro universitario di studi francescani, Assisi, Eco, La metafora nel Medioevo*, in www.doctorvirtualis.it. Cf. also Murphy, *Three Medieval Rhetorical Arts*; Blumenberg, *Die Lesbarkeit der Welt*.
51. *De concordantia catholica*, III, 465. "Imperatorem fidei defensorem potentem esse."

to defend the church against every enemy.[52] However, the emperor should not consider himself superior to the priesthood[53] and should be aware that his services are nothing comparing to the eternal goods.[54] Consequently, Nicholas asserts, in order to achieve an eternal concordance it is necessary to avoid any conflict. Indeed, the church is like the union of soul and body: the Holy Spirit lives through the concordance, and all the Christians should live together peacefully. To maintain this harmony the pope must elevate himself above all the bishops, so he can exercise his rightful and necessary power.[55] The pope's objective is to keep the vital concordance of the church through holy canons and canonical sources, which derive from the source of Holy Spirit.

The seat of soul is the center of heart; from this blood the vital spirits flow through all the arteries, to make body healthy and alive. By using the metaphor of the body and blood vessels, Nicholas explains that the canons envelop the body of the church, including the head, pressing the limbs with sweet and vital bonds. Then, just as a vein begins from the liver and spreads throughout all the body, becoming tangled in the flesh, in the same way the canonical synod lives through the liver (synod committee), where all the veins flow together (constitutions). Furthermore, just as small veins sprinkle different zones, bringing vital strength to the soul through constant connection; in the same way all the statutes of provincial councils must be always pursuant to the general canons of the church.[56]

Nicholas applies the similitude of the human body to the empire's body and writes that imperial laws connect all the imperial territories just like nerves connect all the parts of the organism. Even the supreme head, therefore, must pay attention that nerves are not too relaxed or even tense, for with such excesses, the body can be damaged. The law, Nicholas affirms, must therefore be as tense as a bow-string, that is, not too tense so that the bow is not broken, and not to loose so that the bow is useful.

---

52. *De concordantia catholica*, III, 465. "Agit pro eius tutela quaecumque possibilia et quantum eius vires sufferunt. Non vi capit, non repetit donata, sed defendit et nutrit sacerdotium, quod solum ut dignissimum veratur."

53. *De concordantia catholica*, III, 466.

54. *De concordantia catholica*, III, 466.

55. *De concordantia catholica*, III, 468.

56. *De concordantia catholica*, III, 469.

8. Emperor as Physician

The emperor must be aware that nerves stick strongly to the bones even when flesh is putrefied. In like manner, the laws of the empire must be kept incorruptible. Nicholas compares the empire to the bones that contain the marrow and hold the flesh: since men are less lasting and they sin because of weakness and ignorance or inconstancy of human nature, the emperor must be like a father, dispensing and punishing according to what is best for the health of everyone. Furthermore, it is necessary that the particular laws, comparable to the small veins, are pursuant to general law, made for the common good, as well as to the fundamental principle of laws, the natural rational right. Indeed, if a particular law is against the common law, it is like a disease that corrodes limbs and all body. [57]

The emperor, therefore, like a skilled doctor, must be able to keep healthy all parts of the social body in order to keep united the vital spirit and the body. If the body exceeds or lacks in the four humors,[58] the result is monstrous. It may become gloomy because of a melancholic temperament, which is a source of avarice that sows in the organism several pests such as usury, fraud, deceits, theft, robbery, and all sorts of activities devoted to the acquisition of riches. For the empire, this would inevitably lead to damnation. Or the body may become feverish and ardent because of an irascible temperament, and this would lead to wars, conflicts, and divisions. It may become swollen because of a bloody temperament that breeds pomposity and lust. The body may also become bloodless and soft because of a phlegmatic temperament, and this would breed general sloth with respect to all sorts of virtuous actions and in economic activities. According to Nicholas, in all these cases the emperor must find a medicine, following the suggestions of books and the advice of expert doctors of the empire. Furthermore, the emperor must formulate laws. Just as a medicine is evaluated through taste, sight, and smell, so the law must be written for the people and must be judged by a committee of judges. This committee, like a medicine coursing through a body, could spread the law into each part of the kingdom. The emperor, for his part, should not ablate a member; he must prove every remedy, and if the remedy is ineffective, he must cut off the infected member.

57. *De concordantia catholica*, III, 472. "Debet itaque citharoedus rex esse, et qui bene sciat in fidibus concordiam observare, tam maiores quam minores, nec nimis nec minus estendere, ut communis concordantia per omnium harmoniam resonet."

58. Gaia, *Opere religiose*, 544, footnote 32.

9. Conclusions

Nicholas of Cusa can be defined both as a humanist writer and as a medieval orator. He knows the value of the metaphor, of allegories, and he uses them in his sermons for an illiterate public. Nicholas of Cusa through his organic metaphor especially points out the concept of difference. This concept is fundamental for him and is found in all of his works. It is articulated on multiple levels: metaphysical, ecclesiological, and political. The concept of difference is related to the development of the idea of concordance: difference is the fundamental element inside the social system and exists in different grades that are connected throughout *concordantia*. Pluralism and difference are crucial to understanding the rule of the hierarchy. Indeed, through a hierarchical disposition, all differences can be united. Nicholas represents this process of *concordantia-differentia* through the organic metaphor of the body: each part of the body is likened to a different part of the empire. These parts are social and political, and they must reach peace and harmony in order to keep the vital system healthy.

Ernst Kantorowicz[59] writes that the work of Nicholas of Cusa is the most important example of the transposition of the metaphor of *corpus mysticum* from the church to the empire. Analyzing the organic metaphor in *De concordantia catholica*, we find descriptions of the relationship between 1) the whole and each part; 2) eternity and time; 3) soul and body; and 4) head and members. Kantorowicz considers these four categories to show that, over time, the *corpus mysticum* of the church came to be associated with the political character of the church or likened to a political institution in a secular world. The organic metaphor expresses a deeply rooted vision of political theology and the passage from the ecclesiastical world to secular world. Use of the body as a metaphor has Aristotelian influences and draws upon Thomas Aquinas; its influence can be seen throughout the Middle Ages.

As mentioned previously, in *De concordantia catholica* the organic metaphor describes, among the other things, the difference between eternity and time; use of the metaphor underscored the immortality of the church. Nicholas uses the same metaphor also to write about temporal power. According to the Kantorowicz's theory, the king was the head of the political body but was also a mortal human being. Medieval scholars compared the eternity of Christ's power to the power of emperor to confer

---

59. See Kantorowicz, *The King's Two Bodies*.

some elements of eternity on temporal power, thus effecting a transfer of the organic metaphor from the church to the emperor. This evolution is completed in the work of Nicholas of Cusa; his work is thus an exegetical model of this transformation over time and helps to understand the complex intersections between theology and politics.

Furthermore, as evidenced by the medical metaphor of *De concordantia*, the theme of difference in the essential role of an organism survival is extremely relevant. If hierarchy is absolutely necessary to ensure the harmony of all parts, it is likewise true that difference represents an *a priori* of the existence itself of each part and of the whole body. A pluralistic stance is therefore a consequence of this assumption, which in turn leads to the willingness to reconcile, to combine pluralities within a harmonious unity. Nicholas of Cusa's approach reveals an attempt to find a peaceful resolution to the problem of difference and diversity, an irenistic solution that longs for finding a common and consensual substrate between opposite and clashing positions. In the wake of recent critical comments focused on the substantial continuity of Cusanus' works, *De concordantia catholica* clearly reveals that the irenistic instance is a fundamental element that develops from Nicholas' particular approach to the theme of difference.

3

De docta ignorantia, Identity and Difference

1. Introduction

IN LINE WITH THE issues pointed out in the previous pages, I shall try to explain the method followed by Nicholas of Cusa to enunciate the theme of difference in relation to identity, and the way in which, following this perspective, he comes to formulate a first discourse focused on interreligious dialogue.

As remarked by J. Decorte, basing on the assumption that it is necessary to work in depth to accept and understand alterity,[1] we can interpret the theory on conjecturality expounded by Cusanus in *De docta ignorantia* as a system of thought that proves essential to understand the irenic model of *De pace fidei*, because just in virtue of this metaphysical assumption Nicholas affirms that absolute truth cannot be reached and infinity is incomprehensible to anybody.[2]

Cusanus makes use of different metaphors and figures of speech to describe the conjectural conception of the world, and in particular, the metaphor of the sphere, which leads him to the formulation of a perspective view of reality. Perspective view allows achieving a different knowledge modality comparable to intellect. The human mind knows insofar as it measures things by applying its own measurement standard to an object, by noticing a particular proportion which yet can never reach the truth of things. In this case, this theme becomes particularly interesting if focused on interreligious dialogue and the sharing, among different creeds, of a

---

1. See Decorte, "Tolerance and Trinity"; Duprè, "Spirit, Mind and Freedom."

2. Decorte, "Tolerance and Trinity," 115, writes: "So, the Christian does not have to become a Muslim, and the Muslim does have to become a Christian. On the contrary, both will have to make an effort within their own religious and cultural traditions to convince their co-religionists of the conjecturality of their approach to the absolute Infinite."

single truth in a position to support peaceful coexistence at a theoretical level.

By developing the theme of *concordantia differentiarum* (concordance of differences), Nicholas of Cusa elaborates in *De docta ignorantia* the theme of the *coincidentia oppositorum* (coincidence of opposites).[3]

2. The Model of *De docta ignorantia*

De docta ignorantia opens with an epistle dedicated to the cardinal Giuliano Cesarini (1398–1444), who had been the teacher of Cusanus during his stay in Padua, from 1417 to 1423. When in 1432 Cusanus participated in the Council of Basel, Cesarini was called to take the chair in it and he backed his friend in his action in support of Pope Eugenius IV.

This treatise is presented by Cusanus as a *ratiocinandi modus in rebus divinis* (a way of reasoning about divine matters) and a theological method.

De docta ignorantia clearly reveals an attempt to formulate an original theory, which does not aim at clashing with tradition, but rather at understanding its contradictions and solving them in a synthetically correct way. In his analysis, Cusanus begins from what he has learned and knows, from the texts he studied, and from an observation of the natural things and the world.[4]

He contends that *docta ignorantia* (learned ignorance) is a model not because it represents a mere speculative solution, but because it is an attempt to find a solution to the real problems of contemporary society. When, in his epistle addressed to cardinal Cesarini, Cusanus defines his work as a *via doctrinarum*, he expresses the critical intention to analyze the limits of the dominant scholasticism, both in philosophy and in theology. The *docta ignorantia* method represents an alternative and innovative program that Nicholas wants to offer Cesarini, and through him, to his contemporaries, so that it may be spread.[5]

---

3 This chapter adapts my article, "The Interreligious Dialogue in *De docta ignorantia* of Nicholas of Cusa," (*Medieval Encounters*, 2014). I thank *Medieval Encounters*' editor for permission to use the article here.

4. *De docta ignorantia*, I.14–19.

5. Watts, *Nicolaus Cusanus*, 34.

The meaning of "learned ignorance" is already explained in the first chapter: it is the "most perfect" doctrine, and for this reason, Nicholas intends to provide its theoretical pattern.[6]

The "perfect doctrine" theory is expounded starting from the concept of *maximum*, which is similar to the concept of *unitas*; all things are different though they belong to the same universe. The numerical system of signs and the quantity measurement provide Nicholas with a symbolic support to expound the construction of his method. "Learned ignorance" is illustrated through the resort to images and mathematical formulas, and Nicholas makes also use of references to the logical and cognitive system. In chapter 4 of the first book, Cusanus argues about the evidence of the existence of the "maximum" by expounding the first theological argument, through which he intends to affirm the substantial unity of the divine being, in which every multiplicity of the sensible world contracts.[7]

Chapter 7 includes the description of the three attributes of God the human being can quite imperfectly perceive in his worldly experience: unity, equality, and connection. From these attributes, Nicholas begins to develop his method. As Santinello remarks:

> By taking words and geometrical examples in a figurative way (*transumptive*), in a transcendent proportion (*transumptiva proportione*), it is possible to establish a symbolic ratio (*symbolicae*), a concealed and incomprehensible proportion (*occulta et incomprehensibile proportione*) between visible things—the creatures—and the invisible creator. Incomprehensible comprehension is the one existing between a symbol and a symbolised thing. Appealing to Pythagoras, to the Platonists, to Aristotle and, among the Christian philosophers, to Augustine and Boethius, Cusanus thinks he can use mathematics in a symbolic manner.[8]

Cusanus establishes the rules for a symbolic use of mathematics: the geometrical figures he refers to in the following chapters are: the line, the triangle, the circle, and the sphere. The *modality* through which Nicholas makes use of mathematics in order to connect concepts deriving from

---

6. *De docta ignorantia*, I.I.19-24. "Nihil enim homini, etiam studiosissimo, in doctrina perfectius adveniet quam in ipsa ignorantia, quae ipsi propria est, doctissimum reperiri; et tanto quis doctior erit quanto se sciverit magis ignorantem. In quem finem de ipsa docta ignorantia pauca quaedam scribendi labores assumpsi."

7. *De docta ignorantia*, II; *Praefatio*, 1-9.

8. Santinello, in *Nicola da Cusa, La dotta ignoranza e le congetture*, 86.

different disciplines, such as theology or philosophy, can be defined as a symbolic system.

Cusanus explains the way in which this system of signs can be translated to understand the maximum line, and therefore, infinity. The sources are explicitly and repeatedly cited, especially Dionysius the Areopagite who, in Nicholas' opinion, explained in his work the real essence of the divine, which is minimum and maximum at the same time.

Nicholas continues his definition of the "learned ignorance" theory, and develops the theme of *maximum* related to *unitas* (unity): he examines in what alterity and inequality consist, and goes as far as to show that both are subsequent to unity and equality. Nicholas paraphrases Dionysius' theory and mentions Moses Maimonides' philosophical theory.[9]

The system constructed by Cusanus is connected to the general discourse of the use of metaphors as a cognitive instrument.[10] In his opinion, an individual is metaphysically and epistemologically formed by God. In his cognitive approach to the world, which takes place through the symbolic thought, the human being makes use of an essentially metaphoric system referring to what exists in nature. In this sense, images and symbols have always a disproportion and error margin. In connection with this conception of the metaphoric nature of the symbolic thought, man also believes that God remains concealed and that it is possible to talk about the divinity only though paradoxes.[11] The philosopher Nicholas in his symbolic theory refers to is, in fact, Pythagoras. Cusanus' knowledge of Pythagoras derives to a great extent from Boethius' writings and from the adaptation of John of Salisbury's doctrine.[12]

Nicholas clearly declares in the dedicatory letter of *De docta ignorantia* that, in its general structure, his work is focused on the speculative method, and throughout the conceptual development of this work, he makes clear how this method works.

Nicholas employs the mathematical system of signs, and therefore he makes use of a system of signs, which belongs to established tradition. In this sense, Nicholas makes use of a set of canons derived from mathematics, consisting of rules and paradigms, to establish his theological theory.

---

9. *De docta ignorantia*, I.XVI.13–16.

10. See the article by Nicolle, "Quelques sources philosophico-mathématiques de Nicholas de Cues," 47–59.

11. This theory if extensively developed by Nicholas in his work *De Deo abscondito*.

12. See Watts, *Nicolaus Cusanus*, 34.

Cusanus avails himself of the mathematic system and transfers its semantic value to an upper significant level by means of analogy and figures of speech, such as metaphors and similes, to construct its epistemological assumptions. This assumption should be acknowledged as well-grounded, and it should therefore refer to a system already rooted in the mechanism of knowledge transmission, mathematics in this case. Cusanus aims at giving a common answer to the number of political and religious problems of his time arising from ideological differences, economic and political interests, and from the changes occurred in the social structure.

3. Identity (Sameness), Difference and Diversity

Nicholas puts forward one of the issues his "learned ignorance" method is grounded on by beginning to wonder about the nature of God's name and the possibility to know something of the divine substance, though man is immersed in the plurality of reality.[13]

He deals with the problem of plurality resorting to categories derived from the negative theology.[14] According to the theologian Cusanus, "the divine being is the simplest unit as it exists in a single universe, and consequently, ... the plurality of things is in God through the mediation of a single universe."[15] Resuming Anaxagoras' theory that each thing includes only a minimum part of all the things, Cusanus argues that similarly, there is a sort of reflection of the universal substance in each individual. This statement can be fully understood only if we do not consider an actual, but a potential thing. Any one thing, indeed, cannot be present in all things, except as an idea, as *in potentia*: the diversity originates from the different explication of the idea in the actual thing. The diversity of things depends on their connection.[16]

Cusanus explains the reasons that have led to the existence of idolatry. The Gentiles named their divinities by similitude. Gods were hypostizations of natural phenomena, but nonetheless, in Cusanus' opinion, heathens worshipped only one God. Heathens' error consisted in that they wanted

---

13. *De docta ignorantia*, II.III.16-23.
14. *De docta ignorantia*, I.XVI.
15. *De Docta ignorantia* in Nicholas of Cusa, *Opere*, Italian translation by G. Federici Vescovini 123.
16. *De docta ignorantia*, II.V.

to attribute positive names to this endless, unknowable, and inscrutable being. Nicholas then explains his negative theology:[17] through the philosophical method derived from the Pseudo-Dionysius, the names of God are denied, and by denying any name to the divine being it is not possible to fall into idolatry. Besides the Jewish Tetragrammaton (YHWH), the only name we can attribute to God is Infinity.[18]

The foundations of the learned ignorance method consist in the *maximum absolutum, presupposition,* and *repraesentatio* principles.[19] These three subjects form the body of Cusa's philosophical theory. He develops these principles in the doctrine of the *coincidentia oppositorum,* which is a completely new way to comprehend the non-contradiction principle.

The separation of the opposites is the Aristotelian principle to be discussed: we can debate whether this dispute means the way out of the Middle Ages and the autumn of scholastic philosophy or not, but in this case our interest is focused on the meaning the theory of the union of contradictions takes in Cusanus' explanation.[20]

Aristotle looks for a prime principle laying the foundations of science, which may be certain and well-grounded, and formulates the following proposition: this principle cannot both be and not be. An evidence of this principle is therefore impossible, as it should be based on a higher principle, which has to be found. For Aristotle, the foundations of all knowledge rest therefore on the axiom of the non-contradiction principle.[21]

Cusanus develops instead his theory of knowledge by adopting the concepts of unity, itness (*iditas*), and sameness:[22] unity and identity are

---

17. *De docta ignorantia,* XXVI.

18. Arfè, "Nicola Cusano interprete dell'Asclepius." Nicholas chooses the Tetragrammaton, the traditional Jewish name of God; its abstractness suits the divine being not based on some relation with the creatures, but in virtue of its own essence. "The first translation of the Tetragram is the hermetic syntagma *unus-omnia.* This hermetic denomination of God is the base of a terminological ascent that going through the subsequent statement *omnia uniter,* culminates in the more appropriate term of non-numerical *unitas.*" Ibid., 141.

19. Riedenauer, *Pluralität und Rationalität,* 208. The construction of this method takes place through symbols, and sets the goal of approaching the absolute, of understanding in some way the transcendent truth.

20. Stammkötter, "*Hic homo parum curat de dictis Aristotelis* Der Streit zwischen Johannes Wenck von Herrenberg und Nikolaus von Kues," 244.

21. Aristotle, *IV Metaph.*

22. About the concept of identity in Cusa's work, see the essay by Beierwaltes, *Identität und Differenz,* 106 and ff.

conceived, through the concept of absolute identity, as the limit of all coincidences[23] and of the *una est ergo praesentia omnium temporum complicatio*.[24] From this conceptual tangle, the theologian Cusanus can develop his theory of the *coincidentia oppositorum* (coincidence of the opposites) as the highest expression of thought. Since God is simultaneously the absolute maximum and the absolute minimum, God is, in Cusa's opinion, the *coincidentia oppositorum*. This conception is an attempt to counter the logic of the scholastic philosophy and of the natural philosophy inspiring to Aristotle.[25]

This *coincidentia oppositorum* transcends the late-scholastic notion of *potentia absoluta*. Through his absolute power, God can do any thing, and even infringe the law of non-contradiction, this "violation" being a sign of his infinite power.[26] *Coincidentia* can be considered a metaphoric figure, as it indicates the divine power and the Creator's infinite freedom, and is the main theme the doctrine of the *docta ignorantia* is grounded on.

Coincidentia is a theological method, which aims at providing a well-constructed understanding of Christ's nature.[27] According to Nicholas, theologians should not infringe the paradox of the coincidence of the opposites, because the incarnation, which is the primary and original coincidence, establishes the limits of the logical patterns and determines what can be referred to the concepts of distinction and reconcilement.

According to Cusanus, the human nature is a mean nature compared to all the others existing in the universe. In its contraction, it can summarize all the natures towering above, as angels or intelligences, and those below it, as the animal and the vegetable kingdoms. The divine person, the Son, can unite human nature, which being a microcosm, sums up the whole created world: it is an event we can pre-represent in a future scenario, in which the human essence and the divine essence would coexist in the same form.[28]

Nicholas' idea is supported in this work by a number of metaphors, patterns, similes, and references to three different fields: the biblical, the

---

23. *De docta ignorantia*, I.9. See Haubst, *Das Bild de Einen und Dreien Gottes in der Welt nach Nikolaus von Kues*.

24. *De docta ignorantia*; II.III.4–6. "Ita identitas est diversitatis complicatio, aequalitas inaequalitatis, est simplicittas divisionum sive discretionum."

25. Watts, *Nicolaus Cusanus*, 140.

26. Arfè, "Alberto e Cusano interpreti dell'Asclepius," 144.

27. Bond, "Nicholas of Cusa and the Reconstruction of Theology," 81–94.

28. *De docta ignorantia*, III.

mathematical, and the logical fields. The biblical field essentially refers to the problem of God's name. The mathematical field is extensively dealt with in the first book of *De docta ignorantia*, and is summarized by the figure of the sphere, which is the most perfect form exactly conforming to the metaphor of the divine. The logical field, instead, concerns the problem of identity.[29] As Lawrence Bond remarks, attributing to the absolute being the power and the action (*possest*) means in some way translating what is written in Exodus 3:14: "I am that I am."

In each of these metaphors, regardless of the ambit they belong to, there is always an attempt to communicate something of God's infinity.

In the First Book, the Author expresses in what "learned ignorance" consists: it is a method through which we can understand the divine truth.[30] Though it is impossible for man to judge whether a name can be attributed to God or not, yet he can have an idea of what God cannot be. In this perspective, religious culture, the different kinds of worship, and faith intertwine at a discursive level. For Cusanus[31] the problem of the human being consists in having the inborn desire to know the truth but in always having the frustration of not having access to it. Learned ignorance is the first step that can lead man to become fully aware of this impossibility, and therefore, paradoxically, to a first knowledge of truth.

Another fundamental concept is developed by Cusanus, who will systematically use it in *De Pace Fidei*: the *praesuppositio*.[32] A *praesuppositio* is much more than a premise, it is a "methodical transcendence." A *praesuppositio* can be considered an important part of the *manuductio*, a text interpretation process analyzed in particular by Rudolf Haubst in his essay "Die Wege der christologischen manuductio." Haubst identifies just in *De docta ignorantia* the primary theological and philosophical conceptual nucleus that has led to the creation of the *manuductio* method used by Nicholas of Cusa. Ludwig Hagemann[33] too, affirms that this method is one of the bearing elements of Cusanus' theology.

The *manuductio* (guidance) process allows intellectual understanding to be guided step by step through the logical-rational discourse, even if a person who wants to understand the sense of things in depth must elevate

29. Bond, "Nicholas of Cusa and the Reconstruction of Theology," 90.
30. *De docta ignorantia*, I.XXVI.
31. Watts, *Nicolaus Cusanus*, 60.
32. Ridenuaer, *Pluralität und Rationalität*, 196.
33. Hagemann, *Christentum contra Islam*.

the intellect over the power of words and not remain fixed to their immediately understandable meaning.[34]

4. The Metaphor of the Sphere: The Perspective

In Cusanus' opinion, man is, as the Scriptures teach, a creature made in God's own image and likeness:[35] therefore, man is not a passive reproduction of the Creator,[36] but instead an active and creative image.[37]

Though the first book of *De docta ignorantia* does not extensively raise any problem concerning the debate on human nature and man's abilities, it includes, however, the premises which allow us to understand a fundamental aspect of the metaphysical and epistemological contexts within which Cusanus develops his conception of man. Desire is the drive that moves man towards truth, and also in the dedication to Cesarini, desire is a central theme, which is only preceded by the astonishment on wonder from which the will to understand originates. But this drive of life also creates the human tragedy since, though man was created by God, he is also a mortal creature. He lives in finiteness, but longs for infinity. The centrality of man's tragedy in Nicholas' work was remarked by Stadelmann[38] and is one of the themes which undoubtedly link Cusa's thought to the ideas of the forerunners of humanism.[39] The same theme can be found also in *De Pace Fidei*, in which the representatives of all religions are joined by the desire to have access to a common truth.

---

34. *De docta ignorantia*, I.II.12–17.

35. *De docta ignorantia*, III.I.4–13.

36. Arfè, "Nicola Cusano interprete dell'Asclepius," 148. As Pasquale Arfè remarks: "the creativity of the intellectual activity of the mind mediates, on the one hand, the relation with the divine, and on the other, the relation with the world. Man places himself in front of God as a *secundus deus*, and in front of the world as a *humanus mundus*. The typical idea of man-microcosm develops in this way in connection with the theme of an intermediate position in the universe. Man is a microcosm not only because he gathers and resumes in himself the different regions of the world, but, above all, because he is placed in the middle between the sensible and the intelligible nature, in the horizon of time and eternity, a universal connection between worldly and divine things."

37. *De docta ignorantia*, III.III.28–1; 1–6.

38. Cf. Stadelmann, *Vom Geist des ausgehenden Mittelalters*.

39. On the theme of individuality and subjectivity in Cusanus, see Gómez and André, "Coincidencia de opuestos y concordia," 163–76.

According to Cusanus, man creates the conjectural world, that is to say, he constructs representations of reality similar to the way in which God created the real world. Metaphor is the instrument man has at his disposal to create the conjectural world, the visible mark of his divine nature. The metaphor of the microcosm is directly connected with the metaphor of the divine being represented as a sphere. Nicholas introduces his reflections with a very simple experiment: man is not aware of motion unless it is related to something stationary. Similarly, if a person did not know that water flows, and did not look at the banks of a river from a boat, how would he know that the boat is moving?[40]

Therefore, we cannot affirm that the earth is the center of the universe, because it would mean stating something we do not know at all. Likewise, the universe has not center because it is endless. In this case, the hierarchical vision of the universe crumbles away. Cusanus' speculation presupposes a certain interest in the phenomenon of perspective.[41] He wants to know not only all that we can see, but also to understand the conditions that allow us to see. These conditions are changeable, depending on how an observer's position changes. Therefore, there can be different points of view and different visions concerning an object.

The perspective theory developed in its original formulation by Alberti and Brunelleschi is strictly related to a different way to describe objects. The invention of perspective as a theoretical form had enormous consequences not only on arts, but also on other fields of knowledge. The Aristotelian space theory was rejected: the space is an endless field in which we can perceive countless forms and shapes of the same matter. Therefore, the metaphor of the divine being as a sphere should be interpreted in the light of this connection with the perspective theory.[42] Cusanus formulates his metaphor referring to Meister Eckhart's writings in the first book of *De docta ignorantia*,[43] and in chapter 12, Book II, he revises the metaphor of the sphere transferring it to the cosmos. Harries argues that:

---

40. *De docta ignorantia*, II.12.

41. Harries, "The Infinite Sphere," 5–15.

42. Ibid., 7. See Euler, who compares an anonymous fifteenth-century painting kept in the Franciscan monastery of Santa Maria della Pace in Sassoferrato, called "The Three Representatives of the Three Monotheistic Religions Talking together" with Nicholas of Cusa's *Cribratio Alkorani*, in: "An Italian Painting from the Late Fifteenth Century and the *Cribratio Alkorani* of Nicholas of Cusa."

43. *De docta ignorantia*, I.12.

> Cusanus' transference of the metaphor of the infinite sphere from God to the cosmos, far from being "astonishing" was suggested by the metaphor itself. . . . The metaphor expresses thus not only God's transcendence, but also the transcendence of man's intellect. . . . Cusanus would have us understand the cosmos as the infinite mirror of its Creator. But this understanding is only the shadow of another: the comprehended cosmos is the infinite mirror of its creator, of man.[44]

The use of the perspective vision is therefore one of the keys (the *Prinzip der Repräsentation*) for understanding *De docta ignorantia*.[45]

As a principle of knowledge, it recurs in many texts of Cusanus, and is one of the main philosophical themes connected with the influences of mystical philosophy on his thought.[46] The perspective vision allows achieving a different modality of knowledge, which can be considered similar to the intellect. According to Nicholas, knowledge can be either rationally or intellectually achieved, and this process takes place through the *coniectura*. The human mind knows insofar as it measures things by applying its own kind of measurement to the object, and by acknowledging a given proportion, which never attains the intrinsic truth of things.[47] This theme is important in the case of interreligious dialogue and of the sharing among different creeds of a truth capable to support, at a theoretical level, peaceful coexistence.

5. Interreligious Dialogue in the *De docta ignorantia*

The act of knowing moves from the desire to understand reality in its numberless facets, and a paradigmatic example of the plurality of reality is provided by the number of existing religions. In fact, peoples have different faiths,[48] different ways to worship the divine being. However, in Nicholas' opinion, these peoples, as the Gentiles, and so on, were mistaken—*omnes qualiter seducti sint et longe fuerint a veritate praemissa ostendunt*—as all

---

44. Harries, "The Infinite Sphere," 15.
45. Ridenauer, *Pluralität und Rationalität*, 208.
46. See Cuozzo, "Mystice Videre."
47. Riedenauer, "Pluralità di prospettive finite nell'orizzonte dell'infinito." In addition, see Santinello, *Il pensiero di Nicolo Cusano nella sua prospettiva estetica*.
48. *De docta ignorantia*,I.XXV.4–20.

these ways avert them from truth.[49] In the third book of *De docta ignorantia*, Cusanus resumes some themes he had already dealt with: order, harmony and unity. Multiplicity and differences reach their contraction only in infinity. Similarly, individuals, too, are "contracted," or placed on a scale by degrees, where transitions take place according to a hierarchical sequence, from the bottom to the top.[50]

The uniqueness of the human mind lies also in the fact that it is angelic and brutish at the same time, though it is evident that the former definitely stands above the latter.[51]

The human element of the person of Christ transcends intellectual knowledge: the human intellect is potentially in all things, while the divine intellect is in all things in its actual form. Though the human intellect is able to reduce the elements of possibility and contingency in its abstraction process, yet it cannot understand and grasp the highest intellect. Through the person of Christ, man can instead have access to the aspect of both the human and the divine being.

This conception of man's nature, grounded on the firm belief that mind and intellect can understand these different aspects involves also believing that the body has not much to do with the most profound essence of the human being, as its real essence is actually determined by the intellectual and not by the corporeal aspect, according to Cusanus.

It is just the intellectual element which allows the reception of religion. And one of the most debated theses of the intellect concerns the name of God, a discussion that belongs to the sphere of positive theology. Heathens and Christians have always wondered about the names to attribute to the divine and the divinity. This can easily be inferred from the fact that heathen temples are dedicated to a desirable characteristic or to a positive idea like peace.

In Cusanus' vision, this worship base might be often connected with idolatry, especially among common people, who are used to worship the human images of Christ and the saints instead of truth. For most early philosophers this kind of approach to the sacred had to be avoided, as it clearly results from heathen philosophy, in particular from Cicero's *De natura*

---

49. *De docta ignorantia*, I.25, The source of this excerpt is, as Cusanus states, Cicero's *De natura deorum* in which we find: "Vidistine igitur ut a physicis rebus bene atque utiliter inventis tracta ratio sit ad commenticios et fictos deos." Cicero, *De natura deorum*, II, 28, 70.

50. *De docta ignorantia*, III.I;

51. *De docta ignorantia*, III.I.21-27.

deorum. One of the main reasons of the difference between the religious experience of an ordinary man and a philosopher's experience consists in that all religions have two different levels of spirituality: on the one hand, each religion has a more popular level and its rituals; on the other, there is the level of true faith.[52] Cusanus thus finds an essential common characteristic among different religions by shedding light on the element of social cohesion characterizing the religious phenomenon.

6. Conclusions

I tried to explain the way in which Nicholas of Cusa resumes, changes, and in some respects strengthens his pluralistic positions stated in *De concordantia catholica*. If this work shows more evident political traits and tones, *De docta ignorantia* is instead a purely philosophical treatise in which Nicholas develops his ideas on difference and identity by means of the so-called coincidence of opposites. The structure of this treatise as a "conflict-dialogue" (basing on Ritter's definition) is revealed by the positions of Cusanus' opponent and brings to light the profoundly contradictory dynamics at the base of any work written in dialogue dealing with different and opposed philosophical, historical and religious stances. The method through which a system of thought forms is realized using text exegesis, and the themes emerge in the consolidated repetition and in the changes brought by the author throughout his work.

In *De pace fidei*, the themes of difference and identity are further developed and elaborated to converge in the well-known formula "a variety of rites within a single faith."

---

52. Nicholas of Cusa's position about this dual theological understanding level can be found also in his sermons. Some sermons by Cusanus are divided into three parts: one for the men of letters and learning, one addressed to less cultivated persons, and a third part devised for illiterate persons. This different approach emerges in particular in the *exempla*, examples of good behaviors mostly addressed to illiterate persons, and in the references to sources, juridical texts, the Bible, etc. This division of the sermons leads the author to use different styles, different *figurae*; a great deal of *images*, metaphors, similes, analogies. Recent studies on Nicholas of Cusa's sermons are included in "Mitteilungen und Forschungs-Beiträge der Cusanus-Gesellschaft" MFCG, *Die Sermone des Nikolaus von Kues Merkmale und ihre Stellung innerhalb der Mittelalterlichen Predigtkultur, Akten des Symposions in Trier vom 21. bis 23. Oktober 2004*. See also: Costigliolo, "Predicazione e Metafora; il sermone XXI di Nicola da Cusa."

— 4 —

De pace fidei and the Interreligious Dialogue

1. Introduction

IN THIS CHAPTER I shall analyze the sources referring to the Muslim religion Nicholas of Cusa drew from in writing his treatise *De pace fidei*. Of great importance was the use he made of the translation of the Qur'an into Latin and of the anthology of Western writings that studied the Islamic traditions known under the name of Toledan Collection (*Corpus Toletanum*). Availing myself of Thomas Burman's research on Robert Ketton and Mark of Toledo, I aim at pointing out some differences emerging between Ketton's translation of the Qur'an and the use Nicholas of Cusa made of it, for the purpose of underlining the resulting textual misunderstandings, and consequently the misinterpretations of the Islamic culture and civilization. Furthermore, my study continues my previous investigation of the themes of difference and identity tackled by Cusanus, which here intertwine with the concepts of equality and unity. In fact, through the paradigm "unity, equality, and connection," he intends to express not only the trinitarian essence of divinity, but also God's unknowableness. By reverting to one of the most important paradigms contained in *De docta ignorantia*, Cusanus comes gradually to the formulation of ritual-free expression. I shall also point out the different semantic levels in which the text is structured, namely an anthropological, a theological, a philosophical, and a political level, and an analysis of the text will also reveal the *manuductio* method used by Cusanus. Although this methodological process is of the utmost importance, it is even more important to follow, through its modifications and repetitions, the development and the evolution of the concept of difference in Cusanus' works, because, as he affirms, the *manuductio* process is exegetically inherent in the structure itself of the text.

The Western world received in 1453 news of the fall of Constantinople at the hands of the Turks. The climate of general confusion caused by the fall of the *metropolis* profoundly damaged the foundations of the European identity.[1] Enea Silvio Piccolomini,[2] in a letter filled with desperate tones, describes this event as the greatest plague to befall humankind.[3]

2. Sources of *De pace fidei*

Marshall McLuhan states: "the medium is the message."[4] This might describe the new approach to the Islamic religion and culture as an object of in-depth studies, which began developing as soon as the first translation from Arabic of some treatises of science and mathematics began circulating in the Western world.

---

1. Daniel, *Islam and West*, 187–97. "We can still see this mechanism at work in our time. Cracks in identity are best mended by closing ranks against the one, ultimate and common, truly devilish enemy: in this case "the Turks." It becomes an unparalleled, ultimate, almost cosmic struggle: a struggle for life and death, a struggle between (absolute) good and (absolute) evil." It is all the more surprising to hear a conciliatory voice calling for dialogue amidst the cries of dismay and the calls for revenge. Nicholas writes his *De pace fidei* a few months after the fall of Constantinople, almost immediately after he has been told about it. He feels personally and historically-theologically involved, because of his trip to Byzantium for the purpose of achieving a possible reunion between Rome and the Orthodox Christians. This prompts him to write a dialogue pleading for dialogue."

2. Enea Piccolomini, *Der Briefwechsel des Eneas Silvius Piccolomini*.

3. Piccolomini's reaction can be easily understood: from the fall of the Roman Empire, Byzantium had played the role of spiritual center for Christendom. Byzantium was also a multi-cultural and multi-religious city, in which the Greek-Roman culture, Judaism and Christianity lived together: the fall of Constantinople was symbolically intended as the fall of Christianity, which was then going through a difficult period due to the rise of a number of heretical movements and schisms. Cf. De Libera, *La philosophie médiévale*. On the fall of Byzantium, De Libera argues: "On 4 April 1497, the Arabization movement of European culture comes to its first institutional standstill: Nicholas Leonicus Thomaeus (1456–1531) came to Padua to hold the chair of philosophy and for the first time in Europe, Aristotle was taught based on the original Greek text. There is something in common between the fall of Granada and the recovery of the Greek Aristotle: Arab, whether person or language, is wiped out of our heritage. But this movement does not stop here. The expulsion of the Jews wipes out Toledo. There is no more any external debt. Byzantium has died. Greece is still there, *unimpaired*. On these three disappearances, the Renaissance can build its new identities."

4. Cf. McLuhan, *The Gutenberg Galaxy*.

Among the authors who wrote outstanding works focused on the relations between Islam and Christendom, we shall discuss[5] in particular Abelard[6] (1079–1142) and his *Dialogus inter philosophum, Judaeum et Christianum*, and Ramon Lull (or Llull) (1235–1315), who wrote the *Liber de Gentili et tribus Sapientibus*.[7]

Abelard, like Cusanus, wrote his dialogue in a period of conflicts and violence. De Libera defines this dialogue as "a great intercultural work . . . which marks a turning point in the history of Latin philosophy. For the first time, an Arab philosopher argues with a Jew and a Christian, while the author himself acts as an arbitrator."[8] Like *De pace fidei*, Abelard's dialogue is a work of the author's maturity that deals with the theme of rational and intellectual knowledge as an instrument of confrontation between different confessions.

In his *Dialogus inter philosophum, iudaeum, et christianum*, Peter Abelard discusses a problem similar to the one expounded in *De pace fidei* concerning rituals: the practice of faith is expressed in a different way, as the Jew emphasizes in the dialogue with the philosopher.[9] The Jew complains that several precepts, and especially circumcision, are the cause of the isolation and the labors his people must tolerate within the community. The community, in fact, does not consider the practice of circumcision with benevolence, as well as all the prohibitions concerning food Jews impose themselves to comply with their Law. Then, the philosopher asks why do Jews insist on observing the precepts imposed to them, and the Jew answers that these precepts mark the separation between his people and Gentiles, and just for this reason they must be observed.[10] Circumcision prevents marriages between Jewish men and heathen women, and consequently

---

5. This paragraph adapts my article in www.revistamirabilia.com/issues/mirabilia-19-2014-2. I thank *Mirabilia*'s editor for permission to use the article here.

6. Concerning Abelard, see Pinzani, *The Logical Grammar of Abelard*. Orlandi, "Per una nuova edizione del Dialogus di Abelardo."

7. For the Italian edition of Abelard's dialogue, see Abelardo, *Dialogus inter philosophum un giudeo e un cristiano*. For an edition of Lull's works, see Bonner, *Selected Works of Ramon Lull (1232–1316)*. The influences of this issue on later authors were recently studied by Blum, "Salva fide et pace," 527–28.

8. De Libera, *La philosophie médiévale*, Italian edition, 302 ff.

9. Abelard, *Dialogus inter philosophum, iudaeum, et christianum*, 240–46. "Fidem tecum de unius Dei veritate communem habeo; eque ipsum fortassis, ut tu, diligo, et ex operibus, que tu non habes id in super exibeo. Quid mihi hec opera, si non prosint, officiunt, etiam si non sint precepta, quia non sunt prohibita?"

10. Abelard, *Dialogus inter philosophum, iudaeum, et christianum*, 579–85.

ensures that social groups remain divided[11] without any cultural contamination. In Abelard's dialogue, the physical mark of circumcision has therefore a double value: one in connection with tradition, and the other in connection with social and political distinction. Jews distinguish themselves from the rest of the community through an intimate bodily mark weighing on another aspect of life, sexuality, which is particularly intertwined with precepts, obligations, and prohibitions of religious origin. The rite of circumcision clearly shows how some invasive, though intimate practices, do not only have an individual relevance, but also have a broader and extensive significance, being expressions of exercised and suffered powers, dynamics of bio-powers. As Mary Douglas argues: "Rituals mark the form of social relations, and in giving these relations a visible expression, they enable persons to know their own society. Rituals influence the political structure through the symbolic medium of the physical body."[12]

The Jew emphasizes once again the need to observe the precepts, referring to the passage of the Leviticus which reads: "If you walk in my precepts, and keep my commandments, and do them, I will set my tabernacle in the midst of you, and my soul shall not cast you off."[13] The Jew comments: "since our Lord wanted to separate us from the infidels so that we were not corrupted by them, He ordained that we observed those precepts and rites."[14] The Jewish people differentiates itself from the infidels (*infidelibus*) through its precepts (*operum ritibus*), and rites have the power to guarantee our access to salvation and true beatitude, because the prohibitions imposed by the Law aim at preventing sin.[15] Salvation is certain for those who are free from sin, and this purification can be achieved through ritual practices and the observance of precepts. The blessing of the Old Testament is the source of all good things, and the loss of this blessing involves falling into disgrace and danger. In order to try to understand the abominations of

---

11. Cf. Platvoet and van der Toorn, eds., *Pluralism & Identity, Studies in Ritual Behaviour*.

12. Douglas, *Purity and Danger*, 203. "The body is a complex structure: the functions of its different parts and their relations with each other provide a range of symbols for other complex structures. We cannot interpret the rituals concerning excrements, mother's milk, saliva and so on, if we are not prepared to consider the body as a symbol of society, and to see the powers and dangers the social structure is based on reproduced in miniature in the human body."

13. Leviticus 26:3–11.

14. Abelard, *Dialogus*, 843–45.

15. Ibid., 870–73.

Leviticus it is necessary to start from texts, and to understand that the opposition between holiness and abomination is at the base of precepts.[16] The concept of holiness includes also the concepts of separation and integrity: all that is holy is free of contaminations and is pure. Therefore, the Jewish strict dietetic rules aim at preserving purity, and one could even consider these prohibitions as "symbols which every time drove believers to meditate on the unity, purity, and completeness of God. Through the norms of abstention, holiness receives a physical expression at any encounter with the animal kingdom, at any meal."[17] As to Lull's work,[18] its sources cannot be easily determined, and in this case, the identification of sources becomes even more complex because in the prologue the author declares his intention to "follow" the model of the Arab book of the "Gentile." Maybe these words make reference to an Arabic version written by Lull himself, but it seems more likely that the author refers to the work of a twelfth-century Jewish author, Judah Halevi, who wrote the book *Kitab al Khazari* (*Sefer ha-Kuzari*, in Hebrew), which is considered one of the most polemical and well-known medieval works.[19]

Although written in Arabic, the style of this polemical Jewish book is quite different from that of the *Book of the Gentile*, being more closely linked to the style of the *Book of Religions and Philosophical Sects*, written by the twelfth-century Persian historian Muhammad Shahrastani, author of a dialogue among a Muslim, a Jew, and a Christian.[20]

Some passages of Lull's writing seem to draw inspiration from Abelard's *Dialogus inter philosophum, Judaeum et Christianum* and in any

---

16. Douglas, *Purity and Danger*, 94.

17. Ibid., 104.

18. Bonner, *Selected Works of Ramon Lull (1232–1316)*: "To take the second aspect first, it was only natural that Judaism, Christianity, and Islam should feel defensive in each other's presence. All the three were of Near Eastern Semitic origin, all three were revealed religions (or religions "of the book," as the Muslims put it), and all three had major struggles trying to assimilate Greek thought. Moreover, ever since the Jewish diaspora and the Muslim conquest of so much of the Mediterranean basin, they lived in close proximity to one another or, as in the case of Spain, actually intermingling. The intent to convert others was natural under such circumstances." See also: Fidora and Rubio, *Raimondus Lullus*; Johnston, *The Evangelical Rhetoric of Ramon Lull*. On the relation between Cusanus and Lull, see Fidora, Bidese, and Renner, *Ramon Llull und Nikolaus von Kues*, in particular: De La Cruz Palma, "Polemica antiislamica in Lullo e Cusano," 24–40.

19. Yehuda-ha Levi, *Il re dei Khazari*.

20. Shahrastani, *The Book of Religious and Philosophical Sects*. See Fine, *Judaism in Practice*.

case, Lull's dialogue fully belongs to a consolidated tradition.[21] Lull lived in thirteenth-century Spain, a period in which the political and social situation of the country led to an upsurge of apologetic works, as in the span of twenty-two years (1226–48) the Muslim possessions grew so much as to occupy one third of the Iberian peninsula, concentrating in the area of the kingdom of Granada.[22]

Lull did not belong to the Parisian scholasticism, but he undoubtedly knew the *Summa contra Gentiles*, as he declares in his work *Liber de acquisitione Terra Sanctae* written in 1308, though the way in which he succeeded in coming into possession of it is unknown. He had undoubtedly a profound persuasive ability grounded on his firm belief that rhetorical arts are a powerful conversion instrument, and the *Book of the Gentile and the Three Wise Men* is based on the methodology of Art.[23]

This treatise, according to the typical method and structure of the rhetoric art, is an anthology of apologetic arguments. It does not include any particular symbolic references and the mechanism of the text is completely supported by Lull's literary ability and continuous attempt to emphasize the humanity of the four main characters. The book opens with the lamentations of the Gentile and ends with an expression of joy. The moaning of the Jew is caused by the state of slavery of his people, and the statements of the

---

21. See Fidora, Bidese, and Renner, *Ramon Llull und Nikolaus von Kues*.

22. Bonner, *Selected Works of Ramon Lull*, 93–95: "This sudden absorption of new lands had a different effect on the crown of Aragon than on Castile. In the latter, a nation of 3 million conquered some 300,000 people in Andalusia, with the resultant increase of only 10 percent in population; whereas Aragon and Catalonia, with a combined population of half a million, found that in Valencia alone they had taken on 150,000 people, representing an increase of 30 percent. Ideologically, the reaction to this situation in the Crown of Aragon was a peculiarly specific one, set in motion by the Dominicans, as the instigation of their third master general, St. Ramon de Penyafort, and his disciple, Ramon Martì. A brief table of their activity in the field of missions, polemics, and apologetics should give some picture of the situation." Lull was certainly acquainted with the teachings of Ramon Martì, though he did not share his missionary method.

On Muslims' presence in Spain, see Anawati, *Islam e cristianesimo*; Tedeschi, *Cristiani, ebrei e musulmani nel basso medioevo spagnolo*. See Zonta, *La filosofia antica nel Medioevo ebraico*.

23. Bonner, *Selected Works of Ramon Lull*, 97: "Rather than give a general outline of this dependence here, I suggest the reader turn to the introduction to the *Ars demonstrativa* for an idea of the components of the Art, and then use the notes I have provided to the text here for specific points of comparison. In this way he will gradually become aware of how the gentile is built on the structure of the Art, how it uses the Art "to confound the erroneous opinions of unbelievers by means of cogent reasons."

Muslim concern the power the precepts of the Islamic religion exert on life on earth, which is proved by Muslims' possession of the Holy Land.

The dialogue proceeds in a cordial atmosphere. In this sense, Lull intends to offer a discussion pattern, or—as Bonner argues—"perhaps he also hoped in this way to make his Christian convictions more acceptable to his Muslim and Jewish adversaries. His tact even leads him to introduce an ending most surprising in a piece of medieval polemical literature."[24]

Lull's skillful use of rhetoric and his literary and psychological abilities run throughout this work: the resort to the rhetorical art is more evident in book one and book three, while in book two and book four the author's considerations on Islam and Judaism prevail.

As well as the *Book of the Gentile*, Lull wrote other works in defence of the Christian faith, in which he countered the Islamic and Jewish theological theories. However, none of them does jointly consider the three Abrahamic religions as the *Book of the Gentile* does. He undoubtedly judged this work extremely important, as it can be inferred by the number of times he recommends its reading in his later works.[25]

There are different hypotheses on the period in which the *Book of the Gentile* was written.[26] According to Bonner, it was written between 1274 and 1276.[27] Several analogies between the two dialogues *De pace fidei* and the *Book of the Gentile* can be found both as regards their philosophical approach characterized by a considerable openness towards the "other," and by their political and ecclesiastic commitment, though the two books show substantial differences mostly depending on the different periods of their composition. But nonetheless, they share a deep interest in the potential unity of the three different religions, which—as Euler writes—express "a single truth in different networks of the universal space."[28]

The idea of writing a dialogue in which a representative of Islam participated was not a new one in fifteenth-century cultural production, but

---

24. Bonner, *Selected Works of Ramon Lull*, 98: "The Saracen's final description of Paradise, for example, is surprisingly beautiful when one considers that it was written by a man horrified at such a purely sensual conception of Heaven."

25. Ibid., 99: "That his disciple Thomas le Myesier shared the same conviction is evidenced by the pivotal role the work plays in the Electiorium, where it forms the centre piece of the central seventh part, toward which the rest of the anthology is directed, and which deals with "the knowledge and love of god and the salvation of all men."

26. See Fidora, Bidese, and Renner, *Ramon Llull und Nicolaus von Kues*.

27. Bonner, *Selected Works of Ramon Lull (1232–1316)*.

28. Euler, *Unitas et pax*, 160.

undoubtedly, within literary production, dialogues belonged to a minor genre. Muslims were considered by the same standard as heathen peoples, infidels. Their evangelization was therefore considered necessary, and the Crusades called for reconquering the Holy Land and other Christian properties were envisaged as legitimate wars aimed at getting back "stolen" lands. In Muslim lands, Christians' explicit attacks on Muhammad were not very frequent, as the *sharia* prohibited any offence to the Prophet and punished those who offended him by death. In the Christian view, martyrdom suffered under those circumstances might prove even more effective than any evangelization action through sermons. "These attitudes may help explain Christendom's endemic laxity in the deployment of missionaries."[29]

The texts that spread in the Western world the holy writings of Islam are part of the Toledan Collection (*Corpus Toletanum*) dating back to twelfth century. Rober Ketton (1110–1160), archdeacon of Pamplona, completed this collection in 1143 by adding the complete translation of the Qur'an as well as some significant treatises: *Fabulae Sarracenorum, De generatione Mahumet et nutritura eius, Doctrina Mahumet,* and *Risalat*, attributed to Al-Kindi.[30]

No other translations of the Qur'an into Latin were made in Toledo in the following sixty years, and only in seventeenth century was a new and more literal translation published.[31]

Robert Ketton and Mark of Toledo (fl.1193–1216) were the first authors of unabridged translations of the Qur'an from Arabic into Latin.[32]

In 1142, Peter the Venerable, one of the main sources of Cusanus, commissioned not only the Qur'an, but also the apology of Al-Kindi written by an anonymous Middle-East Christian author, and a set of collections or anthologies belonging to the Islamic tradition.[33] Robert Ketton was a member of the team of scholars gathered by Peter the Venerable to prepare

---

29. Izbicki, "The Possibility of Dialogue with Islam in the Fifteenth Century," 178.

30. On the translation of the Qur'an made by Peter the Venerable's team, see: Martinez Gasquez, "Las traducciones latinas medievales del Coran," 491–503.

31. Burman, *Reading the Qur'an in Latin Christendom, 1140–1560,* 14.

32. Ibid. The other translations analyzed by Burman were written in fifteenth and sixteenth century by Gabriel Terrolensis and Egidio da Viterbo (1469–1532), and by Flavius Mithridates (1475–85).

33. Peter the Venerable's work, known as Toledan Collection (or *Corpus Toletanum*), includes *The Apology of Al-Kindi, Chronica Mendosa, Doctrina Mahumet, Liber generationis Mahumet, Summa brevis.* Burman, *Reading the Qur'an in Latin Christendom, 1140–1560,* 15.

the Latin version of the Qur'an, which was entitled *Lex Mahumet* and was drawn up with the help of an almost completely unknown Muslim called Muhammad.[34]

Ketton's translation survived in about twenty-five medieval manuscripts, and was printed first in 1543 and again in 1550.[35] It is of paramount importance to consider that Ketton's version remained the best-known translation in the intellectual circles of Christian Europe until the seventeenth century.[36]

Juan de Segovia,[37] who wrote the first commentary to Ketton's Latin translation, identified several mistakes the author had made in his work, pointing out, for example, that Ketton had inverted in some parts the order in which the Qur'an had been written by overturning the opening words of several passages, and vice versa, that he had distorted the meaning of some Qur'anic terms, and often ignored the explicit sense of the text to express in his translation the sense he considered implicit.[38] In his translation of the Qur'an, Ketton closely followed the most important manuals of rhetoric of his age, and in particular Cicero's *Rhetorica ad Herennium*. Numerous figures of speech are in fact included in the text, such as anaphoras, hyperboles, and a number of parallelisms and similarities. Ketton's translation was considered by contemporaries a work characterized by a high stylistic level.[39]

Ketton was fully aware of the high literary value and elegance of the Arabic language used in the Qur'an. Juan de Segovia studied Ketton's translation and deeply esteemed its style. Over the centuries, Ketton's translation continued to be commended, even if its contents were condemned.

It included some passages derived from the Islamic tradition, among them the texts by Al-Tabarsi.[40] An example of this influence can be found in the translation of Sura 2.192 on the *jihad*, which reads "but if they desist, since God is merciful," whereas in Ketton's translation it reads: "when the

---

34. As repeatedly stressed by Burman, this version of the Qur'an into Latin soon became the most widespread one in the Western world.

35. Burman, *Reading the Qur'an in Latin Christendom*, 89.

36. Ibid., 90.

37. Ibid., 9.

38. Ibid., 93.

39. Ibid., 26–41.

40. Abu Ali Fadal ibn Hassan ibn al-Fadl al-Tabarsi, born in the year 468 of the Muslin calendar, wrote a celebrated commentary to the Qur'an. See Mahmoud Ayoub, *The Qur'an and Its Interpreters*.

enemies shall return to God, he will offer them his pardon." This translation derives from Al-Tabarsi's commentary to this Sura, in which this interpreter argues that the verse "if they desist" should be interpreted as "if they return to God." The same interpretation is supported also by Al-Baydawi and Ibn Kathir.[41]

By the end of the first half of fifteenth century, Juan de Segovia contributed to write a new translation into Latin of the Qur'an, which is contained in a manuscript including two versions of the text, one in Arabic and the other in Castilian.

Both Juan de Segovia and Robert Ketton tackled the Qur'anic text in a quite different way from any other contemporary author who wrote polemical treatises against Islam. A fairly widespread procedure consisted in focusing the attention only on some verses considered particularly relevant, while the rest of the text was usually overlooked.

Robert of Ketton, an English theologian, came to Spain in 1123, driven by his desire to study the Greek and Arab classics who had written on sciences and mathematics. He completed the translation of the Qur'an by 1143, adding a dedicatory letter to Peter the Venerable written in prose and in a very elegant style.

Ketton briefly explains the method used for translating the Qur'an: he wants to provide the raw material (the translation of the Qur'an) on which Peter the Venerable will be able to construct an apologetic work in defense of Christendom, adding that he does not intend to provide a literal translation of the Arab holy book, but rather a translation capable to convey the general sense and significance of this work.[42]

Three generations after Ketton, another translator, Mark of Toledo, undertook a similar project. The archbishop of Toledo, Rodrigo Jimenez de Rada and the archdeacon Mauritius, commissioned Mark to write a new translation, probably because, at that time, Ketton's translation was no longer easily available.

Their request had political aims, as Rodrigo intended to fight against the Arabs established in Spain, and to subject the Iberain peninsula to his authority. Mark was not familiar with the works of the Muslim thinkers, except for some translations of the works by Ibn Tumart (1082–1130).[43]

---

41. Two thirteenth-century commentators of the Qur'an. Burman, *Reading the Qur'an in Latin Christendom*, 38.

42. Ibid., 92.

43. See Constable, *Medieval Iberia*.

Though evidencing a scarce knowledge of the Muslim culture, this Latin version enjoyed some popularity in the Middle Ages, and survived in seven manuscripts, six of which are entitled *Liber Alchorani*.[44] It is important to note that both Mark's and Ketton's translations did consider the Qur'an a holy book, but also a complex work that needed to be tackled through a philological method.

By analyzing the translation method employed by Mark of Toledo (but also by Flavius Mithridate, who lived some centuries later[45]), which may be defined as "literal," as well as the method used by Robert Ketton, which in most cases is one of paraphrase we can better understand Cusanus' approach to the Qur'an, because he had to content himself with those translations, since he did not know the Arabic language.[46]

Concerning the vision of paradise, for example, Christian writers perpetuated an idea of the Muslim paradise as a place of orgiastic practices,[47] because Robert Ketton translated in Sura 22 the word *jiin*, which indicates spiritual beings, with the term "demons."[48] Though Mark of Toledo, too, made a number of translation mistakes, his misinterpretations were however mostly due to his imperfect knowledge of Arabic. Despite his polemical approach, Mark's translation method does not seem particularly affected by his theoretical stance, but rather by the actual problems inherent in a translation from Arabic into Latin.[49]

In Burman's[50] opinion, Mark of Toledo was a great translator, and his translation is compared to the translation of Plato's works made by Leonardo Bruni for the Christian readers.

---

44. Burman, *Reading the Qur'an in Latin Christendom*, 124.

45. Flavius Mithridates was a Jew originating from Sicily, who had converted to the Christian religion. He was one of the teachers of Pico della Mirandola and translated many works from Hebrew into Latin. Burman, *Reading the Qur'an in Latin Christendom*, 18.

46. *Acta Cusana*, Book I, 3.

47. Burman, *Reading the Qur'an in Latin Christendom*, 127.

48. Gardet, *Les hommes de l'Islam. Approche des mentalités*, 35: "God wanted three kinds of beings provided with intelligence: men, jinn, genie, or spirits, elementary beings created of pure fire, the Qur'an reads, and angels created of light, according to the hadith. The Qur'an, word of God, true image of the eternal Qur'an written on the table kept by God, is addressed first of all to men, to teach them all that they must know and practice if they want to fulfill their fate. This could be considered a Qur'anic anthropology."

49. Burman, *Reading the Qur'an in Latin Christendom*, 129.

50. Ibid., 133.

Ketton's translation pursued the same goal. For example, while at verse 12:31 the Qur'an writes that when some Egyptian women saw Joseph, they "exalted him" (in Arabic: *akbarnahu*), Ketton translated this verse into "when those women saw him, they were are menstruating." Ketton deliberately distorts the meaning to stress something disgusting to the eyes of Christian readers, in order to give his translation an apologetic character,[51] thus clearly evidencing the author's strong polemical intentions.[52]

In handling the original Qur'anic text, both Robert Ketton and Mark of Toledo made use of commentaries belonging to the Islamic tradition, and this practice should be brought back not only to explain the meaning of the Qur'anic text, but also to recall the typical medieval habit of studying ancient texts jointly with their commentaries. Thus, the Bible was studied together with the *Postillae* by Nicholas of Lyra, and Aristotle was read jointly with Ibn Rushd's commentaries.[53]

3. Difference and Diversity

Nicholas of Cusa opens his treatise *De pace fidei* (1453)[54] with a strong image. He tells about a man[55] who is informed of the cruel actions and tortures committed by the sultan of the Turks in Constantinople.[56] After few days this man had a vision that made him understand how it was possible to reconcile all the differences that were creating so many deep and painful splits between the world's religions, and how it was possible to obtain peace among religions.[57] To prevent his considerations from getting

---

51. Ibid., 28.

52. Burman sees in Ketton's work an "astonishing ambition," ibid., 23–28.

53. This method was followed also by Cusanus. See Machetta and D'Amico, *El problema del conoscimento en Nicolàs de Cusa*.

54. The Latin quotations have been drawn from the critical edition by Klibansky and Bascour, in Nicolai de Cusa *Opera omnia. De Pace Fidei*, vol. VII.

55. Gaia explains that it is the same Nicholas Cusanus who in 1437 stayed in Constantinople, while the pope's envoys invited the emperor to attend the Council of Ferrara for the unity of the church. Gaia, *Opere religiose*, 619, n.2.

56. This event is the seizure of Constantinople on 29 May 1453, reported in some letters written by Cardinal Isidore of Kiev, who witnessed it, and by Cardinal Bessarion to the doge Francesco Foscari (Bessarionis Epistulae, n. 29, in: Mohler, *Aus Bessarions Gelehrtenkreis*, 475–77), as well as by Enea Piccolomini, bishop of Siena: Gaia, *Opere religiose*, 619, n.1.

57. *De pace fidei*, I, 4: "in religione perpetuam pacem convenienti."

lost, that pious man decided to record the fruit of his vision so that those who had the power to decide on such important matters could treasure it and bear it in mind.

Nicholas begins his narration by explaining that the protagonist had been brought through his vision to a region beyond this world, where the deceased, gathered in the assembly of the "heavenly beings" and before the throne of the Almighty, were discussing whether an agreement among all the different religions was possible on earth. Listening to their words, the King of Heaven and Earth said that some messengers had reported to him that the oppressed suffered many pains and that the cause of such suffering depended, in most cases, on the differences among religions. Therefore, the King called to the front of the assembly those blessed beings who had reported those laments. Immediately all those beings hurriedly responded to the call of their heavenly sovereign, appearing in the vision as spirits and guardians of each nation and religion of the world.[58]

As soon as the assembly met, an archangel offered an invocation in which he asked the King of the Universe what was lacking in every creature to which He had given a rational spirit, "*ut in eo reluceat ineffabilis virtutis tuae ymago* (so that in it the ineffable virtue of Thy image may shine)." These creatures, the archangel observes, seemed incapable of understanding the end of their life, although they could develop it through an act of supreme love capable of bringing them back to their natural home, next to their Creator. The archangel explains that among the great crowd of men who populate the earth, only a very scant minority of them have time and ease to use the freedom granted to them to get back to their origin; all others, who represent the majority, are obliged to live troubled lives, full of worries and misery, and cannot devote themselves to reflection.[59] Therefore, a way in which persons can seek the hidden God is needed, that is to say, a path by which they are able to understand God's unknowability. Human nature is inclined to defend customs and habits as truth, and this hinders humankind's ability to observe and think. Thus, everyone considers his own tradition or religion the best.[60]

The central theme of the dialogue—the problem of difference and diversity—already emerges in the first chapter of the first book of *De pace fidei*. The difference in rites and confessions generates conflicts and war,

58. It is an image drawn from the Old Testament (see Deut 32:8; Dan 10:13).
59. *De pace fidei*, I, 5.
60. *De pace fidei*, I, 4–5.

which inspires Nicholas's interest in understanding the origin and mechanisms of differences. Nicholas's modernity consists in his analysis of diversity from a social and political point of view. Indeed, not only does he develop his discourse from a theological and philosophical point of view but he also includes different semantic levels in his treatment. According to Nicholas, the concept of diversity and difference in the social reality can be expressed by the following relation: diversity and difference are constitutive and necessary for the community, and *varietas* is nothing but the consequence of *diversitas*. These two aspects of the community originate in the creation of groups, because the human being needs to join his fellows in order to guarantee his own survival. "What does a living being seek but living? And what does the existent seek but existing?"[61] Nicholas refers to this basic principle, rather than to the "social nature" of man, to guide his readers to understand the meaning of *varietas*. There are lots of men, they are a multitude: their proliferation on earth (their capacity to reproduce in spite of wars, calamities, and illnesses) is made possible by the survival instinct within each of them. *Diversitas* is unavoidable and in fact necessary. It is realized both inside and outside the community, or between different communities, because—in Nicholas' opinion—God initially placed at the head of his people different kings and regents, in whom he infused the gift of prophecy. Many of them, in the exercise of the office assigned to them, were responsible for educating the uncultured people and making the people accept the laws imposed upon them. The archangel speaking in Nicholas's work ends with the observation that God also sent different prophets and masters to different nations and periods, and this gave rise to differences of opinions.[62]

The archangel then urges the Creator of the Universe to rescue humankind, which finds itself in such a difficult situation because of the love all people feel for Him, in whom everyone identifies the good and the true. Through the words of the archangel, Nicholas goes as far as to claim the possibility of coexistence of different rites within a single religion.[63] There is only one God and, even though it is impossible to remove the difference in rites, because their variety itself represents a boost to devotion, we must nevertheless recognize the existence of a single religion.

61. *De pace fidei*, I; Italian translation by Gaia, 622.
62. *De pace fidei*, I, 6.
63. *De pace fidei*, I, 7. "Si sic facere dignaberis, cessabit gladius et odii livor, et quaeque mala; et cognoscent omnes quomodo non est nisi religio una in rituum varietate."

After the archangel finishes speaking, Nicholas continues his account of the vision. All inhabitants of heaven unanimously bowed down before the Almighty King who, sitting on his throne, begins to speak. He explains that he had created man and provided him with freedom so that, through it, he could finally rejoin Him. But man chose another way and became ensnared by the ignorance of the prince of darkness; man gave himself up to the impulses of sensible life, which unavoidably made him depart from his spiritual and divine path.

4. Wisdom

Nicholas continues his account by relating what these various representatives said. The Greek speaks first, after the Word. He begins with the observation that God is the only one who can bring all religions back to a peaceful and harmonious unity. He maintains that all representatives of all nations must be taught about the way in which religious unity can be achieved, bearing in mind how difficult it is for any nation to accept a different faith from that it had traditionally professed and supported. The Word responds by saying that it is a question not of changing one's faith but, rather, of assuming a single identical religion in all religions. So just as a single original wisdom existed, there was also a single original religion, because before any plurality there is unity.[64]

The Greek and the Word agree on the existence of a single Wisdom. They agree that all that man can behold has come by virtue of that Knowledge, which is the origin of all sensible things and the perpetual nourishment of the intellect.[65] In fact, though the spirit can approach truth and become increasingly close to Wisdom, this truth and Wisdom remain absolute and never attainable by a human being. In Nicholas of Cusa's account, this first discussion ends with some considerations of the Word, which affirms that its interlocutors have entered the straight and narrow path to reach the goal to which everybody should aspire. Though professing different religions, they assume in this difference a single reality they call Wisdom.

After the Word's speech concludes, Nicholas has the Italian speak. He maintains that there is no word outside Knowledge, which encloses all things. The Word then asks the Italian whether maintaining that all things are created by Knowledge or by the Word has the same meaning.

64. *De pace fidei*, IV, 11.
65. *De pace fidei*, IV, 13.

The Italian replies that ultimately, Word and Knowledge are equivalent.[66] The Word then asks whether the kind of Knowledge all are talking about is God or a creature. The Italian answers that since all creatures originate from Knowledge, the Creator necessarily coincides with Knowledge.[67] The discussion continues up to the moment in which both the Word and the Italian man agree that Knowledge is eternity and that, since there is unity before plurality, there is no possibility that several eternities may exist. This leads them immediately to conclude that since Knowledge is God, "*simplex, aeternus, principium omnium* (the simple and eternal principle of all things)," and all agree on it, they must therefore necessarily agree on the faith in a single God.

Nicholas lets then the Arab "come on stage."[68] The Arab in fact agrees with the conclusions of the Word and the Italian man. He adds that, in his opinion, all men by nature long for Knowledge, because it is the life of the intellect, which in turn can keep alive only if it feeds on truth and on the word of life, that is to say, on its intellectual bread—Knowledge. The Word follows the Arab in his reasoning and ends by saying that men assume the existence of a universal Knowledge, which coincides with a single God.[69]

Subsequently, the Arab introduces a new question. He refers to the possibility for those who worship many gods to reconcile their polytheism with the theses of the philosophers who believe instead in the existence of a single God. The Word replies that those men who worship many gods in fact unconsciously adore the Divinity those gods represent, namely, a principle which pre-dates those gods. This Divinity is a single—not many-sided—principle for all gods. The Arab expresses his agreement, adding that it would be absurd to believe in several prime principles, an error no people has ever incurred, because even polytheism assumes a single prime cause.[70] It is difficult to abolish the worship of gods, however, especially

---

66. *De pace fidei*, V, 13.

67. *De pace fidei*, V, 14.

68. As Gaia argues, the Arab, and then, in particular, the Persian, the Syrian, and the Hindu represent the philosophic schools of Islam. We should remember that the great Middle Eastern philosophers were not Arab but were Persians, such as Alfarabi, Avicenna, and Al-Ghazali. Gaia, *Opere religiose*, 629, n.15.

69. *De pace fidei*, VI, 15.

70. *De pace fidei*, VI, 16–17. In this regard, the Word argues that "si igitur omnes qui plures deos venerantur respexerint ad id quod praesupponunt, scilicet ad deitatem quae est causa omium, et illam uti ratio ipsa dictat in religionem manifestam assumpserint, sicut ipsam implicite colunt in omnibus quos deos nominant, lis est dissoluta."

because the people believe they can attain salvation through their cult. The Word replies that a remedy can be found: educating the people to pursue their salvation in the Creator.

5. Equality and Unity

Nicholas of Cusa next brings into the dialogue a Hindu, who asks about the proper attitude towards statues and sacred images.[71] The Word answers that when sacred images do not distract or prevent people from worshipping the only God, they should not be condemned; but when they induce belief that these sacred images made of stone include something of the Divinity, they must be destroyed. The Hindu agrees with the Word but provocatively adds that, in his opinion, it will be easier to demolish idolatry than to convince idolatrous peoples of the dogma of the Trinity. The Word replies that unity lies in eternity and in equality, and through this very simple connection it is possible to understand the Trinity, the prime principle of everything.[72] Through the example of the Trinity, as presented by the Word, Nicholas proves the plurality intrinsic to the divine nature itself. The Word talks about the divine nature as an endless, eternal, single and triune entity. God, the principle of the universe, is one, while creatures are numerous, separate, and differ from one another. The multiplicity of creation must be brought back to the one and eternal prime principle, and hence every inequality is rooted in the eternal and creative equality.[73] Nicholas has his protagonists argue the problem of equality from a theological and "creatural" point of view: equality is connected to a human condition that is "equal" for all subjects: if men are "creaturely" driven to their self-preservation, they perpetuate the difference inherent in social groups, because otherwise they would either live isolated, and consequently perish, or they would kill each other and disappear. Therefore, it is unavoidable not only to accept *diversitas* but also to create and produce different forms of existence, different religions, different usages and customs, and different ceremonies and rituals.

The Hindu then remarks how difficult it is to divert the people from their deep-rooted idolatry, because they believe that idols can really offer responses. The Word replies: responses come not from the idols but,

---

71. *De pace fidei*, VII.
72. *De pace fidei*, VII, 21.
73. *De pace fidei*, VII, 21.12–15–1; 4.

rather, from the priests.⁷⁴ Priests formulate a response based on the motion of the heavenly bodies and show the worshippers this result as if it were a divine answer. This statement reflects Nicholas's own position: the moral uprightness of a reformer, a man who aims to root out the heresies and non-orthodox rites that were spreading in his age. Some words in Nicholas's work recall very closely Gerson's stylistic rigor and a continuous attempt to refer any behavior and any word to the strict orthodoxy of the *sola fide* (faith alone).

Nicholas makes critical use of the works of Eusebius and Hermes Trismegistus to express in a convincing manner the trinitarian nature of God. God is the principle of the universe, and this universe comprises multiplicity, inequality, and a division of roles. This mathematical pattern derives from the school of Chartres⁷⁵ and can be turned into the scheme *unitas-aequalitas-nexus*,⁷⁶ its sources being Pseudo-Dionysius the Aeropagite's works and Moses Maimonides' *Dux neutrorum*.⁷⁷

Through the paradigm of unity, inequality, and connection, Nicholas aims to express not only the trinitarian essence of the divine but also God's unknowability. In *De docta ignorantia*, Nicholas had earlier argued about the trinity of the universe. In his opinion, everything descends from the divine unity. Possibility descends from the divine unity, as do mutability and alterity. The unity itself of the universe is triune, because it is formed by possibility, necessity, and connection. These terms are Nicholas's reformulation of all that can be philosophically turned into the triad: power, act, and connection.⁷⁸ Nicholas had also stressed the incomprehensibility of the trinitarian dogma in his sermon *Dies sanctificatus* (delivered in Mainz in 1445), where he stated that "we believe that God is one and triune, but its unity and trinity are incomprehensible to us."⁷⁹

At this point in the dialogue in *De pace fidei*, Nicholas calls a Chaldean⁸⁰ into the discussion. He underlines that the arguments expressed in

---

74. *De pace fidei*, VII, 19.1–7.
75. *De pace fidei*, Italian edition, n.634.
76. *De pace fidei*, VII, 21.9–15; 1–15.
77. Gaia, *De pace fidei*, Italian translation in *Opere religiose*, 20.
78. *De docta ignorantia*: II, 7.
79. *Dies sanctificatus*, 680.
80. The Chaldean represents a conception close to the Arabs' one (and in fact, Chaldeans live in the Islamic region of Mesopotamia). He has nothing to do with the Christian Chaldeans Cusanus talks about in the *Cribratio*. Gaia, *Opere religiose*, 635, n.23.

the dialogue he has just listened to may be easily understood by learned men but might at the same time prove very difficult for ordinary people. He then asks the Word whether God is one and triune in power. This question offers Nicholas the opportunity to make the Word reply that God is the absolute power of all powers, since He is almighty. Affirming that His power is triune means that God himself is triune, in the sense that power and reality are the same thing in God. God, ultimately, contains unity, which is the entity, the equality, and the connection between them. The power of unity, as Nicholas makes the Word explain, gives all existing things their unity; the power of equality makes all existing things become equal to themselves, that is to say, it fixes all things in their form; while the power of connection unifies and connects anything.[81] Once again, Nicholas reverts to the concept of unity as the prime concept of anything, explaining through the words uttered by the Word that, since man is evoked from not being, there is, by order, first the unity of man, then the equality of that unity or entity: if there is no other equality but the unity of equality, and no other connection but the connection of unity and equality, as a consequence there is no essential distinction in the Trinity. The only difference would consist in the relation existing among unity, equality, and connection. Therefore, those who maintain that God is triune do not deny that He is one when they understand that this Trinity is connected to the simplest unity.[82]

After hearing the Word's explanation, the Chaldean, declaring himself satisfied and convinced, introduces a new doubt about the ability of Arabs to understand the simultaneous presence of the Father, the Son, and the Holy Ghost. The Word replies that some people call the Father unity, the Son equality, and the Holy Ghost connection,[83] and that the endless fecundity of the uncreated Trinity is expressed in it. An image of the Trinity can be found in the unity of the essence of the human mind, which includes mind, knowledge, and love or will. The mind can develop intelligence and knowledge by itself, and will and love derive from them.[84]

The discussion between the Chaldean and the Word reveals Nicholas's understanding of the difficulty most ordinary people have in understanding

---

81. *De pace fidei*, VIII, 23.

82. *De pace fidei*, VIII, 24.

83. As Gaia explains, Nicholas expresses here the Christian Trinity based on the philosophical pattern of *unitas, equalitas, nexus*, developed in particular by the School of Chartres, in which this formula played a relevant role. Gaia, *Opere religiose*, 638, n.29.

84. *De pace fidei*, VIII, 25–26.

these matters. Being obliged to deal with their mere survival, most ordinary people do not have time to devote themselves to speculative activities.[85] How is it possible, the discussion continues, to make this understanding, which is so noble but also so difficult, available to all? The Chaldean argues that the topics he is discussing with the Word can be understood only by learned men, as they go beyond the cognitive capabilities of ordinary people (*communem vulgum*). The Trinity is a difficult subject also for scholars to understand, and it is a matter of much discussion and debate. Nicholas uses the metaphors of love and the lover to illustrate the divine Trinity. Here he constructs the text in the way he constructed his sermons, the third part of which was always dedicated to the people and completely focused on parables, *exempla*, and/or ornamental figures of the discourse, because he deemed it necessary to resort to a figurative way of reasoning to communicate his theological concepts to the common people (*communem vulgum*).

Continuing his exposition of the trinitarian dogma, Nicholas adapts some texts of the school of Chartres, of St. Thomas Aquinas, and of Albertus Magnus to illustrate the theme of *potentia* in relation to *unitas*.[86] Once man is created, he expresses his nature through the form of unity. Unity, in turn, expresses itself through equality, by which man's unity is evoked.[87] All this must be brought back to the primary idea that God, being almighty, is the absolute power of all powers.

The discourse of *De pace fidei* is not easy to understand, despite Nicholas of Cusa's efforts to divulge the mysteries of faith. It assumes, in fact, an in-depth knowledge of theological, philosophical, anthropological, and historical matters, and from this point of view, the work is addressed to a restricted sphere of scholars. Therefore, in this case, we can talk about an internal communication style for a select audience, quite different from the communicative structure of his sermons, which were often addressed to an audience of illiterate believers.

6. The Metaphor of the King

In the dialogue with the Persian, intended to be a representative of Islam, Nicholas tackles the problem of Trinity. How can God—the Muslim asks—become a non-God, a man? The eternal cannot be temporal, the infinite

---

85. *De pace fidei*, I.
86. See Chenu, *La Teologia nel dodicesimo secolo*.
87. *De pace fidei*, Italian edition, 636.

cannot be finite. Christians too, he asserts, wonder about this issue, and admit that the coexistence of two opposing entities is not possible.[88] The Christians the Persian is talking about are the Nestorians of eastern Syria, who belong to the Persian Empire, and the Monophysites of western Syria. The presence of Nestorian Christians in the Islamic Middle-East had already been reported by Marco Polo. Moreover, Nicholas would later (1460–61) deal with the problem of Islam in his *Cribratio Alkorani*, by arguing that the Muslim religion derives from the heretical Nestorian sect.[89] In *De pace fidei*, Nicholas has the dialogue continue from a Christological point of view. He has the protagonists point out affinities between Christianity and Islam, because the latter, though it considers Christ a sublime prophet, does not admit he is the Son of God, in that God is one and undivided. To exalt the prophetic role of Christ, the Persian resorts to a simile on regality.[90] Through this political metaphor, the Persian wants to underline that Christ's nature cannot become divine but remains human, just as the word of God is spread by many prophets but belongs only to God. In the latter case, the human essence of the prophets does not turn into divine just because they speak God's word. Peter replies that although this simile is quite appropriate, we must not think of Christ as just words, but must think of him as similar to the king's heir. The Persian replies by stressing that father and son are not a single person but two different persons, and therefore it is impossible to consider God and Christ as a single entity.

Nicholas resolves this paradox by resorting to the concept of *potential*, which derives from Thomas Aquinas' theology.[91] Through an analogical way of reasoning, Nicholas maintains that adoption is based on the principle of filiation or sonship, and because of this principle an adopted person can participate in the inheritance of the kingdom. An adopted son is not separated from but exists in the same hypostasis with a natural son. This concept of filiation and adoption is advanced also by Nestorians, but, unlike Nestorians, Nicholas supports the divine nature of Christ and not only his participation in the divine through grace. This metaphor makes use of a cognitive process in which there is a definite margin of difference between sensible things and the thing in itself. This

---

88. *De pace fidei*; XI, 30 10–15

89. Gaia, *Opere religiose*, n. 44, 644.

90. *De pace fidei*; XI, 32.6–12.

91. Tommaso d'Aquino (Thomas Aquinas), *Summa theologica*, III, q. 2 a. 2. ad 3. *De pace fidei*, XI, 34.7–11.

process is expounded in *De docta ignorantia*,⁹² as well as in *De filiatione Dei* (1445) and *De visione Dei* (1453).⁹³

Human nature is placed at the top of God's sensible creation and slightly below the angelic nature. This happens, in Nicholas's opinion, because the human nature contains the intellectual and the sensible nature; it encompasses all possible worlds. Therefore, the ancients called it a microcosm. The meaning of microcosm has a strong spiritual value in Nicholas; it refers to the hypostatic union process, which is the assimilation of the human with the divine. Using the concept of hypostasis in connection with that of *potentia* (power), Nicholas affirms that the *potentia* of the king is a substantial idea from which it is possible to draw real and hereditary power. It is indeed necessary to disregard the difference between the regal dignity of the father and regal dignity of the son, because there is only one regal power.⁹⁴

In the dialogue with the Persian Nicholas introduces another theme concerning the Arabs' perception of the figure of Christ. Muslims recognize that Christ raised the dead, and performed many miracles.⁹⁵ Nicholas knew that those legends came to the Arabs through the apocryphal Gospels, and he will later resume this issue in his *Cribratio Alkorani*. This process is part of the *manuductio*, which disclose affinities with the position one wants to defend in the doctrine expounded by an interlocutor.

7. The Psychological Foundations of Faith

At this point in the dialogue presented in *De pace fidei*, the German intervenes, objecting that the considerations expounded up to that moment were certainly excellent, but all of them had considered neither happiness nor the different opinions about it. Therefore, he explains, the Arabs' law written in the Qur'an makes carnal and eternal promises, while the Gospel promises men that they will take on an angelic form, and the law of the Jews makes temporal promises concerning sensible goods. Peter then asks him whether, in his opinion, there is a good in this world for which desire does not diminish but instead continuously grows. The German answers that desire for the goods of intellect never weakens, unlike desire for temporal

---

92. *De docta ignorantia*; III.III.3–4–12.
93. *De filiatione Dei* is included in Nicolai de Cusa *Opera omnia*: Opuscula 1.
94. See Benveniste, *Le Vocabulaire des institutions indo-européennes*.
95. *De pace fidei*, XI, 41.1–4.

goods, in pursuit of which men miserably belittle themselves. Reverting to the example of the Qur'an, Peter points out that many of the pleasures it promises should be understood symbolically, not literally, and many of them, such as floods of wine and honey or lots of beautiful women, were only conceived as a way to dissuade people from idolatry and drive them to long for heaven. Furthermore, the Qur'an not only does not condemn but even praises the Gospel, thereby conveying that the happiness promised by the Gospel is not less than corporeal happiness.

To conclude, Peter says he finds no insurmountable obstacle to the attainment of an agreement in those different opinions about happiness. Having heard those words, however, the German brings forward the example of the Jews, who do not understand the promise of the kingdom of heaven, but only the promise of temporal things. He asks how it is possible to convince them of the opposite. Peter reassures him by explaining that, as a matter of fact, Jews deny neither eternal life nor the possibility to attain it, because otherwise none of them would die for the law. But the happiness they expect is not expected for the deeds of the law—because their law does not promise happiness—but rather for the faith that assumes Christ.[96]

The German raises then the question of the idea of happiness in the different religions: for Muslims, for example, the happiness of heaven is a carnal reward. Peter answers that we must try to rightly understand the Qur'anic metaphor, as it shows that in the state of blessedness, all desires are satisfied. Muhammad expressed himself in this way so as to allow even ordinary people to understand the truth concerning conditions in the afterworld. He continues to explain that desire drives the subject to long for truth as the expression of the happiness in eternal life. Happiness results from its union with truth, in agreement with Thomas Aquinas' perspective.

The Islamic description of heaven was one of the most difficult aspects for medieval Christians to understand, because it is described as a place of sensuous pleasures. In *De pace fidei*, the German raises the question of the difference between the Christian and the Muslim conceptions of afterlife. He asks, "Why does the Qur'an condemn during our life the sensuous pleasure it promises in heaven?" The Christian medieval tradition used this contradiction against Muhammad and the Qur'an. But according to

---

96. *De pace fidei*; XV, 50.1–5. Religion has its origin in man's longing for happiness. In this longing the problem of religious differences is grounded. We read, in fact, in the dialogue with the German who argues about happiness: the Gospel promises the taking on of an angelic form, that is to say, it promises that men will become like the angels, who have nothing carnal.

Nicholas, the Qur'anic text intends to prove that ordinary and uncultured persons need a description of heaven capable of attracting them towards religion. Nicholas quotes Avicenna, who in any case preferred the intellectual happiness of the vision of God and truth,[97] and returns to this theme also in his *Cribratio Alkorani*.[98]

Nicholas affirms that the hope for happiness in the afterlife is so strong "that it goes beyond all that can be described or said."[99] It is the ultimate desire beyond which there is nothing more desirable, and this is not a problem that will preclude agreement among all religions. In *De docta ignorantia* Nicholas wrote that men's belonging to different religions contributes to form different opinions. All that is praiseworthy according to one opinion may not be considered praiseworthy from another point of view,[100] but the hope for happiness in the afterworld represents a common point of extraordinary cohesive strength.

8. Rituality: The Different and the Ridiculous

At this point, Nicholas introduces a new interlocutor, the Tartar, who notes a number of differences among the diverse religions. He mentions, for example, that for some people it is possible to marry only one woman, while others admit concubinage; or that some people practice circumcision and others scar their face with burns. One of the habits the Tartar considers especially abominable[101] refers to the Christians who, in their sacrificial act, go as far as to eat and drink the body of the one they worship. The Tartar asks how is it possible to make religious persecutions cease when the difference in rites, which is a real and necessary thing, creates enmity, hatred, and wars.[102] Paul, who is defined as *doctor gentium*, speaks after Peter and replies that it is necessary to prove that the salvation of the soul can be achieved not by virtue of what a man has done but by virtue of his faith. Only in this way will the difference in rites cease to be a problem, since it will be interpreted only as a tangible sign of the truth of faith.[103]

97. Avicenna, *Metaphysica* X, 3.
98. *Cribratio Alkorani*, II, 18.
99. Gaia, *Opere religiose*, 661.
100. *De docta ignorantia*; III.8.
101. *De pace fidei*, XVI, 51.
102. *De pace fidei*, XVI, 51.
103. *De pace fidei*, XVI, 52. "Signa autem mutationem capiunt, non signatum."

Nonetheless, the Tartar is not completely satisfied. So Nicholas, through the Tartar's questions, gives Paul the opportunity to solve another problem: how can faith lead to salvation? Paul's answer is long and complex and starts from the assumption that when God grants something he does so on grounds of pure liberality and grace. Those who receive grace do so because the Almighty gives to those who want precisely what they want, on condition that all who receive a gift from God believe in him. The Tartar then points out to Paul that when God promises, he must keep his promises, and this makes the believer be justified more by the promise than by faith. This is not true, Paul replies. He mentions, as an example, the promise God made to Abraham, according to which all his descendants would be blessed. But if Abraham had not believed in God—Paul continues—he would have obtained neither the justification nor the promise. The Tartar agrees with Paul in this regard, and asks "what God actually promised Abraham?"

Paul reminds him that God promised to give Abraham, through Isaac, an offspring in which all the peoples were blessed, and this promise was made when it was impossible that his wife Sarah could become pregnant and give birth to a child. After this promise was made and thanks to his faith, Sarah gave birth and Abraham could hug his firstborn, Isaac. Later on—Paul continues—God asked Abraham to offer his only heir in sacrifice. Abraham agreed to do so, being sure that God would have kept his promise despite the death of his son, who would have come to life again. Thus Abraham was rewarded for his faith through Isaac's offspring.[104]

When the Tartar asks which such offspring was, Paul promptly answers "*Christus.*" From Christ, indeed, all nations receive God's blessing, which leads them to the hope of attaining eternal life. Here the author of *De pace fidei* closes the loop of his reasoning and makes Paul affirm that, by promising in Christ the blessing of eternal happiness, God drives us to believe in Him, as Abraham did, so that, through faith, we can achieve eternal life.

The Tartar certainly seems impressed by Paul's words, but he nonetheless expresses his doubts on the possibility to lead the Tartars, whom he defines as an uncultured people, to understand this truth and to believe in Christ as the only way to achieve happiness. Faced with the Tartar's perplexity, Paul answers that both the Arabs and the Christians believe in the

---

104. *De pace fidei*, XVI, 53.

figure of Christ as prophet of the peoples.[105] Finally, the Tartar declares that he is absolutely convinced and satisfied with Paul's explanations. But he has still doubt about whether faith is enough. Paul replies that without faith nobody can be liked by God, and this faith must be shaped, or expressed, through observance of the commandments. The Tartar objects, however, since each religion maintains that it has received its commandments through its messiah—Moses for the Jews, Muhammad for the Arabs, and Jesus for the Christians; he asks whether therefore, it is possible to reach a common harmony.[106]

God's commandments, Paul reminds, are few, and they are known and shared by all peoples, who, in fact, agree upon believing in God and allowing their behavior to be guided by love for their neighbors. Though agreeing upon both issues, the Tartar replies that the rites of the various religions differ considerably from each other, and those who do not practice circumcision will hardly be able to contain their laughter at those who do practice it. Circumcision is not necessary to salvation, Paul counters, although it certainly helps believers to preserve their faith.[107] Since the greatest part of the world does not practice circumcision, he advises the minority to conform to the majority "*(ad) pacem servandam* (to keep peace)." If this adaptation is too difficult, it would be acceptable to tolerate different rites.

Decorte analyzes part XVI of *De pace fidei*, where Nicholas describes the dialogue between the Tartar man and Paul. Decorte focuses on the term *deridere*; this verb indicates, in his opinion, a crucial point in the treatment of the comparison between religions quite different from one another—in this case, the Christian religion and the monotheistic religion of the Tartars, who deride the rites of the Christians, the Arabs, and the Jews, namely the Eucharist, circumcision, and baptism. Decorte writes:

> Amidst the deafening cries for revenge in the form of a crusade against the Turks, Nicholas is a lone voice crying for peace. During his very first intervention, of all people he has the much-hated Turk say the simple Tartars do worship the one God as the supreme Being, but that they laugh at circumcision, and are appalled at the Christians consuming the body and blood of their God: "They devour Him whom they worship." The problem of tolerance is not that we have different opinions, but that we think of the

---

105. *De pace fidei*, XVI, 54.
106. *De pace fidei*, XVI, 55.
107. *De pace fidei*, XVI, 56.

other as incomprehensible, i.e., either as ridiculous or appalling and abhorrent.[108]

Nicholas analyzes the principle of recognition of differences and diversity through the method of dialogue and exchange of opinions. He begins his argumentation by pointing out some rituals of the Christian people, such as marriage and baptism, which are laughed at by followers of other religions.[109] Ridiculing, belittling, and laughing are all modes that concern a very common attitude towards alterity, an "inborn" mechanism of defense. According to Nicholas, however, there is no "best" rite, because it expresses the religious thought of an individual or a community.[110]

From a highly speculative point of view, we should remember that the theory of conjecturality is decisive for Nicholas's model. Man must be aware that he cannot attain absolute truth, because truth is incomprehensible for the human being, insofar as he is finite mortal. Nicholas's theory leads to the paradox[111] that the value of a position or an idea is in inverse proportion with the possibility it is understood. As a consequence, a creed assumed as infallible is false just because of such a position. In addition, an absolute claim to be the truth leads to conflict and intolerance, because, according to the Aristotelian non-contradiction principle, if A detains the truth, and B differs from A, then B is false. Claiming to hold the truth is at the base of an attitude of distrust and fear of the "other." If people became aware of the ineffability of absolute truth, then they would also understand the arbitrariness of such a stance. Through this awareness, it is therefore possible to come to a stance according to which it is unnecessary that Christians become Muslims and vice versa. Conversions cannot solve the problem of religious conflicts. It is sufficient that the followers of both

---

108. See Decorte, "Tolerance and Trinity," 109.

109. *De pace fidei*; XVI, 54.15–20; 1.9.

110. Decorte, "Tolerance and Trinity," 113: "The animosity or bad intent of the other is no longer a characteristic coming from the other but a characteristic that falls to the other because he takes it from me. The other directs himself to me. René Girard appears to be a pronounced representative of this type of thinking about peace and war, with his theory about the mimetic origins of desire that necessarily lead to conflicts and violence. According to this theory my will and that of the other collide, not because they are different, i.e., because the other is the source of a will that wells up in him and differs from my will, which leads to conflict. It proposes that my desire and that of the other collide because they are the same, i.e., the other is not the source and the origin of his own desire, he only mimics my desire. He copies my desire, he wants the same things I want and this causes conflict."

111. Decorte, "Tolerance and Trinity," 115.

religions mutually commit themselves to attain the consciousness of their "learned ignorance," that is to say, a conjectural approach to truth without believing they can completely detain or attain it.

9. Tolerance

Nicholas had already expressed his idea of tolerance towards other religious confessions in his letters focusing on the Hussite problem.[112] The same idea of tolerance is expressed also in *De concordantia catholica* (1433).[113] But what does tolerance mean?[114] Can we talk about the concept of tolerance during the Middle Ages in the same way as we intend it today? The meaning of this word underwent many semantic changes over time. It originally derives from the Latin verb *tolerare* (to suffer), but it is also in semantic connection with the verb *tollere*. In the specific case of Nicholas's work, it is perhaps incorrect to talk about tolerance with the meaning that has come to us as from the sixteenth century, after the Reformation and the religious wars. According to Vescovini,[115] the concept of peace and faith in Nicholas cannot be referred to any one of the most common ideas of tolerance accepted today—from the general concept by which we define the peaceful coexistence of different confessions to the statement of individual freedom of conscience of the so-called spiritual relativism. J. Koch[116] underlines that tolerance is the child of Enlightenment and is based on a rational natural religion and indifference towards all positive religions. According to Koch,

---

112. See Nicolai de Cusa, *Opera Omnia*, Opuscula III, Fasciculus 2 Bohemica.

113. See Watanabe, "Nicholas of Cusa and the Idea of Tolerance": Watanabe argues that the theme of tolerance can be found also in other works by Cusanus, and not only in *De pace fidei*. This seems to confirm the thesis of Cusa's work project grounded first on cosmological and philosophical, and then on political and religious bases in relation to the problem of dialogue and comparison among different religions and cultures. "This paper is not primarily concerned with the question whether Nicholas was or not an advocate of religious tolerance, nor does the writer wish to minimize the influence Nicholas of Cusa exercised on the later thinkers on the question of tolerance. It will rather then stress the fact in any examination of his views on religious pluralism and tolerance, not only his ideal expressed in the *De pace fidei*, but also his other writings and the ecclesiastical and political situation in which they were written must be taken into consideration."

114. See: Quillet, "La paix de la foi: identité et différence selon Nicholas de Cues."

115. Vescovini, "Cusanus und das wissenschaftliche Studium in Padua zu Beginn des 15. Jahrhunderts," 109.

116. Koch, *Der Sinn des zweiten Hauptwerkes des Nikolaus von Kues De coniecturis*.

we should wonder whether or not Nicholas can be really considered a forerunner of the relativistic tolerance of Enlightenment.

It is in any case unquestionable that the term *confraternita*, used by John of Segovia, and Nicholas's concept of tolerance mean an exchange of opinions through dialogue and comment. As underlined by Decorte, we should "understand Nicholas in his debates with the Hussites, the Byzantine Orthodox and the other religions, particularly with Islam" from this point of view.[117] Nicholas wonders whether religious war can be prevented; the answer is to be found in the formula "*religio una in rituum varietate* (one religion in a variety of rites)," in the agreement of all peoples on a single orthodox faith, even in a plurality of rites. Therefore, tolerance in rites is possible, but it is not possible in the sphere of faith.[118]

The debate between the Tartar and Paul having come to an end, Nicholas introduces a new interlocutor, the Armenian,[119] who continues the discussion on the difference in rites and puts forward the issue of baptism, which Christians consider necessary to reach salvation. Paul obviously defends baptism as a sacrament of faith, thus necessary to achieve a justification in Christ. Considering that Christians, Arabs, and Jews all take cleansing baths to express their religious devotion, neither the adults nor the children would have difficulties to accept this institution.

The Bohemian then enters the debate,[120] arguing that it will be very difficult to achieve agreement on sacrifices, referring in particular to the

---

117. Decorte, "Tolerance and Trinity," 166. See Arduini, "Ad hanc supermirandam harmonicam pacem, Riforma della chiesa ed ecumenismo religioso nel pensiero di Nicolò Cusano: il *De pace fidei*," 234–35: "In our opinion, *De pace fidei* has considerable importance, especially from the viewpoint of that religious tolerance, which in Cusanus found such a noteworthy expression in the perspective of the ecumenical unification attempts which had already historically expressed themselves in St. Francis' preaching to the Saladin in 1219, in the treaty with Al-Kamil signed by Frederick II Hohenstaufen on 11 February 1229, in Adam Marsh's peroration in favor of a no longer bloody but persuasive crusade, in Gilbert of Tournai's pamphlet written for the purpose of educating kings and princes, in the spirit of St. Francis, aimed at peacefully settling centuries-old doctrinal quarrels, in the cultural crusade and in the revolution of learning preached and testified by Roger Bacon, in the university innovations of Raymond of Peñafort, in the Opusculum written by William of Tripoli, and finally, in the ecumenical action perspective of Ramon Llull." Arduini also mentions the works by Abelard and Llull as the ideal models of *De pace fidei*.

118. Koch, "Der Sinn des zweiten Hauptwerkes des Nikolaus von Kues De coniecturis."

119. *De pace fidei*, XIII.

120. The Bohemian is introduced because in Cusanus' age, heated discussions were

Eucharist sacrament and to the change of bread and wine into Christ's flesh and blood, which are devoured by the worshippers—in his opinion, a form of sacrifice many peoples consider *insaniam*.[121] Paul replies that the Eucharistic sacrament means that the grace of God finds in Jesus Christ the nourishment of eternal life, as our body is nourished by wine and bread. Therefore, if we believe that Christ is the nourishment of our soul, we can accept to receive Christ under the kinds of food that nourish our body.[122] But the Bohemian does not seem fully convinced and insists on the difficulty of making all peoples believe that in the Eucharistic sacrament the substance of bread is changed into the body of Christ.

Faced with the Bohemian's doubts, Paul does not hesitate to answer that it is necessary to believe in the Eucharist as an act of faith, because Christ took the promise of our immortality upon himself by taking the bodily form of the Son of God. Therefore, Paul continues, we must consider the substantiation of bread and wine into the flesh and blood of Christ in the same way. Here Nicholas gives further voice to the Bohemian's perplexities. Despite Paul's explanations, the Bohemian continues to doubt the conversion of the substance of bread. Paul replies that this conversion is only spiritual[123] and that it must be intended and accepted from this point of view. The Bohemian thanks Paul for his explanations, though he continues to believe that uncultured persons will hardly be able to understand this sacrament. Paul concludes that this would not be a hindrance to men's salvation, since the main thing is that they have faith.[124] The heads of the church will establish the directives which, depending on circumstances, they will judge more appropriate for each religious sect concerning the reception and the rites of Eucharist, provided that faith is always kept.

At the end of Paul's long explanation, Nicholas introduces the Englishman, to whom he assigns the task of asking what will happen in the case of the other sacraments, namely marriage, holy orders, confirmation, and extreme unction. Paul answers that it will be necessary to keep a sympathetic attitude towards men's weakness, but he is certain that an agreement

---

taking place in Bohemia (within the Hussite movement with the moderate Ultraqists' faction) concerning Eucharist both in its doctrinal and in its administering aspects Gaia, *Opere religiose*, 669, n.80.

121. *De pace fidei*, XVIII, 58.
122. *De pace fidei*, XVIII, 59.
123. *De pace fidei*, XVIII, 60.
124. *De pace fidei*, XVIII, 61.

on those matters will be surely reached. The Englishman then asks what will it happen in the case of fasts, divine offices, abstinence from food and drink, prayers, and other similar rites. In this regard, Paul explains that if unity in practice of these religious acts cannot be reached, people should be allowed to continue their own devotions and ceremonies, on condition that peace and faith are kept.

The discussions on these themes with the wise men of all nations having come to an end, Nicholas prepares himself to conclude his dissertation. He mentions some of the most famous authors who wrote in any language on the religious habits of the ancients, especially Marcus Varro for the Latins and Eusebius for the Greeks. He ends his discourse by affirming that an examination of those books shows that differences concern rites rather than the cult of the one and only God.[125]

Nicholas of Cusa puts at the end of *De pace fidei* the image of a heaven in which agreement among religions is rationally discussed. The King of Kings orders these wise men to go back to the earth in order to lead the various peoples to the unity of the true religion. He entrusts the angelic ministers with the task of guiding and assisting the wise men and commands the wise men to go to Jerusalem, the center of the universe, for the purpose of accepting, in the name of all nations, the only faith and grounding on it perpetual peace.[126]

10. Peace

Nicholas of Cusa devises some hypotheses for establishing peace among the different religions.[127] According to him, variety in rites must be understood in light of the truth of faith. The Tartar wants to know how this faith can lead to salvation: Paul answers that God does not justify each living being according to the works he has carried out, but according to grace. "The Almighty gives those who want what they want," Paul says. Faith is what makes men worthy to achieve the fruits of grace, through which they can receive God's blessing and, hence, happiness and eternal life. The different rites, such as circumcision, may be accepted based on a majority or a minority principle. According to Nicholas, if the people practicing circumcision are a minority, they have to conform to the majority to keep the

125. *De pace fidei*, XIX, 62.
126. *De pace fidei*, XIX, 63.
127. Gaia, *Opere religiose*, 662.

peace, and thus they must renounce this rite. Extending his argumentation, however, Nicholas also affirms that the opposite position—the majority following a rite of the minority—could be plausible, in order to strengthen peace through mutual exchange.

Nicholas firmly stresses the theoretical presuppositions of his argumentation and underlines that rites are the external phenomena of a particular confession. Dialogue and "mutual exchange" are based on an intellectual discussion focused on theological matters, through which, thanks to the interpretation of the sources and the mutual knowledge of customs and habits, it is possible to recognize theoretical affinities and, consequently, common practices. In fact, Nicholas, though acknowledging the difficulties of a "conversion" agreement upon different rites, consolidates his idea that it is possible to lay the foundations for peace on faith, through tolerance of the religious habits of each rite. The conceptual core of Nicholas's discourse is always focused on the relevance of faith, which must be formed, or shaped, by the charity that drives man to action.[128]

Nicholas also deals with this topic in *De docta ignorantia*.[129] There he explains that salvation can be achieved through faith, which is the faith of all those who believe in God, whether Jews, Arabs, or Christians. "The soul of the just shall inherit eternal life." Rites are, for Nicholas, signs that may change, but the truth expressed by these signs is unchangeable.[130] He also uses this argument in the *Cribratio Alkorani*:[131] to make the promise of eternal happiness come true, we need to have the same faith as Abraham, and we must rely unconditionally on God. Only through faith can eternal life be achieved.[132]

The theme of sacrifice is another fruitful ground for dialogue among different confessions. Each religion interprets the idea of the divine in a different way, and rites and sacrifices are so much more than just external signs. How is it then possible to convince all peoples about the value of the Eucharist? It is not a question of convincing—Nicholas argues—but rather of understanding that the signs of the Eucharist are an expression of the faith that leads to salvation. Since the Eucharist has, above all, a

---

128. *De pace fidei*, XVI, 58.22; 59.1–9.
129. *De docta ignorantia*, III; 6.
130. *De pace fidei*, XVI, 55.12–15; 1–4.
131. *Cribratio Alkorani*, III; 12.
132. *De pace fidei*, XVI, 57.22–28.

symbolic value; in practicing this rite, each people will therefore follow its own rules.[133]

In Nicholas's *De concordantia catholica*, too, we can see that sacrifice takes a different meaning in comparison to the uniqueness of Christ's sacrifice. In this case, sacrifice means "sign," evidence of the sacred, rite. Only through these signs of faith can we attain the glory of the Resurrection, in order to behold the divine eternal light face to face.

Nicholas believes that the main barrier between Christendom and Islam consists in the doctrine of the Trinity. Therefore Haubst, in his famous essay,[134] focuses his analysis on the problems concerning understanding the divine Trinity. Anawati,[135] in this regard, notes that for this reason the French, Spanish, and Turkish speakers in *De pace fidei* raise objections concerning some fundamental issues of the Christian doctrine, such as the resurrection of the dead and the death and resurrection of Christ. The German asks questions about eternal happiness, the Tartar about the difference in rites. Anawati denies this possibility without hesitation.[136] Referring also to the *Cribratio Alkorani*, he argues that in order to objectively evaluate Nicholas's works dealing with a comparison of different religions, we should consider the notion of dialogue to imply indeed a friendly and hearty exchange, respectful of the interlocutor's opinions and of his beliefs, ideas, and doctrines and aimed at revealing the truth. According to Anawati, the dialogue thus intended is a modern acquisition, and we therefore cannot expect to find it in Nicholas's works. Roger Friedlein[137] argues that medieval dialogue should not be mistaken for the Platonic dialectical process. The former concerns the very concept of dialogue in the Middle Ages, which means, above all, comment, paraphrase, interpretation, not only intellectual exchange between two or more interlocutors. The latter refers instead to the complexity of the dialogue between different religions, a complexity that unwinds itself through many concepts and problems: identity, difference and diversity, and equality are some of the conceptual foundations upon which multi-religious and multi-cultural dialogue is grounded.[138]

133. *De pace fidei*, XVIII, 63.1–12.
134. Haubst, *Die Christologie des Nikolaus von Kues*.
135. Anawati, "Nicholas de Cues et le problème de l'Islam."
136. Ibid.,143. "Et ceci nous amène à répondre à notre troisième question: Nicholas de Cues peut-il nous être utile pour le dialogue Islamo-chrétien?"
137. Friedlein, *Der Dialog bei Ramon Lull*.
138. Anawati, "Nicholas de Cues et le problème de l'Islam," 173.

Watanabe's reflection remains, in my opinion, essential.[139] There is no doubt that in Nicholas's *De pace fidei* the problem of relation between Christendom and Islam could be only solved in a peaceful way. But it is also unquestionable that Nicholas does not grant an identical status to Christianity and to the other religions. The superiority of the Christian religion being undisputed, *De pace fidei* cannot be easily classified as a work really focused on interreligious dialogue.

11. Identity, Difference, Unity

In *De pace fidei*, Nicholas does not put theologians or experts on the stage, only wise men. These characters, identified as "wise," meet to discuss whether or not a single universal religion is possible. If each religion can be handed down and testified to through the mediation of prophets more or less inspired by the divine truth, it goes without saying that their message can become the subject of a discussion among wise men.

As Jeannine Quillet[140] argues, referring to the problem of the different meaning of the term *dialogue* in different historical ages, Nicholas's irenics goes through many of the theological disputes of his age and comes to a foundation represented by the theme of wisdom. The relationship between identity and difference is also a conceptual reference to understand the problem of religious difference.[141] Man himself participates in the unity of the light and in the alterity of the bodily darkness. There are differences and agreements among men. There are contemplative men who speculate, as well as those who keep only to sensible things. There are a number of shades among them, but the common element for all is that no human being can be completely without reason.

Only speculative sciences allow man to accede to understanding[142] the mystery of relationships in diversity and identity, thanks to the coincidence of love and knowledge. God is not the cause of division within diversity; on the contrary, division and difference assume unity and identity, as difference and diversity cannot exist without identity. The Greek man, who represents the philosopher par excellence, tackles the problem of wisdom

---

139. See Watanabe, "The Idea of Tolerance."
140. Quillet, "La paix de la foi," 249.
141. Ibid., 245.
142. *De coniecturis*, II, 167.20–26.

and opens the discussion of *De pace fidei*.¹⁴³ As a representative of rational and philosophical thought, he proposes an irenic solution based on a rational knowledge process.¹⁴⁴

The dialogue with the Arab man includes for the first time the application of the principle of learned ignorance. In fact, according to Nicholas, the Qur'an is a "savoir ignorant"¹⁴⁵ (ignorant knowledge) because it contains many truths which confirm the Gospel. As a matter of fact, Nicholas argues, Muhammad's doctrine does not clash with the trinitarian doctrine. All expressions and manifestations of the divine, if justly interpreted, reflect the proportion of the divine essence within the religious symbolism typical of every creed. Nonetheless, the power of intellect allows discovery of the non-contradiction between identity and difference within the thought process.¹⁴⁶

To come to civil and religious peace, we need to postulate the fulfillment of unity in order to integrate differences within a reasonable concordance. To achieve religious peace, it is necessary peacefully uniting all persons within the same faith, bearing in mind the peculiarity of their specific rites and considering the manifestations of faith as contingent expressions of a truth to which we can only approximately have access. The project developed in *De pace fidei* postulates a free agreement, thanks to a philosophy shared by all men, whether Christian, Jewish, Muslim, or Tartar, based on the essential truth of a single religion, on the difference of rites and habits. This religion is not only the law of love, but also the trinitarian dogma, and Christ is the mediator, God and man, who combines absolute infinity and the unlimited cosmos.

Nicholas had already tackled he problem of concordance in *De concordantia catholica* and had defined it as profound *divina ecclesiae armonia*¹⁴⁷ (divine harmony of the church), in the general sense of a place in which it is possible to reconcile plurality and unity, and vice versa. Concordance is created not only as a typical figure of human, political, and ecclesiological order, but also as the general principle of the economy of the universe,

---

143. *De pace fidei*, I.
144. Quillet, "La paix de la foi," 246.
145. Ibid., 249.
146. Ibid.
147. *De concordantia catholica* I, I, XIV. Concerning the role of Christ and the role of the church in *De concordantia catholica*, see Alberigo, *Chiesa Conciliare, Identità e significato del conciliarismo*, 239.

which encloses the harmony of the *concordantia differentiarum*. *De concordantia catholica* is a major political and ecclesiological effort, which aims to find the lines—the connections—that join the church to God through the mediation of Christ. The church is the bride of Christ and develops at different levels: the visible or *coniecturalis* church; the *Ecclesia ipsa*, or the church in itself; and the militant church, which gathers those who are inwardly joined to Christ *in spiritu* and belong to it as members.[148] The concept of *Ecclesia coniecturalis* is of paramount importance for understanding *De pace fidei*,[149] which contains the principle according to which the unity of the church does not exclude ritual particularism but, on the contrary, is open to different forms of worship, provided that the unity of faith is preserved. At the base of the program of *De concordantia* there is an irenic perspective: the church is a sort of large federation based on election and consensus, which allows settlement of disputes and establishment of harmony. There is a price to pay to obtain peace, however, and it consists in the concordance of all rational spirits. To attain civil or religious peace it is necessary to postulate the fulfillment of unity for integrating differences within a reasonable concordance. This concordance is not the result of a more or less effective compromise, as it assumes a common reflective capacity completely shared by human beings who are equally endowed with the same intellectual power. It also assumes a speculative approach to relationships within unity-plurality, identity-difference or diversity, in its attempt to join all peoples under the same faith.

What does "identity" mean? In *De docta ignorantia* it is defined as all that forms the very essence of unity. All the things of the world participate in the unity, which shines the same way in all individuals. Identity means a search for diversity, and it is unity in plurality. The art of conjecture[150] allows harmonizing the principle of unity with the principle of alterity. Within the divine *complicatio*, all things coincide without any difference. One of Nicholas's key themes is proving the trinitarian nature of God's unity. Unity is eternal: it precedes any alterity and combines both of them. It is the same thing as equality, in which any subsequent inequality can be resolved. Finally, connection is what unites: it precedes all divisions, and generates alterity. Consequently, it is eternal. Connection proceeds from

---

148. See chapter 2 of this book.
149. Quillet, "La paix de la foi."
150. *De Coniecturis*.

unity to equality, and unity is equality.[151] Therefore, multiplicity, diversity, and heterogeneity do not clash at all with unity and universality but, on the contrary, are necessary expressions of both of them.[152] If it is true that all religions teach that God is one, even if in different aspects, it is indeed true that learned ignorance, that is to say speculative wisdom, can teach God's uniqueness.

The third part of *De docta ignorantia* develops some themes of *De pace fidei*, in particular the relation between macrocosm and microcosm, in which the relation between identity and difference reaches its climax. Human nature encompasses the whole universe; it is the union between singular and plural and can be understood through the doctrine of learned ignorance. It is necessary to understand the relation existing between reason and faith to have access to the doctrine. Only faith allows the prime principles to be established, and by acknowledging our ignorance we can reconcile ourselves with the truth men cannot reject, because all men are provided with reason and intellectual intuition capacity. João Maria André[153] argues that *De pace fidei* is the ethical and political rendering of the principle of learned ignorance, and through the philosophical foundations of this doctrine a theologian can construct his theory of multicultural dialogue, which includes of three different levels: epistemological, anthropological, and ethical. From an epistemological point of view, Nicholas refers to the theory of the conjectural nature of knowledge.[154] God wanted to create differences as positive elements, as the foundation and possibility of unity itself. The anthropological level is marked by the vision of any indi-

---

151. See Alberigo, *Chiesa Conciliare, Identità e significato del conciliarismo*, 242.

152. Quillet, "La paix de la foi," 243.

153. Andrè, "L'actualitè de la pensée de Nicholas de Cues, La docte ignorance et sa signification herméneutique, étique, esthétique," 191.

154. Counet, *La contribution de Nicholas de Cuse au Lexique philosophique*, 421–36. According to Nicholas of Cusa it is impossible for men to precisely understand the essence of things. Men are bound to approximation, to conjecture. The reason that assembles in a word, which grasps an essence within a number of perceptions cannot therefore come to truth. Cusanus says that the terms produced to describe the essence of things are never exactly suited. "Leur précision relative est toujours marquée par le plus et le moins et à ce titre pour un terme d'une précision donne on peut toujours en forger de plus précis, sans jamais bien entendu atteindre le maximum de précision, ce qui serait en saisir la vérité, mais celle-ci demeure, nous l'avons déjà dit, hors d'atteinte."

Concerning the studies on Cusanus' language, see: Apel, *Die Idee der Sprache bei Nikolaus von Kues*. See also Meier-Oeser, "Die Prasenz des Vergessenen. Zur Rezeption der Philosophie des Nikolaus von Kues vom 15–18 Jahrhundert."

vidual who encloses "humanity" in himself, that is to say, all the common elements of humankind. Yet if we want to talk about an anthropological level of this text, we should refer to the attention Nicholas shows to the differences in rites and habits existing among peoples. His study and observation of the "other" seem to be more significant from an anthropological point of view than the exposition of the theory of contraction into a single individual, which in our opinion belongs to the typically philosophical speculation of Nicholas. Vansteenberghe affirms that[155] *De pace fidei* represents a "*magnifique complément*" of *De concordantia catholica*. He remarks that Nicholas wrote the work at a moment when Christendom was in danger, like St. Augustine did with his *De civitate Dei*. The striking points in common with Augustine's thought are underlined also by De Libera, who remarks that the work Nicholas wrote after *De pace fidei*, the *Cribratio Alkorani*, follows a process quite similar to the one used by Augustine in his epistles 3.22 and 12.35.[156]

12. Freedom

Concerning the ethical and political level of this work, the problem of freedom plays an essential role.[157] Nicholas of Cusa was fully conscious that there are considerable social differences among men:[158] "You know that a great multitude of men cannot exist without great differences, and almost all are obliged to live a troubled life, full of worries and misery, and to be submitted with servile subjection to the kings who rule on them. Therefore only few of them have sufficient time and opportunities to profoundly know themselves making use of their freedom."[159] Freedom allows man to achieve knowledge, and through knowledge it is possible to reach a form of intercultural dialogue. Thanks to *libertas*, which derives from intellectual faculties, it is possible to have access to a particular interpretation of the holy books, and, subsequently, to compare the different positions on rational grounds. We could therefore talk about hermeneutic interreligious dialogue. The central problem consists not in conversion but in the acknowledgment that there is a common truth in each religion. The

---

155. Vansteenberghe, *Le Cardinal Nicolas de Cues*, 229.
156. De Libera, *La philosophie médiévale*, 454.
157. Vansteenberghe, *Le Cardinal Nicolas de Cues*, 193.
158. *De pace fidei*; I.V.
159. *De pace fidei*, I.V.

question is assuming the same *sapientia*, which is based on rational knowledge made possible by the faculty of *libertas*.[160] The concept of *libertas* in Nicholas's thought is of Christian origin: it does not mean a legal status as in the Roman age but, instead, means what Paul calls *libertas spiritus*, which underlines the independence of one's internal status in spite of oppression exerted by external powers. "And the Word covered itself with humanity to enlighten the man, whose free will can be educated, so that he can see that he has to proceed not as an external man but as an internal man."[161] *Libertas* is God's gift to men, and for this reason, a subject can decide his spiritual direction basing on intellect and reason, irrespective of the directives of the institutional power. Freedom and *sapientia* are concepts linked to one another, emerging also in the dialogue of the Word with the Greek and the Italian, which focused on the concept of *sapientia* in relation to the concept of the length of time. Wisdom is connected to the idea of eternity[162] *De pace fidei* includes another key concept: *veritas*. In fact, tolerance towards non-Christian religions is essentially based, for Nicholas, on the fact that human relations are connected to truth itself. Starting from the concept of truth as God's indispensability.

Nicholas of Cusa finds some affinities between the Christian doctrine and Avicenna's thought. In his *Metaphysica* Avicenna writes: "The happiness of the afterlife can be achieved making the soul free and exempt from the bodily pleasures that clash with the real causes of happiness." Truth and the vision of God differ from happiness intended as satisfaction of one's desire, as truth has a strongly liberating nature.[163]

But in what concerns earthly life, the human condition can hardly approach truth. Nicholas writes, that the earthly human condition has this characteristic: viz., that longstanding custom, which is regarded as having passed over into nature, is defended as the truth. In this way there arise great quarrels when each community prefers its own faith to another faith. *Diversitas* and *varietas* in the forms of life, in beliefs, habits, and customs, are unavoidable and can generate conflicts, but are the product of free will.

The ritual and ceremonial process of each religion will become the expression of the inborn *diversitas* of the human essence and of any social structure. The *libertas* upon which the dialogic method is grounded

160. *De pace fidei*; IV, 10.11–14.
161. *De pace fidei*; II.
162. *De pace fidei*; V, 14.6–7.
163. *De pace fidei*, V.

becomes also the theoretical outcome of the discussion among the eighteen religious representatives. Each of them shall be free to profess his faith according to his cults, being sure that they are the manifestation of a truth that, insofar as it is one and only, belongs to all. In this irenic conclusion lies the originality of this work. Nicholas of Cusa, though he gets the problem of *libertas* from the early Christian tradition, transforms this concept, moving it toward the modern concept of personal religious freedom, as an individual right to profess one's faith. Freedom, in relation to the problem of religious struggles, becomes a part of highly speculative discourse which aims to establish the possibility of a real interreligious dialogue. We should, however, consider that the meaning Paul gives to the term *libertas* already includes *in nuce* the modern sense of religious freedom. In fact, religious freedom can also be primarily intended as independence, responsible freedom to decide opposed to an outer domination claim. We should also consider that precisely in the typical dialectic core of freedom, duty, and service an essential feature of freedom survives, which belongs to the early Christian and early ecclesiastical conception. In any case, this German theologian remains a medieval thinker. As such, we cannot attribute to him the religious tolerance doctrine that asserted itself in Europe only after the disintegration of the traditional idea of Christendom in sixteenth century.

13. Conclusions

Through an analysis of some central concepts which recur in Cusanus' works, I intended to show the process through which he comes to the formulation of the phrase *religio una in rituum varietate,* or concord among all peoples within a single orthodox faith, although in a variety of rites. Cusanus definitely asserts the theoretical presuppositions of his argumentation underlining that rites and rituals are external phenomena of a religion. Dialogue and "mutual exchange" are grounded on intellectual discussions on theological matters, and basing on them, thanks to the interpretation of sources and the mutual knowledge of habits and customs, it is possible to recognize theoretical affinities and reach consequently common practices. I examined the affinities existing among *De concordantia, De docta ignorantia* and *De pace fidei,* to prove that the subject of difference is thematized in all these works and is continuously subtended to deep irenistic instances. Another theme emerging from these works is freedom, which allows man to know, and through knowledge, to reach a sort of intercultural dialogue.

Thanks to *libertas*, which derives from man's intellective faculty, it is possible to come to one particular interpretation of the sacred texts or to another so as to compare different positions basing on rational foundations. I therefore suggest following a line of research based on what we might call a hermeneutic interreligious dialogue, since an exegetic approach to a text aimed at pointing out its intrinsic continuity and also the use of sources, can bring some significant contributions to a correct understanding of the structure of a system of thought. In this case, the themes of alterity/otherness and religious difference are of paramount importance, and it is just on these issues that Nicholas of Cusa focuses his *Cribratio Alkorani*.

5

Cribratio Alkorani, The Change of the Perception of Islam

1. Introduction

CONTINUING MY ANALYSIS OF the sources used by Nicholas of Cusa, as well as the Toledan Collection, another source proved essential in the composition of the *Cribratio*, Riccoldo (or Riccoldo) of Montecroce and his book *Contra legem Sarracenorum*. Cusanus seems to have slavishly followed the polemical line against Islam of this work, which remained one of the major reference texts for any Western author who intended to confront Islamic culture prior to the end of seventeenth century.

An exegesis of the *Cribratio* reveals another methodological assumption used by Cusanus to *cribrare*, or critically examine the Qur'an: the *pia interpretatio*, a method he had already used in *De pace fidei*.

Nicholas of Cusa devotes each book of the *Cribratio Alkorani* to a specific theme. In the Prologue and in the first book, he tries to demonstrate that Islam derives from the Nestorian heresy. In the second book, Cusanus' analysis is focused on the theme of paradise, while in the third book the central theme is Muhammad's persecution of the Christians.

Basing on Thomas Burman's studies,[1] according to which also the strong critical and polemical intention of the writings on Islam and on religions other than Christianity is an integral part of an ever-growing keen interest shown by Western thinkers in the religion and culture of the Islamic civilization, I intend to highlight and stress Nicholas of Cusa's deep knowledge of the Muslim world. A knowledge however mediated by translations and commentaries written by Western authors, which, like Riccoldo's work, are imbued with harshly polemical tones.

---

1. Burman, *Reading the Qur'an in Latin Christendom*.

Cusanus remarks on the differences between the Gospel and the Qur'an. I shall show that the themes of difference and unity emerge also in the *Cribratio Alkorani*. Intertwining with the problem of difference, some other themes are dealt with, such as sin, paradise, and afterworld life. In addition, I intend to develop the discourse on the misinterpretations of the Qur'an included in Riccoldo's work, particularly those concerning the use of violence. In my analysis, I shall also point out that the problem of difference is structured into three different discursive spheres: one based on theological foundations (the Trinity), a second level developing through the argumentation of the difference between the holy books of the Qur'an and the Gospel, while the third level concerns ritual differences (circumcision) and the conception of the afterlife.

2. Sources of the *Cribratio Alkorani*

Nicholas of Cusa wrote the *Cribratio Alkorani* in 1461, three years before his death. This work is dedicated to Pius II, who is urged, like his predecessor Pope Leo, to consider the "Mohammeddan sect" as originating from the Nestorian heresy and, consequently, to be in error and able to be rejected.

In the *Prologus*, Nicholas writes he decided to commit himself to studying the Qur'an as soon as he had the opportunity to read it in Basel in the translation made by the abbot Peter the Venerable,[2] along with the *Disputatio*. Nicholas adds he also had the opportunity to study other pamphlets in depth, including a biography of Muhammad, another booklet concerning his twelve successors in the reign, and finally, the "Doctrine" of the hundred questions.[3] Later, Nicholas decided to send his book to the theologian John of Segovia, who had been at the center of several disputes with the "Moors" focused on the Trinity and the incarnation. Nicholas also

---

2. The abbot Pierre de Cluny (1156) was a friend of Bernard of Clairvaux, and a tenacious opposer of the heretics, the Jews, and the Arabs. Mandonnet, "Pierre le Vénérable et son activité littéraire contre l'Islam." See Piazzoni, "Un falso problema storiografico," 469.

3. These three pamphlets were translated by Herman Dalmatin: *De generatione Machumeti et nutritura eius* (Muhammad's genealogy, which goes back to Adam and Eve, and history of his birth and childhood); *Cronica mendosa et ridiculosa Saracenorum* (History of Mohammed and the first caliphs); *Doctrina Machumeti* (an imaginary account of the visit made by four wise Jews to Mohammed in Medina in order to pose him 100 questions). Hagemann, *Christentum contra Islam*, 102–3. See also Gaia, *Opere religiose*, 718, n.4.

visited Constantinople, where he had the opportunity to consult a copy of the Qur'an in Arabic. When he moved to Pera, a small suburb of Constantinople, situated on the eastern shore of the Golden Horn, he found in the monastery of Saint Dominic another copy of the Qur'an, identical to the one he had consulted in Basel, and he became acquainted with the work of John Damascene,[4] coeval with the writing of the Qur'an and the only thinker of his age who had taken an interest in the Mohameddan "sect."

As Nicholas reports, the news that a foreigner was collecting some information on the Qur'an soon spread, and a merchant named Balthasar de Luparis[5] told him about a very learned man, famous among the Turks, who had secretly studied the Gospel of John and wished to meet him, hoping that Nicholas would help him to secretly meet the pope. Nicholas never met this man, however, because he died of plague, but Nicholas does indicate that he became acquainted, through Balthasar, with the fact that all their men of learning fervently love their Gospel and prefer the book of their laws (*omnes doctos eorum evangelium valde amare et libro legis eorum praeferre*).[6]

Nicholas then reports how he succeeded in convincing the monk Denis the Carthusian to write against the Qur'an and to send a copy of his writings to Pope Nicholas, and recalls that in Rome he had the book of Friar Riccoldo,[7] who belonged to the Dominican order, in his hands. He goes on with a list of writings, including Thomas Aquinas's book *On the Reasons of the Faith against the Saracens, Greeks, and Armenians, to the Cantor of Antioch*[8] and the book entitled *Contra principales errores perfidi*

---

4. See Rozemond, *La christologie de saint Jean Damascène*.

5. Denis Ryckel (1402–71).

6. The Latin quotations are drawn from the critical edition by Hagemann, in *Nicolai de Cusa opera omnia. Cribratio Alkorani*, vol. VIII, (Cribratio Alchorani= *Cribratio Alkorani*, P, 6). This edition includes a Prologus (P) and an Alius Prologus (AP).

7. Riccoldo de Monte Crucis was prior of the Dominican cloister of Santa Maria Novella in Florence; from 1291 to 1310 he went on several long missionary journeys in the East, and learned Arab in Baghdad going as far as translating the Qur'an into Latin. Riccoldo is the source from which Nicholas drew most of the material, usually polemical, concerning Muhammad and Islam. Gaia, *Opere religiose*, 719, n.10. See Merigoux, "L'ouvrage d'un frère Precheur."

8. Aquinas, *De rationibus fidei contra Saracenos, Graecos et Armenos ad Cantorem Antiochenum*.

Mahometis,[9] written by Juan de Torquemada,[10] which convincingly refuted Muhammad's heresy and errors.[11]

Nicholas ends this first prologue by reaffirming his intention to critically examine Muhammad's book in the light of the Gospel of Christ and to prove that the Qur'an includes some things that confirm the Gospel in an unequivocal way. Furthermore, in the passages in which Muhammad's text disagrees with or departs from the words of the Gospel, it proves the ignorance of the person who wrote it.[12]

At the beginning of the *Alius Prologus*, Nicholas tells the story of a monk, Sergius, who after having been thrown out of his monastery, came to Mecca, where he found two peoples: the idolater and the Jew, to whom he preached the Christian faith in the form supported by Nestorius.[13] The monk succeeded in converting all the idolaters, including Muhammad, who therefore died as a Nestorian Christian. Nicholas of Cusa continues: *tres astutissimi Iudaei*[14] (three extremely cunning Jews) joined Muhammad to lead him astray so that he was not able to become perfect, going as far as to suggest him *varia mala* (various tricks). When Muhammad died, all of them returned to their original sect, and those who had led him astray joined Alī, son of Abū Talīb, to whom Muhammad had entrusted his book of writings, convincing him to proclaim himself prophet and to reshuffle to his liking the book Muhammad had left in legacy.

Nicholas relates that Muhammad had first received from Sergius the foundations of the Christian faith, but the Jews moved him from his original faith when they introduced into the Qur'an some passages presenting

---

9. Iohannis de Turrecremata, *Tractatus contra principales errores perfidi Machometi et Turcorum sive Sarracenorum*.

10. Biechler, "A New Face towards Islam: Nicholas of Cusa and John of Segovia," 201. Torquemada's work is characterized by a profound and rigorous rationalism and a precise awareness of his task. The same tenacity that governs his monarchic conception of ecclesiology dominates his exposition on religious errors. The book includes also a description of the twelve reasons why Christianity is superior to Islam, and his reasoning proceeds with an explanation of the reasons why several regions of the world are under the domination of the heretical religion of Islam. Though Nicholas knew Torquemada's *Contra principales errores*, he preferred to adopt a different approach for his *Cr. Alk.*

11. *Cribratio Alkorani*, P, 7. I will use P, AP, or Book & Chapter of *Cribratio* always followed by section number

12. *Cribratio Alkorani*, P, 12.

13. Gaia reports that Nicholas drew this story from the *Disputatio*. Gaia, *Opere religiose*, 723, n.16.

14. *Cribratio Alkorani*, AP, 13.

Muhammad as a prophet of their religion and a believer in the Old Testament. The Noble Arab,[15] who is Nicholas's main source, however, reports that Sergius convinced Muhammad to introduce in the Qur'an the statement that the Christians, especially monks and priests, are better friends than the Jews. Nevertheless, Muhammad was swept away and began to mock the Christians, describing them as "Lords," a term that could be used to describe nobody else but God. As written in Deuteronomy, "The Lord is our God."[16]

Nicholas explains his primary objective from the very beginning, by giving chapter 1, Book I of his work the title *De Alkorano et quod deus verus non sit auctor eius* (On the Qur'an and Why the Real God is Not Its Author). The book of the Arabs' law, he adds, is called Qur'an because it is a collection of rules, and it is also called *Alfurkan* because of the detailed division of its chapters. This division, however, may change depending on the regions in which it is read. In fact, while Western commentators affirm that after the prayer "Mother of the Book,"[17] the text divides into 123 chapter or Suras,[18] Eastern commentators maintain that the first Sura spreads as far as the Amram Sura, which represents the fifth chapter of the book circulating in the Spanish regions. Nicholas explains that the version read in Spain is the same as the Latin one we usually refer to, but in his opinion this is an apocrypha, as *huius auctor videtur apocryphus*[19] (its author seems apocryphal). Some Arab authors affirm that it was written by Muhammad himself, a man from Arabia belonging to the lineage of Ishmael, but other commentators maintain that Muhammad himself indicated the names of seven men as authors of this work, whereas still other commentators report that four different and clashing versions of the Qur'an existed, all written after Muhammad's death by as many authors

---

15. Riccoldo da Montecroce (Ricoldus de Monte Crucis).

16. Deut 6:4.

17. "Mother of the Book" or Mother of the Writing is one of the names given to the first Sura, which praises God and invokes his aid. It is the official prayer of Islam, summarizing the fundamental principles of the faith in one God and in the final judgment.

18. As Gaia explains, the numbering of 123 Suras (instead of 114, as in the Arabic Qur'an) refers to the Latin translation made by Robertus Retenensis (Robert Ketton), who did not include the first Sura into the account, and divided the long Suras 2–6 into 16 chapters, considered as many Suras. Differently from what Nicholas believes, the Arab tradition ignores the existence of a different number of Suras either in the Western or in the Eastern world. Gaia, *Opere religiose*, 730–31, n.3.

19. DC, I, I, 20.

struggling with one another. Some other authors maintain that the book was written by Marwān, son of Al-Hakam, and finally, there are some commentators who talk about a certain Al-Haggāg, a powerful man, who would have removed eighty-five verses from the original text and replaced them with as many verses to his liking.

In Nicholas of Cusa's opinion, the different conjectures on the genesis of the Qur'an do not end with the legends about its author, because the "Chronicle of Muhammad and the kings who succeeded him" tells many other stories about the caliphs, as for example the story of 'Umar, the second caliph after Muhammad, who would have commanded to say prayers in each temple and to read the Qur'an during the month of Ramadān; or also the story of his successor, 'Uthmān, who is supposed to be the first caliph who gathered the whole collection of the book of the Arabs' law. At a certain point, Nicholas affirms:

> Nonetheless, we intend to critically examine, basing on the Gospel of Christ, Muhammad's book, and prove that also that book includes some things, which would notably confirm the Gospel, should it need to be attested, and wherever it disagrees with the Gospel, it was caused by ignorance, and consequently, by perversity in Muhammad's intentions, who did not pursue the glory of God and the salvation of man but rather his own glory.[20]

The Qur'an confirms the truth of the Gospel: Nicholas's comment does not admit any possibility of textual hermeneutics, because he declares he already knows the outcome of his analysis, that is to say, the assertion of the Gospel word through an analysis of the Qur'an. Nicholas wants to sift (*cribrare*), to thoroughly and critically examine the Qur'an: to do so, he makes use of the *pia interpretatio*[21] (pious interpretation), a method

---

20. DC, I, I, 22.

21. Hopkins, *A Miscellany of Nicholas of Cusa*, 45: According to Hopkins, the five objectives of the *Cribratio* are:

An attempt to interpret the Qur'an to make it compatible with the New Testament. Where the text cannot be made compatible with the New Testament, it is wrong and misleading.

An attempt to interpret the Qur'an so as to make it self-consistent.

Wherever there are conflicts *prima facie* between the Qur'an and the NT, it is necessary to interpret the metaphors and the symbology used by Muhammad as religious propaganda addressed to unlearned persons.

To interpret the Qur'an as an intention to praise God without questioning the centrality of Christ.

To work as close as possible with the interpretation the wisest Arabs attribute to the

he had already used in *De pace fidei*. He begins his argumentation from a conceptual evidence he had "conquered" just in the dialogue written in 1453. There is only one truth, the truth of the Gospel, and there are no other possibilities to make any comparison without starting from this presupposition. However, *praesuppositio* is not used in the *Cribratio* to prove the uniqueness of truth though in a variety of rites but, instead, to assume the wicked intention of the author, Muhammad, who is perverse because he subverted the order of truth of the Gospel. For this reason, some parts of the Qur'an cannot highlight the points in which it agrees with the Christian text. "We think we should say that ignorance is the cause of error and ill will: in fact, nobody who knows Christ can disagree with him or diminish his glory,"[22] Nicholas affirms.

The first reference to the Qur'anic text ("As the law could not be observed, God gave the world a law of salvation and made the commandments easier through the Qur'an"[23]) is introduced by Nicholas to underline that, according to the Qur'an, God gave laws and commandments in order to make things become easy, not difficult.[24]

Then he examines the style and the structure of the Book:

> It will not be difficult to find the truth of the Gospel in the Qur'an, though Muhammad himself was far away from a real understanding of the Gospel. And we should not neglect that the chapters of the collection of the aforementioned book of the Arab's law are not connected with one another, but each of them is a whole in itself, and has a particular rhythm and a perfectly measured poetry. The compiler placed the utmost care so as to attract everyone through the charm of his style and arouse astonishment to make his sayings seem divine. Therefore, you have to excuse me if, in discussing the contents of this very confused book, I do not seem to keep a convenient order everywhere.[25]

The problem pointed out by Nicholas refers to the origins of the Qur'an and to the circumstances of its composition. The handling undergone by

---

Qur'an, and prove in this way that their interpretation implies the Christian doctrine.

22. *Cribratio Alkorani*, I, II, 24.

23. "But Jesus, son of the Virgin Mary, the Christ whose coming had been announced by Moses and the prophets, came, and knowing all, he clearly revealed this way, as witnessed by Muhammad." Many passages of the Qur'an present Jesus as the Messiah: Suras 2.87, 136, 253; 3.45, 53, 84; 4.157, 163, 171.

24. *Qur'an*, Sura 5, 82.

25. *Cribratio Alkorani*, Alius prologus, 16, 1–6.

the Qur'an has to be brought back to what is written in the *Disputatio*, in which it is affirmed that its different versions depend on the various interventions and changes[26] brought by Ali, Abu Bakr, Uthman, and Umar.[27]

Nicholas remarks that in the Qur'an, the statement that God the Creator is the only author of the Book is frequently repeated. Nicholas affirms, however, that the Qur'an is a collection of precepts that in no way could be attributed to God, because a collection of writings cannot be a divine work. In Nicholas's opinion, Muhammad made two mistakes: the Prophet seems to have misunderstood or not to have known the real importance of the revelation of the word of Christ, or instead might have known but denied it out of mere wickedness of intentions.

3. Structure of *Cribratio Alkorani*

Nicholas devotes each book of the *Cribratio Alkorani* to a particular theme: in the prologue and in the first book, he tries to prove that Islam derives from the Nestorian heresy. In the second book, his analysis is focused on the theme of heaven, while the third book is devoted to Muhammad's persecution of the Christians.

The analysis of the first book focuses on the style of the Qur'an for the purpose of proving that it is not God's work. Nicholas considers the disjointedness of the text the most significant feature that proves what he says. He shows himself to be well acquainted with the Qur'anic text, as mediated through the Latin translations, and to have philologically studied in depth the composition of the holy book. Nicholas's working method leads us to make two remarks: he gives his full attention to examining the alleged textual contradictions within the Book. His analysis proceeds in a totally humanistic manner, as he seeks out manuscripts and closely examines their substance and style. In her article "Renaissance Humanism,"[28] Pauline Moffit Watts underlines that when Nicholas wrote his dialogue *De idiota* in 1450, some time before he was named cardinal by Pope Nicholas V, he had

---

26. Mervin, *Histoire de l'islam: fondements et doctrines*, 32: "The relationship of the Uthmanic text to the revelations received by Muhammad is clouded by the existence of numerous collections of variant readings that have survived, attributed to a number of early scholars who were widely known for their excellence in reading and reciting the Qur'an."

27. About the style and structure of the Qur'an, see: Dammen McAuliffe, *The Cambridge Companion to the Qur' ān*.

28. Watts, "Renaissance Humanism," 169–96.

already established relations with the Italian humanists for several decades. These contacts dated back to 1417, when Nicholas was studying law in Padua and had the opportunity to meet there Toscanelli, who belonged to a circle of Florentine and Roman intellectuals interested in discovering the works on mathematics of the ancient Greeks. This circle of scholars also included Filelfo, Alberti, Brunelleschi, George of Trebizond and the future Pope Nicholas V.[29] Watts identifies, especially in *De docta ignorantia*, the marks of the deep influence exerted by some classic authors as Lorenzo Valla and Ambrogio Traversari, who were the humanists who mainly influenced Cusa's methodology.[30]

In the fifteenth century, the rediscovery and translation of some Platonic and neo-Platonic texts incited an ever-growing number of humanists, philosophers, and theologians to write. Though in all his previous works Nicholas had never tackled the problem of the immortality of the soul, as from 1440 up to his latest writings, he began to deal with these theoretical issues.[31] Both Nicholas and the humanists assumed that all human beings

29. Watts, "Renaissance Humanism," 177: "It is important to remember that the intellectual interests and associations sketched above, focused as they are on Cusanus' connections with Renaissance humanists, provide only a partial picture of the range and the roots of his thinking."

30. Watts, "Renaissance Humanism," 188: "Cusanus' conception of the relations of words of names to thing invites yet another comparison with his friend and colleague, Valla. Nicholas wrote the dialogues during a period when he resided in Rome, and he was in touch with Valla at the point. (As noted, one of the surviving letters he wrote to Valla dates from 1450.)" In his work known as *Repastinatio dialecticae et philosophiae*, written in 1438–39, Valla used the instruments of grammar and rhetoric to deconstruct the scholastic dialectic, and to re-establish the use of the language and logic of subjectivity conceived in a qualitative manner. In the first book of *Repastinatio*, Valla conceives nature as a relation between words and things, and this conception likely influenced Cusanus.

The vision of man in Nicholas is not limited to the real world and to concrete life, but extends as far as to reach afterlife as a distinguishing trait of the individual as a being provided with an immortal soul. As regards this theme, too, Watts identifies a close relation with the Italian humanists: "the *locus classicus* for ancient discussion on the immortality of the individual soul is Plato's *Phaedo*, which Nicholas knew through Bruni's translation); Aristotle nowhere definitively stated that the soul was immortal. As Kristeller has pointed out, there is no place in scripture that speaks of the immortality of the soul. Augustine (who was much influenced by Neoplatonic thought) did develop a doctrine of the immortality of the soul, but it is significant that the medieval scholastics, influenced mainly by Aristotle and his Arabic commentators, did not elaborate the doctrine. Instead, they mulled the interpretations of thinkers such as Averroes, who argued for the immortality of a universal, not an individual, soul."

31. Watts, "Renaissance Humanism," 190.

share a common intellect or are part of a great collective soul. Yet they were inclined to see in the infinite variety of human truths the manifestation of the transcendent One. In Watts's opinion, this tendency results from a non-systematic approach to the *studia humanitatis*.[32] Though they considered Cicero their main model, the humanists drew the inspiration of their thought also from different sources and had to face the difficulty of reconciling the Greek, Roman, Jewish, and Christian teachings. Medieval thinkers had encountered the same difficulties, but in the fifteenth century, humanist thinkers had the great advantage of having at their disposal a number of texts that were completely unknown during the Middle Ages.[33]

Watts carefully examines the influence of humanist thought on Nicholas's work and argues that the underlying idea of *De pace fidei* is rooted both in *De docta ignorantia* and in *Apologia de docta ignorantia*,[34] in which he argues for God's unknowability. Though Nicholas cannot be defined as a humanist in a strict sense, his thought was crucially influenced by the texts translated by the humanists, and the body of his works is crossed by the same themes and same problems that mark the dividing line and the relationship between human and divine, sacred and profane.[35]

Furthermore, the philological method used by Nicholas in *De concordantia catholica* regarding the Donation of Constantine is a peculiarity that undoubtedly brings him closer to the humanists. This method is further developed also in the *Cribratio*, where the examination of the Qur'an is conducted through a careful comparative and exegetic reading.

4. *Manuductio* and *pia interpretatio*

In chapter 19, Nicholas of Cusa deals with the *pia interpretatio* method: he reports that, while he was reading the Qur'an, he noted that "the last judgment, heaven and hell are often mentioned, and always in a different way and through similes. . . . And since I saw that also in the Gospel and

---

32. Ibid., 189.

33. Ibid., 192: "To be sure, these difficulties were shared by their medieval predecessors, but they were greatly compounded by the presence of many texts unknown to the scholastics. Finally (and this is a factor that Kristeller does not discuss in his essay), they lived in period in which Europe was simultaneously expanding and facing incursions. The search for the unity of truth was not therefore simply an insulated academic debate: it was now driven by a kind of existential imperative."

34. Nicolai da Cusa, Vol. II: *Apologia Doctae ignorantiae*.

35. Watts, "Renaissance Humanism," 195.

in the Old Testament, the Kingdom of Heaven is characterized by different similes, I thought to myself that the pious interpretation of the followers of the Book could be justified."[36] Again, in Book II we read: "Hence, it can be inferred, according to a pious interpretation, that the Qur'an intended to reveal these mysteries only to wise men."[37]

The *Cribratio* is based on two key concepts: the *manuductio* and the *interpretatio pia*. The *manuductio* is a theological concept derived from the Neoplatonic tradition, which refers to the method through which the human mind is guided step by step (and "hand in hand") from sensible knowledge to divine knowledge. The Neoplatonic conception of the cosmos is hierarchically structured, and knowledge and love must gradually progress. Nicholas analyzes the Qur'an to find in it the traces reflecting the divine nature. The *manuductio* is the method through which Nicholas tries to convince the Muslims that they misunderstood the Christian creed.

The *interpretatio pia* is one characteristic that marks the *Cribratio* as a treatise completely different from any other anti-Muslim work. The *intepretatio* indicates a hermeneutic principle through which it is possible to understand the Qur'an in a sense close to the Christian doctrine. This method leads us to read the teachings of the Qur'an not as something antithetic to the theology of the Trinity, but rather as criticizing only Christ's crucifixion, and therefore not far removed from the contents of the Bible and from its cardinal points concerning the final judgment, heaven, and hell.[38]

5. The Metaphor of Glass

Subsequently, Nicholas of Cusa prepares himself to analyze the last theme dealt with in the first book of the *Cribratio Alkorani*. Chapter 20 is entitled *Digressio ad manuductionem divinorum*, a digression which opens by saying that the Qur'an calls Christ *ruholla*,[39] a word that, in Nicholas's opinion, was translated by some commentators as "breath of God" and by other

---

36. *Cribratio Alkorani*, II, 820. *Cribratio Alkorani*, II; 86; 1–5. A reference to the *pia interpretatio* is included in the first chapter of book II: "Nunc accedamus ad elucidationem trinitatis, quam in divinitate colimus, et ostendamus Alkoranum pia interpretatione non contradicere trinitati, modo quo nos de ipsa loquimur, qui evangelico inhaeremus."

37. *Cribratio Alkorani*, II, 794.

38. Biechler, *A New Face towards Islam*, 200.

39. Gaia, however, points out that nobody knows the source Nicholas drew this denomination from, as it cannot be found in the Qur'an and combines the Arab words *rūh allāh* = spirit of God. Gaia, *Opere religiose*, 770, n.1.

authors as "spirit of God," "word of God," or "soul of God." Regardless of the kind of translation one prefers to accept, he argues, it is relevant to note that none of the possible accepted meanings would change the truth that God does necessarily exist, and consequently, it would be better to accept the translation "word of God."[40]

To allow even the simplest persons to grasp the meaning of Father, Word, and Spirit, as well as all that follows and proceeds, Nicholas deems it useful to resort to a simile, which refers to a master glassmaker. The art of making glass, he writes, is a work of intelligence, and those who lack intellect cannot learn this art. The glassmaker takes an iron pipe, puts an appropriate material on its end, blows into the pipe, and creates a glass vase in the shape he wants. A breath, Nicholas underlines, which, acting inside the matter, succeeds in molding it.[41]

The intellect—Nicholas continues—expresses with one word the idea and the concept it sees within itself, making it perceptible to sense; as a consequence, the intellectual movement that accomplishes this operation proceeds from the intellect and from its mental word. Returning to the metaphor of the glassmaker, Nicholas underlines that in the glassmaker's blowing, it is possible to discern the presence of the intellective nature, that is to say, the intellect, its word, and its spirit, as well as the movement in both of them. If these elements were missing, the glass-blowing action by itself would never introduce the shape of the vase; thus, the intellect, its word, and their spirit never detach themselves from the glassmaker since they sensibly turn into the blowing action.[42]

We should bear in mind, however, that God is neither in the strong breath that overthrows the mountains, nor in the earthquake that follows it, nor in the fire resulting from it, but rather, *in sibilo aurae tenuis ignem subsequente*[43] (in the feeble hissing produced by fire), and this proves he is a thinner spirit than any breath. Furthermore, his presence is not sensible but spiritual, and therefore it does not take up room, similar to the way intellect is present in discourse. It is, in fact, the Spirit or substantial Motion which creates each substance and each thing, which contains the science or art of

---

40. *Cribratio Alkorani*, I, xx, 68.

41. *Cribratio Alkorani*, I, xx, 69. On the metaphor of the glassblower in *De mente* XIII, nn. 146-47; *De genesi*, III, n. 164.

42. *Cribratio Alkorani*, I, xx, 70. Nicholas of Cusa continues arguing that likewise, all intellectual actions are accomplished, even if not through a bodily blowing action, through the intellect, its word, or through the movement and spirit of both of them.

43. *Cribratio Alkorani*, I, xx, 70.

all things, and the intellect, which is the father of science and art. Therefore, Nicholas argues, it is evident that the substance is spirit and resembles God, who is spirit.

It is worth saying this, Nicholas concludes, to make the uncultivated followers of the Qur'an raise their mind to spiritual things.

6. The Nestorian Heresy

In the *Cribratio Alkorani*, Nicholas of Cusa tackles the problem of the names of God. Muhammad mentions in the Qur'an the ten names of God, among which *Adonaj*, translated as "Lord."[44] Since the Christians called Christ "Our Lord Jesus," and Mary "Our Lady," Muhammad maintained that the Christians used to worship Christ and Mary in the place of God, but he avoided assigning the name of "Father" to God.[45]

According to Nicholas of Cusa, when Muhammad spoke highly of the Christians, he referred, as a matter of fact, to *de vestitis in albo* (those dressed in white), as he called the apostles and the believers in Christ, whom he (wrongly) believed were the Nestorians. Nicholas explains that Nestorius accepted all that the Gospel included and believed that body, soul, and divinity were encompassed in Christ, but was mistaken about the way in which these natures combine. According to Nestorius, body and soul were naturally combined and united to form a real man, but man was united by the divinity of grace, or better, by the fullness of grace. Therefore, the will of God and the will of the man Jesus form a single will. Through this most excellent grace, it is therefore possible to declare that Christ is the Son of God, but it is not possible to admit that Mary is the mother of God, because all that Christ received from his mother was not divine.[46]

Concerning the issue of eternal generation, Nicholas reminds that Muhammad did not intend to write anything against the Holy Trinity and eternal generation; he only wanted to condemn the plurality of gods. However, according to what Muhammad affirms, God sent Christ, the Word of

---

44. Sura 59.23–24.

45. Alius Prologus, 15.

46. Alius Prologus, 16. Thus, Nicholas continues, Nestorius claimed that the human nature was deified in Christ, but, according to the Gospel, the Word of God was made flesh: "ideo hunc sensum damnavit ecclesia in conciliis universalibus tertio et quarto dans matri Iesu nomen theotocos scilicet dei genitrix. Nestoriani autem generationem aeternam confitentur."

God and the son of Mary, because a greater envoy than he was unthinkable. And God covered Christ with *humana natura mundissima*[47] (with the purest human nature), as we can frequently read in the Qur'an. Nicholas closes the *Alius Prologus* with the declaration that he is able to identify in the Qur'an the truth of the Gospel, though Muhammad was far away from really understanding the biblical text. In addition, he reminds us that the chapters of the Qur'an, though connected to one another, are separate and independent and have a particular rhythm, as the compiler was most concerned with this sort of measured poetry.[48]

That having been said, Nicholas informs his readers that in trying to give the book of the Arabs' law an order, he intends to divide his essay into three parts, and each part into several chapters. Before starting his analysis, he lists the titles of the nineteen chapters of the first part, the nineteen chapters of the second part, and the twenty-one chapters of the third and last part.[49] Then, he begins analyzing the first theme.[50]

We read in the *Alius Prologus*: "Now, Nestorius accepted all that we find in the Gospel, and also that in Christ there was body, soul, and divinity, but he was mistaken about their union."[51] Here Nicholas refers to the Nestorian doctrine, according to which body and soul are joined in man, and man is joined to the divinity by means of grace. Therefore, the Nestorians admitted the divine essence of Christ, but denied that Mary was the mother of God. Thus, Nestorius affirmed that the human nature is deified in Christ.

> And since the Gospel declares that the Word was made flesh, and not that the flesh was made the word of God, for this reason the Church condemned that opinion during the third and fourth universal council, giving the mother of Jesus the name of *Theotokos*, or God-Bearer, whereas the Nestorians acknowledge eternal generation.[52]

47. AP, 17.
48. AP, 17.
49. AP, 17–20.
50. *Cribratio Alkorani*, Alius prulugus.
51. *Cribratio Alkorani*, Italian edition, 725.
52. *Cribratio Alkorani*, Italian edition, 725. Vine, *The Nestorian Churches*. See also: Tucci, *Le civiltà dell'oriente: storia, letteratura, religioni, filosofia, scienze e arte*. The name of Nestorius, who lived in the fifth century and was bishop of Constantinople, was often associated with the Christological theory later called Nestorianism, though this religious movement had not been originally founded by him. The creation and establishment of

In his exposition, Nicholas remarks that the term *theotokos* was at the origin of a theological dispute between the Nestorians and the council's fathers. The concept of *theotokos* contains a profound difference in positions concerning the nature of Christ. According to the theses of the Council of Nicaea, the two natures of Christ cannot be confused: the *Logos*, whose divine nature is unchangeable, and the human essence through which it is possible to have access to all human sentiments.[53] Thus, in the person of Christ, there are two different but perfectly combined natures, and what makes the union of these natures absolute and complete is the postulate according to which this fusion process begins from the very moment of the conception. The Virgin Mary, through the conception of Christ, made it possible for the Word to be made flesh.

According to the Nestorian theory, union concerned an *eudokia*, adoption,[54] between the human and the divine nature, rather than a mere union of essence: *eudokia* and not *ousia*. Both natures, the divine and the human, were therefore in conjunction as in a sort of boundary, rather than in a state of real unification.[55] One of the main arguments of the *Cribratio* against Islam concerns the alleged derivation of the Muslim religion from the Nestorian sect.[56]

Chapter 6 includes an extensive commentary on the passages in which the Qur'an is in open contradiction with the Holy Scriptures, and the major differences concern the figure of Mary. For example, in the Qur'an Mary is described as the sister of Aaron and the daughter of Amram,[57] because the holy book also mentions the Old Testament Mary. In this case, too, Nicholas compares the different versions of this subject included in the Qur'an to reaffirm that the Book cannot have a divine origin.[58] When in the

---

Nestorian churches, also called "churches of the East," was a gradual process, which began to develop when Mar Babai, patriarch of Seleucia-Ctesiphon (487–502), declared the complete independence of the churches of Persia—and of other areas of which he had named himself spiritual patriarch—from the Church of Rome.

53. Vine, *The Nestorian Churches*, 23.

54. About the meaning of the term Ευδοκια see *Ep*; 1.5 and also Luke 2:14.

55. Vine, *The Nestorian Churches*, 27. See also Scipioni, *Nestorio e il concilio di Efeso: Storia, dogma, critica*.

56. *Cribratio Alkorani*, Alius prologus, 15.1–5. Cf. Vine, *The Nestorian Churches*, 32. See also Biechler, "Christian Humanism confronts Islam: Sifting the Qur'an with Nicholas of Cusa," 1–14.

57. *Qur'an*, Sura 19, also called Mary's Sura.

58. *Cribratio Alkorani*, I.33.1–3.

Qur'an we find something "beautiful, true and bright, it must be necessarily a glaring beam of light of the Gospel, and this can be easily understood by those who, after having read the Gospel, turn to the Qur'an."[59] A similar argument can be found also in Riccoldo's *Contra legem*, the source to which Nicholas refers:[60] contempt for the world, call for justice, belief that dying for God means earning eternal life, are the elements the prophet Muhammad drew from the Gospel.

7. Textual Differences: The Qur'an and the Gospel

In his second chapter, Nicholas of Cusa examines the theme of *Quid continet Alkoranus secundum eius laudatores* (The contents of the Qur'an according to its praisers). His discussion begins with the consideration that, according to Muhammad's followers, the Qur'an was written with good intentions to make known how Muhammad, an orphan who was idolatrous, poor, ignorant of the Law and the Scriptures, and polygamous, after having gained the mercy of God became rich, enlightened, and famous. God himself has conferred upon him the title of doctor of the uncultured and idolatrous Arab people and has sent him to visit the Arab people as a prophet, however, without giving him the power to perform miracles. His mission was to bring on the straight and narrow path those people miserably fallen into error.

Based on what is written in the Qur'an—Nicholas of Cusa continues—God revealed to Muhammad that he had to accept Abraham's religion and convince the Arabs accordingly, without using any violent compulsion. In addition, he had to preach that God was the one and only Creator of all things and that no other Lord or King of the Universe existed.[61] But the followers of the Qur'an, Nicholas explains, believe that the book of Arab law descended from heaven and that its most genuine foundation is faith in a single God and in all men's return before his dreadful judgment. Some things kept in the book are evidence of that faith, while others are laws the Arab believers are obliged to observe. If they want to obey God, they must worship and remain in his grace so that they can receive heaven as final and supreme reward.

59. *Cribratio Alkorani*, III.VI.41.1–2.
60. *Cribratio Alkorani*, n.41.
61. *Cribratio Alkorani*, I.II.26.

Those who profess this faith are called "*musselmanni*" (Muslims, literally "those who submit to God") or *sanae fidei* ("those who firmly believe"). Muslims believe that those who want to avoid eternal fire and save their souls must necessarily believe in this faith which all the prophets of the past agree upon. Nicholas remarks that the Qur'an does not contradict the prophets but, on the contrary, it approves and confirms the books God gave them, namely, the Testament given to Moses, the Book of Psalms given to David, and the Gospel given to Jesus Christ, son of the Virgin Mary. According to the Qur'an, those who believe in these articles of faith and observe the law written in the books of their religion are freed from hell.

Since Muhammad began his preaching in the year A.D. 624—a period that saw the rise of many heresies, condemned by the synods,[62] about the understanding of the Gospel and the Old Testament—many people joined Muhammad believing that his interpretation of Scripture was more appropriate than others. According to some sources—Nicholas adds—the Jews joined Muhammad in order to prevent him from becoming a perfect Christian. This is why, in addition to his poetic way of writing, the stories written in the Qur'an quite rarely agree with those of the Old Testament and the Gospel. The same sources report that Muhammad reacted firmly, declaring that he was inspired only by God and that "God himself and his blessed spirit had written this highly trustworthy book."[63]

Nicholas explains that not only were some terms found in the Gospel and the Old Testament replaced in the Qur'an, but also the original meaning of some passages was completely upset:[64]

> Among the nonsense preached by the Qur'an, the Author mentions the passages concerning the Virgin Mary, explaining that the Mary the Qur'an talks about had died and was buried in the desert more than thousand years before the Virgin Mary, mother of Christ, who, as it can be inferred from the Qur'an itself, lived at the time of Zachary, father of John the Baptist.[65]

This is not the only passage in which the Qur'an is mistaken, as for example in chapter 35, when the Book tells about Moses' return to the

---

62. In this case, Gaia reminds that Nicholas of Cusa refers to the council of Ephesus (431), Chalcedon (451), Constantinopople I (553), Constantinople II (680), which condemned the Nestorians and the Monophysites. Gaia, *Opere religiose*, 739, n.5.

63. Sura 16.101-2.

64. *Cribratio Alkorani*, I.IV.31 and 32.

65. *Cribratio Alkorani*, I.IV.31 and 32.

Pharaoh who had raised him. This tale, Nicholas explains, is absolutely improbable, considering that the Pharaoh had died long before Moses' return to Egypt, as testified in the Book of Exodus.[66]

Nicholas does not put *Quod evangelium sit Alkorano praeferendum* (that the Gospel must be preferred to the Qur'an) in doubt, as stated in the title of chapter 5. This truth is not even denied in the Qur'an, since in Sura 3 we can read that "God gave men as guidelines first the Testament, then the Gospel, and finally he sent from heaven a truthful book, the Qur'an, which confirms your law."[67] Again in Sura 3, Nicholas remarks that some propositions are very short, for example the prayer placed at the beginning of the text also known as "Mother of the Book," which affirms that men must worship and fear the one and only God and Creator, who is the dreadful judge on doomsday, when resurrection will take place.[68]

The superiority of the Gospel and the Old Testament over the Qur'anic text can be inferred also from chapter 12 of the Book, which affirms that God told the Jews he had sent Christ, son of Mary, to complete their law and had entrusted Christ with the Gospel "which is a light and a confirmation of the Testament, an exhortation and a guide for those who fear God."[69] Moreover, the Qur'an defines the Gospel as *lucidum et aliquando splendidissimum*[70] (bright and most shining), since it contains everything necessary to salvation and supplements the law of the Old Testament with all that remained to be completed.[71] We can find some examples of the Gospel's superiority in the Qur'an itself, Nicholas underlines, reporting the following passage: "The men of the law shall not reach the perfection of any law or faith if they do not observe the precepts of the Testament, of the Gospel, and of this book given by God."[72]

In Nicholas of Cusa's opinion, the author of the Qur'an was undoubtedly acquainted with the Gospel, as evidenced by the numerous quotations of its passages which are precisely and appropriately included in it.[73] At

---

66. See Exod 2:23. *Cribratio Alkorani*, I.IV.33.

67. Sura 3.3–7.

68. *Cribratio Alkorani*, I.V.34.

69. Sura 5.46.

70. *Cribratio Alkorani*, I.V.34; Suras 35.24 (illuminating book) and 3.184 (illuminated book).

71. *Cribratio Alkorani*, I.V.35.

72. Sura 5.68.

73. *Cribratio Alkorani*, I.VI.37.

the same time, Nicholas explains, the Gospel mentioned by Muhammad and from which he drew his quotations was in his time likely kept within some ancient manuscripts in the regions of Arabia before the composition of the Qur'an. Indeed, the Gospel had been written several centuries before Muhammad,[74] but Arab scholars had not cared about studying the Christian truth.

Therefore, all that we read in the Qur'an that is beautiful, true, and illuminated is drawn from the Gospel, in particular the exhortation to justice and merciful acts; God's love for the neighbor; the belief that selling all worldly goods represents the highest profit if it is made for God's sake; the idea that dying for God means living forever for the sake of truth; and prohibitions against usury, homicide, perjury, fornication, adultery, and greed for material things. On the contrary, when the Qur'an[75] refers to sensual pleasures and to the pleasures of flesh, it diverges from the Word of the Gospel.[76]

Then Nicholas begins to examine the literary style of the Qur'an, coming to the lapidary conclusion that the stylistic elegance of this book is no evidence of its divine origin. In fact, Muhammad states that, in virtue of the marvelous elegance of its style, the Qur'an could not have been written by any man or devil but only by God.[77] Even assuming that Muhammad had a gift for the Arabic,[78] it does not mean that all that is written in the Qur'an is really the Word of God.[79]

In addition, Nicholas mentions Muhammad's lasciviousness and wanton interest in women, his marked propensity to pursue material goods, and his inability to perform miracles. Since the Qur'an reports the account of Muhammad's life, this further proves that God did not intend for Muhammad to be compared or preferred to Christ, Moses, and the other prophets.

---

74. *Cribratio Alkorani*, I.VI.37.

75. *Cribratio Alkorani*, I.VI.38.

76. *Cribratio Alkorani*, I.VI.38. In this way, Nicholas of Cusa affirms, it is possible to distinguish those who are guided by the spirit of Christ from those who, like the "lubrico Mahumeto and illis antichristis, hoc saeculum futuro praeferunt et nihil bonum iudicant, nisi huic mundo et eorum concupiscentiis conformetur."

77. *Cribratio Alkorani*, I.VII.38.

78. *Cribratio Alkorani*, I.VII.39.

79. See Suras 7.36; 10.17; 11.18; 29.68. And since, many passages contradict what is written in the Testament and in the Gospel, then "deo ignorantiam et inconstantiam atque mendacium adscribi oporteret, quod tamen etiam in Alkorano pro maximo peccato habetur." See Sura 2, 200–202.

Indeed, if we compare the life and the doctrine of the other prophets with Muhammad's, it immediately emerges that nobody should prefer to follow Muhammad instead of Christ.[80] There are numerous passages in the Arabs' book of law that give evidence of Christ's superiority over any other prophet and include a clear recommendation to follow him before anyone else.[81] Therefore, the Qur'an itself drives us to follow Christ rather than Muhammad, and the Gospel rather than the Qur'an. That said, how could the one who admits several gods really glorify the clearness and the glory of God? In several passages the Qur'an not only seems to blame the expression "Son of God,"[82] but also to maintain that this term implies the existence of a plurality of divine substances (*consubstantialitatem*), which is denied both the in Old Testament and in the Gospel.

In some passages, the Qur'an denies that God gave birth to a Son in a human way, and in this it does not contradict the Gospel, because God is pure spirit and is not made of flesh and blood. In other passages, however, we read that "there is only one God, necessary to all things and incorporeal, who does not generate and is not generated, and does not have anyone similar to him";[83] consequently, this Sura should be interpreted as follows: the Qur'an aims at giving God glory and not at subtracting praise from Christ. In his chapter entitled *Obiectio ex Alkorano et eius solutio* (An Objection to the Qur'an and its solution), Nicholas unravels the problem of the contradiction of the Qur'an with the Gospel concerning the incorporeal nature of God and the divine nature of Christ. God and divinity are the same thing, but since God, being the simplest entity, is absolutely incorporeal and uncreated, when we behold the divinity we cannot see any generation.[84]

8. Unity, Difference, and Equality

The *Liber Secundus* opens with the chapter *De theologia mystica, secundum quam deus est ineffabili* (On mystical theology, according to which God is ineffable). Through the *manuductio*, Nicholas intends to prove that the Qur'an does not deny the Christian Trinity. As in other parts of his essay, Nicholas pretends to answer an objection raised by an Arab. In this case,

80. *Cribratio Alkorani*, I.VIII.41.
81. *Cribratio Alkorani*, I.VIII.42.
82. Sura, 23.92. The Qur'an states that "God did not take a Son."
83. Sura 112.1–4.
84. *Cribratio Alkorani*, I.XIV.55.

the Arab recognizes that Qur'an contains much praise for the Gospel, yet he maintains that—in contrast to Christians who believe in the plurality formed by God the Father and Creator, God the Son, and God the Holy Ghost—Muslims admit the one and only God, Creator of all things, and deny any plurality. Therefore, they prefer the Qur'an to the Gospel, the reading of which is even forbidden in some schools.

In the title of chapter 2, *De theologia affirmativa, secundum quam deus est creator trinus et unus* (On affirmative theology, according to which God is the Creator, triune, and one), Nicholas anticipates the themes he intends to tackle, starting from the consideration that men perceive the visible world differently from what their eyes perceive in a particular moment, since it might be greater or smaller.[85]

Furthermore, just like the intellect, when it is active, must necessarily participate in the performance of any idea or concept (because otherwise it would not know what it is doing and would not be intellect), it must likewise possess that idea in knowledge and art, since if it were lacking in action, it would be ineffective. It must also possess the idea in its will, because the noble intellect does nothing without willing it. In other words, Nicholas warns that we must consider that science and art are also generated by an idea, just as free will results from an idea and from art and science. Therefore, if there were no idea, neither would there be any art, and if there were neither idea nor art, there would exist no free will to choose. Therefore, in his opinion, it is important to bear in mind that all that exists in the operative intellect also exists in art and will; there cannot be one thing in the idea, another thing in art, and another in will, *alias non esset una perfecta operatio* (since otherwise, it would not be a perfect operation).[86] According to Cusanus, that which is in knowledge is knowledge; for in knowledge the known is the knowledge.

Nicholas concludes that the excellence of the intellective nature, which he affirms is free, demands that a mind should not be mistaken for the knowledge it generates, because science, being generated by the idea itself, is not the generating idea or father. Furthermore, this excellence demands that an idea, and the science generated by it, should not be mistaken for the will which proceeds from the idea and art, because all that it produces is not all that it originates from.[87] To better explain the concepts he is going to

---

85. *Cribratio Alkorani*, II.II.75.
86. *Cribratio Alkorani*, II.II.77.
87. Cf. Gaia, *Opere religiose*, 778, n.2.

expound, Nicholas resorts to a new metaphor of the sower who is sowing a field with wheat. The sower must have the idea of the seed of wheat in his mind, the art of sowing in his knowledge, and the intention to sow the wheat in his will.[88]

Since the intellective nature received its essence, excellence, and nobility only from the Creator, it acts in his likeness. Consequently, by creating, it produces real things. Creating, in fact, means "bringing to life," and understanding means "assimilating."[89] Christians call the divine mind in which all creatures have existed since the dawn of time the "Father and Creator," while they call the art of his omnipotence, that is to say, his knowledge and his science, "Son," and the will moving from the Father and the Son, without which nothing can exist, "Holy Ghost." The actions of this Trinity are undivided, because activity and the creation of all things constitute a single act. Both the Gospel and the Qur'an refer to God's creation and activity in the plural, but this does not mean believing in several gods or departing from the unity of God Creator.

In Cusanus' opinion, since Muhammad believes that God is the Creator of all things, he should necessarily agree with what the Christians confess about the Trinity of God. In order to enable every Arab to reach the faith, each man must understand the divine fecundity, generation, and love; he must be able to understand that this world cannot last and exist without fecundity, generation, and love;[90] and he must understand that these qualities belong to a single world that would cease to exist without these qualities. Furthermore, all beings participate in these three elements.[91]

Of course, the world derives its being, necessarily one and simultaneously triune, from its Creator who, like the creation, is one and triune. Through a process of *manuductio de intellectuali trinitate ad divinam*, Nicholas considers the Trinity and affirms that it derives from the uncreated Trinity, like a copy derives from its model and effect derives from cause.[92]

---

88. *Cribratio Alkorani*, II.II.77.
89. *Cribratio Alkorani*, II.III.78.
90. See Gaia, *Opere religiose*, 782, n.1.
91. *Cribratio Alkorani*, II.V.82.
92. *Cribratio Alkorani*, II.V.82–83.

9. Sin

Nicholas of Cusa imagines that a zealous Arab[93] asks to be better informed on how the death of Christ glorifies the Father, Creator of all things. To prevent anybody from questioning this statement, Nicholas continues his argumentation, starting from the statement that sin, as the Gospel reaffirms, brings division between God and man.[94] This is, obviously, original sin, which condemns every man to live in impurity, victim of the sensual pleasure of flesh.[95]

It is not by chance that some of Nicholas of Cusa's most significant thoughts on the theme of original sin were included in the *Cribratio Alkorani*.[96] By underlining the pivotal role, in the Christian faith, of the dogmas of the incarnation, death, and resurrection of Christ, Nicholas defines sin as a separation of man from God. Sin brings division between God and man, your sins have divided you from your God.[97] In mentioning the dual possibility that the *malum mundi* (the evil of the world) might descend either from today's sin or from original sin, Nicholas affirms that in this case we must refer to original sin, because "anyone conceived by his mother in sin was born in impurity and in the sensual pleasure of flesh." Since, beginning from Adam, everyone was conceived in this way by his mother conforming to the will of a man, we were born as children of wrath with concupiscence for the flesh, and from the propensity to evil we feel from our adolescence, we understand that we are not driven by the good Spirit of God.[98] Man, who is placed at the lowest rank among the intellectual creatures, possesses an intellect that is merely potential; he needs another act to help him making the transition from power to act. This perfect act, Nicholas writes, is the divine grace which completely permeated and enveloped the garden of Eden.[99]

Sin, caused by man's act of disobedience, is one of the central themes in Christian theology. Nicholas of Cusa affirms that Islam is a heresy, and

---

93. *Cribratio Alkorani*, II.XVII.114.

94. Isa 59:2: where we read "Your sins have divided you from your God."

95. *Cribratio Alkorani*, II.XVII.114; see Sura 70.19–20: "Man was created unstable; in evil he collapses, in good he is intractable."

96. Cuozzo, "Il tema del peccato originale nella teoria della conoscenza di Nicola da Cusa," 121–22.

97. *Cribratio Alkorani*, II.XVII.114.

98. Cuozzo, "Il tema del peccato originale," 122.

99. *Cribratio Alkorani* II.108.

therefore the subsequent departures of the Muslim doctrine are the fruit of Muhammad's ignorance and the effect of the sin inborn in all men. He argues that both the Gospel and the Qur'an agree that Christ was the only one who was not born as a child of wrath, hatred, or abomination but as the purest man endeared to God and, thus, never divided from Him.[100] The fact that God gave His beloved firstborn and only Son for the salvation of the world is proof of the Creator's love for the world itself, the evidence of which is witnessed in the Gospel.[101] The Qur'an, in contrast, reveals that Adam, since Adam did not at all do what was commanded by God, he became subject to the law of mortality.[102] All those who died in the death of Christ gave God satisfaction and were released from slavery to the prince of darkness. Differently from Abraham, whom God ordered to kill His only son Isaac to please Him, Jesus gave himself up to death for the redemption of mankind, giving proof of the ineffable glory of God the Father in having given to death His Son for the sake of the whole mankind.[103]

We must bear in mind that the spiritual kingdom of heaven is not like the kingdom of the world, of which only a small part is owned by each man. Rather, it is like the intellectual kingdom, which can be owned by numberless intellects and completely by each man. Through knowledge, in which all beings provided with intellect participate, and its teachings in the Messiah, every man can resurrect in Christ. This knowledge did not die when Christ died as a human being, since it does not differ from the knowledge through which God, Father and Creator, created all things. The Qur'an calls it "the soul of God,"[104] as it affirms that the souls of men participate in the soul of God inasmuch as he reduces the knowledge in them,[105] whereas the soul of Christ is joined to the height of God's knowledge.[106] Therefore, the Qur'an states that God offered Christ his soul.[107] Furthermore, the book of the Arabs' law maintains that Jesus received that knowledge already when he was in the womb of his mother,[108] and this is also confirmed by Muham-

100. *Cribratio Alkorani*, II.XVII.115; cf. Sura 3.47; 4.156; 19.20; 21.91; 66.12.
101. *Cribratio Alkorani*, II.XVII.116; Gio., 3.16.
102. *Cribratio Alkorani*, n. 144. Cf. Sura 7.24.
103. *Cribratio Alkorani*, II.XVII.117.
104. See *Crib.*, I, c. 20.
105. See Sura 17.85.
106. See *Col.*, I.19; 2.9.
107. See Sura 2.253: "We have comforted him (Christ) with the Holy Ghost."
108. *Cribratio Alkorani*, II.XVII.119.

mad, both in the "Doctrine" and in the Qur'an, which mentions, as it does the Gospel, the miracles performed by Jesus.

10. Heaven

The doctrine of sin is directly related to the eschatological doctrine. Referring to heaven, Nicholas of Cusa acknowledges that an Arab might raise some objections about the numerous differences existing between the Gospel and the Qur'an on this subject.[109] According to some commentators, the Qur'an did apparently depart from the Gospel in order to lead the uncultured Arabs to believe in a single Creator and make them believe that God would give them in the eternal afterworld a better and more perfect life than that they had on earth. Muhammad was driven—Nicholas explains—to introduce many similes so that not only learned men were able understand them; otherwise, he concludes, the Arabs probably would not have understood God and would have been diverted from pursuing the joy of afterlife.

When Muhammad affirms that "the good shall go to heaven, where they shall forever enjoy the sweetest waters, any kind of fruit-bearing trees, a variety of fruits and the most delightful and pure women, as well as any other good,"[110] we must pay the utmost attention to interpreting the promise of tangible things as the promise of "all the good," which is God.[111] Here, Nicholas maintains that in many passages, the Qur'an refers to the day of judgment, paradise, and hell by resorting to a number of *similitudines* (similes).[112] The Gospel, too, makes use of several similes, and this might induce us to believe that *posse illa pia sequacium libri interpretatione excusari* (this can justify the pious interpretation of the Book given by its followers).[113] The Qur'an praises the chastity of the Virgin Mary,[114] forbids copulation in temples, and prescribes bathing before praying, because

---

109. *Cribratio Alkorani*, II.XVIII.121.

110. See Sura 2.25.

111. *Cribratio Alkorani*, II.XVIII.123. See *Doctrina Machumenti* (Bibl. I.193.29–31).

112. *Cribratio Alkorani*, II.XIX.124. Gaia refers to Cusa's work *De coniecturis*, in particular to chapter I, 12, 12, pointing out that conjecture is a positive assertion, which participates in truth, by approaching it in an always relative and imperfect way. Gaia, *Opere religiose*, 819, n.1.

113. *Cribratio Alkorani*, II.XIX.125.

114. See Suras 3.42–47; 4.156; 19.20 ff.; 21.91; 66.12.

purity is appreciated by God.[115] It also affirms that the good shall behold God and shall be with him in heaven, and that God shall reward them with eternal and incorporeal joy.[116] Through an *Invectio contra Alkoranum* (Invective against the Qur'an), Nicholas continues his reasoning in harsh tones, reminding that in the Book Muhammad affirms that God promised him also the pleasures He forbids the others.[117] Nicholas writes that he cannot understand how Muhammad was not ashamed to swear against God by charging Him with having ordered such a blasphemy (to allow the Prophet to continue to live in adultery). Another evidence of this foulness, according to Nicholas, can be found in the passages describing permissible behavior with women: according to the Qur'an, women can be used and subdued to the will of man,[118] who has the right to practice polygamy,[119] and once their dowry is paid, women become property of their husband, who can do with them whatever he likes.[120]

Nicholas then examines the passages where the Qur'an writes that God ordered Muhammad to become His messenger and chose him to fight the idolatrous Arabs.[121] Since Muhammad's task was exclusively that of announcing to the believers of God a message full of joy, why then—Nicholas wonders—did he not limit himself to executing God's order, that is to say, to being His messenger? Why, instead, did he arrogate to himself the right to be called *doctorem gentium* (teacher of the peoples)?[122] Then Nicholas breaks out in an open censure, charging Muhammad with having preached against the Gospel and the Old Testament and with having claimed to teach a new law and a new book as if it were the task entrusted to him. However,

---

115. See Sura 2.222.

116. *Cribratio Alkorani*, II.XIX.126.

117. See Sura 33.2, in which God sanctions Muhammad's marriage with Zainab, the former wife of his adoptive son, whereas the Arab customs prohibited this practice. *Cribratio Alkorani*, II, xix, 126; see Sura 66.1–2, in which God reproaches Muhammad for having made illicit under oath what he had declared licit (notably, copulating with one's slave woman, such as Mohammed did with Mary the Copt, but having been caught by his wife Hafsa, he swore her he would stop that love affair) and reminds him that a believer can be released from an oath through atonement.

118. Sura 2.223.

119. See Sura 4.3.

120. Sura 4.24. *Cribratio Alkorani*, II.XIX.127; on the perfect law of freedom, see *Giac.*, I.25.

121. See Sura 68.1–3.

122. *Cribratio Alkorani*, II.XIX.128; Sura 68.52.

at the end of the second book of his treatise, Nicholas softens his rebuke and reverts to the similes which make the Qur'an resemble the Gospel.[123]

The hope for happiness in the afterlife is also a recurring theme in *De pace fidei*. Man's hope in heaven is the ultimate desire, beyond which there is nothing more desirable. This should not hinder the achievement of concordance among the different religions. Nicholas writes also in *De docta ignorantia* that the fact that men belonged to different creeds contributes to the creation of different opinions; all that is praiseworthy in one man's opinion may not be such in the opinion of another man.[124]

11. Difference and Diversity

The problem of difference and diversity in the *Cribratio* is focused on three discursive areas: the first is based on theological foundations (Trinity); the second develops by arguing on the differences between the Qur'an and the Gospel; while the third concerns ritual differences (circumcision) and the conception of the afterlife.

As in *De pace fidei*, the intellectual comprehension of the dogmas of Christianity plays a primary role, and in Cusanus' opinion, interreligious dialogue is possible through such comprehension. Nicholas wrote *De pace fidei* in the form of a dialogue, however, while the *Cribratio* is a commentary of the Qur'anic text written with a strong apologetic *intentio*. Though this work is not a real dialogue, the theme of the relationship between Christianity and Islam is central. In the *Cribratio*, the reasoning on Islam is far more extensive than in *De pace fidei*, and Nicholas proves to be well-acquainted with both the Qur'an and Muhammad's biography, as well as with some works of Avicenna and Al-Ghazali. Watanabe affirms that in *De pace fidei*, the superiority of the Christian religion is undisputed. Then in the *Cribratio*, the alleged superiority of the Christian religion over Islam seems even more evident. From this point of view, the continuity between these two works is evident, as are their links to *De docta ignorantia*. The theme of difference and unity, which recurs also in *De concordantia*, for example through the organic metaphor of body and soul as symbolic personifications of the empire and the church, is resumed by Nicholas in *De docta ignorantia*, where difference is the presupposition of the cognitive process, as well as in *De pace fidei*, where the difference between religions

---

123. *Cribratio Alkorani*, II.XIX.128.
124. *De docta ignorantia*, III.8.

and rituals is not considered a hindrance to peace, but rather, a need for the political community. In the *Cribratio*, Nicholas reverts to the topic of difference from several points of view for the purpose of proving the truth of the Christian religion as rationally and intellectually self-evident. The continuity among Cusanus's major works, grounded in similar conceptual paradigms and themes, seems therefore confirmed.

12. Method of Cusanus

The second book of the *Cribratio Alkorani* is focused on three major themes: Trinity, crucifixion and resurrection, and heaven. Nicholas of Cusa decides to deal with these three theological themes because the two religions differ considerably regarding the trinitarian dogma and the Christological sacrifice. The Qur'an affirms indeed[125] that Jesus is the son of Mary and the messenger of God, but it denies that Christ is the Son of God, as God cannot have any son. Starting from the concordances he identifies between the Gospel and the Qur'an, through mystical—or negative—theology, Nicholas aims to demonstrate that we can say nothing certain about God, but we must only admire and behold in silence.[126]

Cusanus' dialectic process is particularly refined. He neither affirms anything certain about the nature of God, nor does he contradict what is written in the Qur'an. Instead, he finds some theoretical affinities between the two scriptures. For example, both the Qur'an and the Gospel consider God transcendent and infinite. The problem of the nature of Christ is therefore subordinated to the inescapable acknowledgment of God's ineffability.

After having demonstrated through metaphors and theological arguments[127] that everything in the world leads to the vision of the Trinity, Nicholas makes use of a statement drawn from the Qur'an to affirm that "all living beings come from water."[128] Just like there are in water a source, a stream, and a pond, so do the three divine elements combine and become part of the Trinity.[129] Nicholas draws the metaphor of water from John Scotus Eriugena and Meister Eckhart and quotes a Qur'anic Sura, which as a matter of fact refers not to the divine Trinity but to the

125. Sura 4.
126. *Cribratio Alkorani*, II.I.88.1–5 and 18.19.
127. *Cribratio Alkorani*, II, chapters 2, 3, 4, 5, 6.
128. Sura 21.30.
129. *Cribratio Alkorani*, II.IX.110.5–9.

generating principle of life. Chapter XI of the second book puts an end to the discourse on Trinity, and Nicholas concludes that "the Arabs must necessarily confess the Trinity."[130]

Nicholas intends to prove the numberless affinities existing between the Qur'an and the Gospel through the *manuductio* and the *pia interpretatio*. Depending on the case, to support his reasoning and beliefs he quotes all the Qur'anic Suras related to the subjects he deals with. If there are so many similarities between the two texts, since the Qur'an writes that "the Gospel is an extremely clear and truthful book," the Arabs (or Muslims) must consequently recognize the evangelical truths, because otherwise they would fall into error and contradiction.[131] As Hageman argues: "Nicholas does never gets tired of searching in the Qur'an for what he likes to define as new possible links that might pave the way to the Christian faith . . . . The themes already tackled in *De pace fidei*—Trinity, the interpretation of Heaven from an eschatological point of view—. . . are presented again in the *Cribratio Alkorani*."[132]

Nicholas aims to lead the Muslim reader to learn the truth of the Gospel. The eschatological problem is strictly connected with acceptance of the dogma of the Trinity. The *manuductio*, as well as being one of the leitmotivs of Nicholas's theology, also groups all his attempts—he calls *manuductiones ad trinitatem*—aimed at explaining to Muslims the concept of Trinity. To achieve his purpose, Nicholas makes use of some frequently recurring concepts developed in his earlier works—unity, equality, and inequality—through an *analogia entis* (analogy of entity) method, but above all, through the conceptual crux *unitas-equalitas-nexus*. Unity generates equality. Equality comes before any plurality, and inequality comes after it and depends on equality; therefore equality is eternal. Nicholas of Cusa resumes the arguments he had developed in *De concordantia catholica*, *De docta ignorantia*, and *De pace fidei*, to support the trinitarian dogma, one

130. *Cribratio Alkorani*, II.XI.1.

131. Biechler, "Sifting the Qur'an," 282: "We must note one other notion that sets the Sifting apart as unusually open-minded and irenic. This is the surprisingly ecumenical notion of *manuductio*. In Nicholas' usage it suggests that Qur'anic teaching opens the Islamic faith to a kind of guidance—a leading by the hand—that leads the human mind step by step through and beyond the sensible world to a knowledge of the divine. Manuductio had along and distinguished Neoplatonic pedigree and in Nicholas' hands he finds in the Qur'an nuggets of truth that reflect divine truth and these then serve as touchstones enabling him to "take the Muslims by the hand" to lead them to an understating to true Christian belief.

132. Hagemann, *Christentum contra Islam*, 100.

of the most relevant themes to be tackled in a comparison with the Islamic religion. This is particularly important not only for studying the structure of the *Cribratio* but also, in general, Nicholas's thought and the intellectual process through which he came to the commentary on the Qur'an after having developed a model of multi-religious dialogue in *De pace fidei*.

The other issues in which Nicholas identifies a clash between Christianity and Islam include Christ's resurrection and heaven. In Book II Cusanus deals with the theme of the resurrection of Jesus starting from the Qur'anic Suras 18 and 19, in which it is written that man will rise again from the dead.[133]

13. Kalam

Muslim theology, or *kalam*, refers to the legal status of the believer and the unfaithful sinner. According to Islamic theology, the act of faith consists of three elements or stages:[134] an inner judgment of truth, the profession of faith expressed in words: the works of faith, that is to say, one's obeisance to God and the prophets; and observance of the law.

Early Mu'tazili and Asharite theologians considered man a living body and considered life and soul to be accidents of the body.[135] The *falasifa*, Arab philosophy deeply influenced by Platonism, defined man as pure spirit, spiritual and immaterial substance, emanated through the gradation of the One and introduced into a material body acting as an instrument of knowledge and action, which waits until freeing itself and joining with the One.[136] The soul, or spirit, is immortal, and death frees the soul from the

---

133. *Cribratio Alkorani*, II, XV.130.5–8.

134. Caspar, *Theologie musulmane*, 16: "The term Islam is usually referred, though incorrectly, to the Muslim religion. As a matter of fact, Islam is one of the terms used by the *kalam* to define the *imam*, or the ways in which faith is expressed. Another element is the *ihsan*, or worship of God. Muslim theological schools differ also as regards their views on the relation between *imam* and Islam. For the Mu'tazili school, for example, there is identity between *imam* and Islam, whereas, for the Asharite school, *imam* refers to the faith of heart, and Islam to ritual practices. Though there are considerable differences among the various Muslim theological schools, they however agree on the meaning of Islam, that is to say, the act of submission to God, which points out the fundamental attitude of faith and the general attitude of all believers."

For an introduction to Islamic theology, see Winter, *The Cambridge Companion to Classical Islamic Theology*. D'Ancona Costa, *Storia della filosofia nell'Islam medievale*.

135. See McGinnis and Reisman, *Classical Arabic Philosophy*.

136. Caspar, *Theologie musulmane*, 22.

body. The Mu'tazilis defined man as a substantial union of body and soul, and death as the separation of these elements. The theologian Al-Ghazali was undoubtedly the first who clearly expressed this concept.[137]

Paradise and hell are often mentioned in the Qur'an. Paradise is named in seven different ways according to seven different ages: the Greek garden or *paradeisos*; the biblical Garden of Eden; the garden of immortality; the garden of delight; the garden of refuge; the home of peace; and the home of majesty.[138] The *falasifa* strongly denies corporeal delights, which are interpreted as symbols of intellectual and spiritual delights, the only possible forms of joy for the souls that have parted from the body. Most Muslim authors, including the Mu'tazilis, are inclined to consider the Qur'anic word a metaphor, whereas other authors, in contrast, support the reality of corporeal delights in paradise, though they underline that such pleasures are not similar to those that can be enjoyed on the earth.[139] This interpretation is also adopted by Nicholas of Cusa, who affirms that Muhammad introduced similes and figures of speech for the purpose of converting uncultured persons, as written in Sura 3.145: "It is impossible that a being dies without the permission of God, the date of his death being established and written by Him; we shall grant afterworld rewards those who want them, and we shall grant worldly rewards those who want them; we shall give all those who are grateful to us their reward."[140]

In chapter 19 of the *Cribratio Alkorani*, entitled "Invective against the Qur'an," several Qur'anic theological concepts are expounded. Nicholas aims to prove that the holy book is extremely ambiguous and scarcely convincing on eschatological and theological matters. Through the *manuductio*, Nicholas guides his readers "hand in hand" to a right comprehension of the Qur'an. Through the *pia interpretatio*, Nicholas comments on Sura 2.25, in which it is written: "But give, Muhammad, those who believe and do good the good news that there are for them Gardens in the shade of which rivers flow, and when they shall eat those fruits every time they will say: 'This is the food we also had before,' but it shall be only apparently

137. Ibid., 165.

138. Ibid., 175.

139. For an introduction to the concept of heaven and paradise in the different religions, see Krauss, *Il paradiso. Storia e cultura*. On Islamic paradise, see Ali, *The Meaning of the Holy Qur'an*.

140. Qur'an, Sura 3.145. The Aristotelian philosopher Ibn Rushd (Averroes) postulated in his writings a distinction between two kinds of interpretation of the Qur'anic text: one for the philosophers' elite, and another for the believers' crowd.

similar to that food; and there, they will have the purest wives and will remain there forever!"[141] Nicholas intends to prove that "any good forever" is nothing but God, though Muhammad does often promise tangible things.

14. Happiness

The theme of happiness is dealt with also in *De pace fidei*, in which the representatives of each religion discuss their different views and positions concerning eternal life and resurrection. In *De pace fidei*, Nicholas goes so far as to affirm that man's aspiration to happiness is at the origin of all religious beliefs, and therefore all confessions are alike,[142] thus providing a "psychological" reflection on the origin of faith. In the *Cribratio* Nicholas' approach is based on an analysis of the composition style of the Qur'an, in which Muhammad made use of metaphors so as to make its comprehension easier also to uncultured persons.[143]

Nicholas of Cusa identifies two textual communication levels: one concerning communication to uncultured believers, and one addressed to men of letters and intellectuals. The latter, in fact, do not need metaphors or figures of speech focusing on the promise of the corporeal delights[144] of paradise, because all Muslim theologians[145] are interested in the possibility to behold God. In particular, the theologians Al-Ghazali and Razi[146] insist on the interpretation of Sura 9.72: "God promised all men and women who believe in Him gardens in the shade of which rivers are flowing, where they shall dwell forever, and good abodes in the gardens of Eden: but God's good pleasure shall be the greatest gift for them."

In Book III of the *Cribratio* there is another reference to the dual level of textual communication of the Qur'an: Nicholas underlines that while

---

141. Sura 2.25.

142. *De pace fidei*, chapter XXI.

143. *Cribratio Alkorani*, II.XVIII.150.9–13.

144. Caspar, *Theologie musulmane*, 179. In Caspar's opinion, there are many eschatological differences between Christianity and Islam. For example, God does not live in paradise and remains inaccessible in his home, and faith persists in heaven, evidencing the oneness of the absent God. The divine vision is discontinuous for the Muslims, who do not envisage an "annulment" of the soul in God's beatitude. For the Christian religion beatitude is God himself. The vision of God is the divine vision and faith dissolves, while charity remains.

145. Caspar, *Theologie musulmane*, 176.

146. See McGinnis and Reisman, *Classical Arabic Philosophy*.

in Sura 3.5 it is written that "nobody can rightly intend the Qur'an, except God and the wise men who hold the divine science," Suras 26.27 and 75 state instead that "the Qur'an is simple and clear."[147] In Book II, Nicholas, as a theologian, justifies the textual differences of the Qur'an, arguing that they were the result of the Prophet's intention to address a stratified audience that included both men of letters and illiterate persons. In Book III, however, the change in textual style is reason for heated controversy, and Nicholas affirms in fact that because the Qur'an so contradictory, it cannot be a work of God.

15. Muhammad's Persecution of Christians

Muhammad's persecution of Christians is a burning question for Nicholas, all the more because the Qur'an contains several statements that clash with each other. In particular, Muhammad often reverts to the theme of the impossibility of conversion, contradicting through this statement what he had affirmed concerning the belief that man does everything because God predetermined that he do it, intending this predetermination as a necessary act. According to Nicholas, this is absolutely wrong and denies any law and judgment, any reward and punishment. Differently from what he writes in write about Muhammad, Nicholas explains that truth is quite a different thing for Christians. Since God in eternity can see all events which follow one another over time as if they were all contemporary, he can also simultaneously see a man's life, death, and in-between course of life.[148] This vision, however, does not necessarily determine the events; God simply sees everything and each single action of man because he knows all in eternity.[149]

Everything included in the Qur'an, Nicholas writes, is shrouded in obscurity. Referring to the book of the Arabs' law, Muhammad declares that "If it were not a work of God, it would contain many contradictions."[150] Nicholas seizes on this declaration to observe that, since as a matter of fact it contradicts itself quite often, the Qur'an cannot be a work of God: *ex deo esse non potest.*[151]

---

147. *Cribratio Alkorani*, III.VII.183.12–14.

148. Here Nicholas refers to God's prescience in the way argued by Boethius in *De cons., fil.*, V, chapters 2–6.

149. *Cribratio Alkorani*, III.VII.147.

150. Sura 4.82.

151. *Cribratio Alkorani*, III.VII.147.

Nicholas of Cusa gives chapter 7 of Book III the title *Quod finis operis Mahumeti fuit sui exaltatio* (The end of Muhammad's work being his own exaltation). Here he argues this statement by pointing out that Muhammad, being motivated by his personal thirst for power decided all things through his sword.[152] Hatred and persecution against the Christians, therefore, do not depend on enmity and are not a dictate of the Qur'anic law. Rather, they are the result of Muhammad's inclination to violence and thirst for domination. In Book III of the *Cribratio Alkorani*, in fact, reference is often made to the violent nature of the Islamic doctrine itself.[153]

16. The Theme of War

Several Suras of the Qur'an refer to war,[154] and there are frequent references to "fighting"[155] or *qital*, and to battle and to *jihad*.[156]

The theme of war and *jihad* is extensively dealt with in Islamic literature.[157] Malik ibn Anas, a scholar of religion who lived between 710 and

152. *Cribratio Alkorani*, III.VIII.148.
153. *Cribratio Alkorani*, III.VIII.184.1–5.
154. E.g., Sura 2.191.
155. Kelsay and Turner Johnson, *Just War and Jihad*, 47.
156. About *jihad* and war in the Islamic culture, see Kelsay, *Arguing the Just War in Islam*; Campanini, *Islam e politica*; Kelsay and Turner Johnson, *Cross, Crescent and Sword*. See also Lewis, *Islam*.

Kelsay and Turner Johnson, *Just War and Jihad*, 48. Peters, *Jihad in Classical and Modern Islam*: "stood apart from all other states, the governments of which were not dedicated to fostering the performance of Muslims' religious duties. As we have seen, by the end of the second century A.H./eight century C.E. the juristic tradition had developed the notion of the 'abode of Islam' *dar al-Islam*, and 'abode of war' *dar al-harb*, as a succinct expression of this political dichotomy." In addition to the Qur'an, Muslims gathered the Prophet's words and ideas into a set of religious laws and doctrines, which were handed down in the form of *hadith*, a concise collection of his sayings and acts.

157. Gardet, *Les hommes de l'Islam*, 66. "Muslim law makes a distinction among personal, community and sufficiency duties. The first ones are corporal acts—the pillars of Islam, the five daily prayers, fasting during the lunar month, legal alms and the pilgrimage to Mecca.

Sufficiency duties do not concern individual believers but the whole community. They consist, for example, in the legal exercise of justice, the maintenance of order and peace, the efforts on God's path to defend and enlarge the borders of Islam through the arms, called *jihad*, which is usually uncorrectly translated as 'holy war.' In fact, this term is not connected with the biblical meaning of holy war as extermination and execration against a region and its inhabitants, since it does not aim at destroying but rather at building the City in which the divine prescriptions shall be observed. This goal can be

796 and specialized in Islamic law, spent the greatest part of his life in Medina and is considered the founder of the Malikite school of jurisprudence (*madhhab*).[158] His masterpiece is *al-Muwatta'*, one of the oldest treatises of Muslim jurisprudence. Malik aimed to codify and organize the law of Medina, thus ensuring its enforceability. Among the different versions of this text, only two have survived: one by Yahya ibn Yahya al-Masmoudi, who died in 848, and one by Muhammad al-Shaybani, who died in 805. Both works discussed Malik's opinions and extensively confuted them according to the Hanafite theory. Both works exalt martyrdom in connection with holy war.[159]

Another important source for learning about the juridical doctrine of the *jihad* is the work *Bidayat Al-mujtahid Wa Nihayat Al-muqtasid*,[160] written by Averroes (Abu al-Walid Muhammad Ibn Muhammad Ibn Rushd). This book belongs to the *ikhtilaf* (dispute) genre, which includes treatises dealing with the disputes of the early jurists, in which the opinions of the different schools are compared. Though their contents are drawn form earlier tradition, the way in which the *Bidayat* is presented is quite original. In arguing each dispute, Averroes critically analyzes the theme, and compares the different positions resulting from different and sometimes clashing interpretations of the Qur'anic verses.[161]

Another author who dealt with the moral and religious doctrine of the *jihad* is Taqi al-Din Ahmad Ibn Taymiyyah (1263–1328), a Syrian jurist belonging to the Hanbali school,[162] who emphasized the example of the pious ancestors (*al-salaf al-salih*) as the highest authority. His intransigence brought him into open conflict with the religious establishment and the political authorities of his age, and thus he spent many years in prison. His conception of the purity of Islam was not only academic, as he participated in several military expeditions against the heretics. In his work *al-Siyasa al-Shar'iyya*, he developed a political theory that on the

---

no longer achieved through the arms, but through persuasion, as some contemporary scholars maintain."

158. See Mahmoud Ayoub, *The Qur'an and Its Interpreters*.

159. Gardet, *Les hommes de l'Islam*, 50.

160. Ibid., 56. Averroes adhered to the Malikite school, the most important Islamic school of Spain, but in his work he compares the different schools rather impartially. About the juridical aspects of Ibn Rushd's thought, see Weiss, *Studies in Islamic Legal Theory*.

161. Peters, *Jihad in Classical and Modern Islam*, 47.

162. Dammen McAuliffe, *The Cambridge Companion to the Qur'ān*, 196.

one hand legitimized the political system prevailing after the fall of the caliphate in 1259, and on the other, emphasized the need to exercise power in compliance with the *Sharia*.

Nicholas begins to tackle the theme of violence in Book III in a way similar to how he handled them in chapter 3. After discrediting Muhammad's prophetic ability,[163] he begins to analyze the Qur'an. He does not avail himself of the Latin translation, but instead follows Riccoldo's text,[164] *Contra legem Sarracenorum*, in which the author writes that Muslims believe they will achieve salvation in spite of any kind of crimes they may have committed.[165] This passage clarifies Cusanus' use of sources for the *Cribratio*: he becomes acquainted with the Muslim world through the texts of some commentators of the Qur'an, who in most cases were apologists for Christianity. He makes use of passages drawn from *Contra legem* and from the Qur'an without making any precise distinctions. The chapter of the *Cribratio*, entitled *Why those who believe in the Qur'an, and whose master is the sword consider themselves saved*, focuses on Sura 21.5-6, which reads: "But they say: 'Vain images of dreams! It is he who invented it, he is the poet; may he bring us a token like he did with the ancients!' And none of the cities We destroyed before them, did believe: shall they believe now?"[166] The version of this Sura reported by Nicholas reads instead: "Thou hast collected dreams, accumulated oaths, or perhaps Thou are a poet. Come at least with a miracle, as the previous messengers did. He answered: 'We have destroyed,' God says, 'the cities of those who did not believe; you would not even believe in miracles, you only believe *in your sword*.'"[167]

Nicholas includes the expression *per gladium*, which is not part of the Qur'an, copying it from Riccoldo's text. This textual procedure was a frequent practice in the Middle Ages: translation, comments, and analysis of the text intertwined to make a precise exegesis almost impossible. Yet this

---

163. *Cribratio Alkorani*, III, II: "What kind of prophet is Muhammad, who does not even know what he himself and the other have to do, apart from what had been previously ordered, and brings as his defense witnesses the Jews; this means that he only explained the previous divine commandments of the Testament."

164. Nicolai de Cusa, *Cribratio Alkorani*, cit., 137, n. 169.

165. *Cribratio Alkorani*, III, III, 169, 7-9. Nicholas of Cusa resumes Riccoldo's argument: "Et ut Arabes dicuntur, tunc intentio Mahumeti erat hanc confessionem facies paradisum intrare, etiamsi fornicatus, latrocinatus et alia peccata fecisset, quia fides salvaret."

166. Sura 21.5-6.

167. *Cribratio Alkorani*, III.III.170.1-7.

procedure highlights at the same time the author's theoretical position and the purpose of his writing. Nicholas of Cusa makes use of Riccoldo's words because he intends to argue the violence of the Qur'anic message and aims to prove its inconsistencies and danger. In Book II, chapter 6 of the *Cribratio*, Nicholas makes use, once again, of the *pia interpretatio* method, reporting some Suras that support the uselessness of violence and constraint.[168]

Through the *manuductio* method, Nicholas intends to prove that the Qur'an includes the necessary reasons for not doing violence to Christian believers. To confirm this, he mentions the passages of some Suras dealing with the theme of law and persecution[169] and, in particular, the passage in which it is written: "no constraint shall exist in faith: the straight and narrow path can be correctly distinguished from error, and those who reject *Tagut* and believe have firmly gripped a hilt that can never be broken."[170] After having quoted Sura 106, Nicholas later writes:

> He does not say you shall do violence to them. On the other hand, in other passages you affirm that the contrasts existing among Jews, Christians and other nations will be settled in the last day. Furthermore, in some parts of the Qur'an you introduce God who praises you for your pity and meekness. Why then, do you show yourself practically opposed to those virtues, and give thus false witness of God? Why did you put your God in contradiction with himself each time you changed your mind?[171]

To answer these questions, Nicholas resorts to the Gospel of Matthew:

> Blessed are they which are persecuted for righteousness' sake, for theirs is the kingdom of heaven. Blessed are you, when men shall revile you, and persecute you, and shall say all manner of evil against you falsely, for my sake. Rejoice, and be exceeding glad: for great is your reward in heaven: for so persecuted they the prophets which were before you.[172]

Nicholas betrays some concern about the conversion power of Islam, and as a matter of fact, he writes the *Cribratio* in a historical period in

---

168. Suras 2.256.

169. On Islam pluralism, see Mervin, *Histoire de l'islam*, 292 ff. See also Bamyeh, *The Social Origins of Islam*.

170. Sura 2.256.

171. *Cribratio Alkorani*, III.VI; n. 180; 2–7.

172. Matt 5:10–12.

which the Turks' advance is progressing and represents a danger for the Western world.[173]

Nicholas also remarks on the great relevance placed by the Qur'an in the day of the final judgment.[174]

17. The Speech to Muhammad II

Then Nicholas of Cusa addresses the Calif of Baghdad[175] and asks him why he arrogates to himself the custody of the law of the Arabs.[176] The sultan was formerly a Christian, but he repudiated his religion in order to be fit for the principality.[177] For this reason he denied that Christ was the real Son of God and had died on the cross.[178] But after having become sultan, Nicholas adds, the sultan began to believe that Amram was the father of Mary.[179] It would therefore be better if he realized that the Jews who helped Muhammad deceived him about Mary.[180]

All that being said, Nicholas tries to find his way to the sultan's heart, leading him to meditate on the fact that some authoritative emperors—such as Theodosius, Marcian, Constantine, and all their successors—tried to enhance the glory of the Virgin Mother of Christ. Surely, he continues, the sultan might object that he never refused to properly pay honor to the Virgin Mary, sentencing to death those who swore at her, but it might escape his mind that Christ was born of the Virgin Mary. Nicholas answers this rhetorical question by affirming that all answers can be found in the Gospel.

Nicholas then asks the caliph of Baghdad,[181] as spiritual and religious leader of Islam and director of the theological schools, whether or not he

173. See Caspar, *Theologie musulmane*, chapter 3; Kelsay and Turner, *Just War and Jihad*, 135.

174. *Cribratio Alkorani*, III.XX.231.1-5.

175. He certainly refers to the Osmani sultan Muhammad II (1451-81), the conqueror of Constantinople, see Toffanin, *Ultimi saggi*.

176. The sultan had no religious authority as guardian and interpreter of the Qur'an (this office was held by the Grand Mufti of the Hanafis, the sheikh el-Islām), but kept watch over the observance of law.

177. As Gaia explains, the alleged conversion of Muhammad II is another legend that spread in the Western world.

178. See Sura 19.23-26. This tale is included in the Gospel of Pseudo-Matthew 20.

179. See Suras 3.33ff.; 66.12; 19.28.

180. *Cribratio Alkorani*, III.XVII.176.

181. At Nicholas of Cusa's time, the caliphate of Bagdad did not exist any more, as it

believes that God is the author of the Qur'an. Before learning his answer, however, Nicholas warns that if the answer is negative, he would not understand why the caliph commands that in the schools of Baghdad great zeal must be devoted to that book. If the answer is positive, we meet with all the contradictions included in the text, which most likely—Nicholas concludes—depend on the fact that, after the death of Muhammad, the Jews brought some additions to the Qur'an, because Muhammad's collectio was in their hands. Nicholas thus makes allowances to the caliph and the Arabs for having been seduced by cunning and perverse Jews, blasphemers of God. Those Jews, who had adhered to Muhammad's preaching, had come into possession of the collection of his precepts. After Muhammad's death, before handing the Book over to Ali (to whom Muhammad had ordered it to be given), the Jews introduced the passages concerning Abraham—whose sons they boast to be—as well as many other things, which remained in the Qur'an.

In the title of chapter 19, Nicholas of Cusa discloses his aim to demonstrate that *sine Christo non posse felicitari* (it is not possible to rejoice without Christ). His imaginary interlocutor is still the caliph, whom he reminds that, as Muhammad affirms, he and all the others shall submit to Jesus Christ without hesitation, because only through conversion they can aspire to eternal life. According to the Qur'an, too, nobody can become immortal by merit or right. Just as a beast, in spite of all its efforts, will never become intelligent, a man, though he may seem closer than another to immortality and God, will never be able to reach divinity. In fact, the Qur'an also agrees that the only man who undoubtedly deserved eternal life was Christ. Christ deserved the kingdom of immortality through the human nature he had drawn from the Virgin, and this could happen because, in roots or hypostasis, he was immortal by nature.[182] Those who listen to his words and follow him are in possession of immortality. Christ, Nicholas continues, is heir to the immortal kingdom of God, where only

---

had disappeared after the conquest of Baghdad by the Mongols in 1258. Nonetheless, the title of caliph continued to be held by several Islamic princes. Cusanus, who was not acquainted with the actual historical and political situation of the East, considers Riccoldo's information on the caliphs of Baghdad a still living matter. Gaia, *Opere religiose*, 870, n. 1.

182. *Cribratio Alkorani*, III.XX.184. "Natura igitur humana in ipso non est facta immortalis solum ex gratia unionis eius cum divina hypostasi, sed etiam ex exercitio virtutis."

God dwells and to which all men aspire. He is the heir to the universe both by nature and by deed of the Father.[183]

To prevent the caliph from falling into error in his thinking of the way in which the human nature is joined to the divine hypostasis, Nicholas affirms that Jesus, as written the Qur'an,[184] is pre-represented by Adam; and he explains that Adam was created by God so that he ruled over the animals as king and messiah. In Adam, indeed, there was a higher intellectual hypostasis than in animals combining with the brutish nature of beasts. Notwithstanding his dual nature, Adam was a single person. However, Nicholas explains, only a partial comparison between Adam and Christ can be made, because Adam's intellectual life combines sensible life, whereas the divine nature of Christ hypostatically combines both the intellectual human life and the divine life, the greatness of which is unlimited. Since hypostasis is infinitely strong, it never abandons the nature it attracted, just as the strength of a magnet never abandons the iron it attracted, but, on the contrary, through the iron it attracted is capable of attracting another piece of iron, and would do so to infinity if its strength allowed. However, as the strength of the magnet neither takes shape in the iron nor penetrates the iron to become iron nor combines with iron to form a third being made of both elements, and their natures do not get mixed, so the iron adheres to the hypostasis of the strength of the magnet and never abandons it, even if it is moved above or below the magnet.

In Christ, the second heavenly Adam,[185] all those who are predestined to the immortal life of the kingdom of heaven are summarized, and receive from him all that is necessary to become citizens and servants[186] of that heavenly and incorruptible kingdom.[187]

---

183. *Cribratio Alkorani*, III.XX.186–87.
184. See Sura 3.59.
185. See 1 Cor 15:45–47.
186. See Ef., 2.19.
187. *Cribratio Alkorani*, III.XXI.190. Then, addressing the Caliph for the last time, Nicholas of Cusa says: "Quae clarius et apertissime sic esse reperies, si deus dignabitur tibi oculos aperire, ut legas et intelligas sacratissimum evangelium, quod tibi concedat deus pius et misericors sempre benedictus!"

18. Conclusions

In the *Cribratio*, Nicholas of Cusa analyzes the differences between the two confessions basing on their common Christian origin. He finds in the philosophical dialectics developed in *De docta ignorantia* the most appropriate instrument to detect the conceptual inconsistencies of the Qur'an, and consequently unmask a truth that is nothing but the truth of the Gospel. If something beautiful can be found in the Qur'an, it surely comes from the Gospel. Cusanus' *Cribratio Alkorani* exhibits two key features: a reliance on medieval themes, including the violence of the Qur'anic law; and the use of *praesuppositio* to guide Nicholas's reading of the Qur'an. By arguing that the Qur'an presupposes the Gospel's truth, Nicholas simultaneously modifies his perception of Muslim by insisting on their ignorance.

Furthermore, I tried to underline the strong textual coherence of the *Cribratio*:[188] coherence with the testament tradition and coherence with the author's system of thought.

---

188. Cf. Assmann, *Das kulturelle Gedächtnis*.

6

Cusanus and Others: The Western Perception of Islam

1. Introduction

IN THIS CHAPTER, I shall explore how, in addition to Cusanus, both Western and Byzantine thinkers sought to deepen their approach to Islam.[1] The exchange between Byzantium and the Latin West intensified as they formed strategic alliances against the Turkish enemy,[2] and the humanist responses to the Ottoman advance have influenced Western views of the Turks and Islam until today.[3] Yet these humanists relied on earlier accounts of Islam, especially the *Contra legem Sarracenorum*, the main source of Cusanus and one of the most widely circulated and influential works about Islam into the eighteenth century.

I shall briefly examine Riccoldo's *Contra legem Sarracenorum*, since Riccoldo's legacy vividly demonstrates both the shifting rhetoric about Islam and Muslims, and the slowly changing perception of Islam from "enemy" to "other."

Furthermore, I trace rich legacy of *Contra legem* as it was translated and used in the works of five representative authors from the fourteenth and fifteenth centuries. Fazio degli Uberti's *Dittamondo* shows that the *Contra legem* was so widely known that it echoes in fourteenth-century vernacular

---

1. Bisaha, *Creating East and West*, 9. See also Jones, "The Image of the Barbarian in Medieval Europe," 376–407; Piemontese, "Il Corano latino di Ficino e i Corani arabi di Pico e Monchates"; and Meserve, *Empires of Islam in Renaissance Thought*.

2. Hankins, "Renaissance Crusaders."

3. See Burman, *Reading the Qur'an in Latin Christendom*; Nederman, *Worlds of Difference*; Bisaha, *Creating East and West*.

This chapter adapts my article "Perspectives on Islam in Italy and Byzantium in the Middle Ages and Renaissance," in *Nicholas of Cusa and Islam*, edited by Ian Levy, Donald Duclow, and Rita George-Tvrtkovic. I thank *Brill*'s editor for permission to use the article here.

poetry. Riccoldo also informs the Byzantine responses to Islam in Demetrius Kydones' *Pro subsidio Latinorum* and *De non reddenda Callipoli*, and in the treatise *On the Eternal Glory of the Autocrat* of George of Trebizond written to Mehmed II. Marsilio Ficino's *De Christiana religione* adapt *Contra legem* to argue that Islam presupposes Christian truth—a truth that Muslims fail to acknowledge. Finally, I analyze the letter of Enea Silvio Piccolomini and I compare the differences with the *Cribratio alkorani*.

2. The *Contra legem Sarracenorum*

The *Contra legem Sarracenorum* is a work structured in the medieval form of *quaestio*.[4] Its tone is aggressive throughout, as Riccoldo seeks to demonstrate the irrationality and insubstantiality of Islam. He describes Muhammad as a persecutor of the divine—that is, Christian—law,[5] and Muslims as persecutors of Christians.

In the first chapter Riccoldo writes that Muhammad's principal intention is to convince readers that Christ is neither a god nor the Son of God, but only a wise man.[6] Riccoldo outlines the affinities between Islam and heresies such as Arianism and Manichaeism. Furthermore, he underlines the lecherous reputation of Muhammad. According to Riccoldo, Muhammad does affirm that beatitude consists in carnal pleasures and in food, in marvelous clothes, and in living in gardens rich in water. In the Qur'an Muhammad aims to eliminate everything that is difficult to believe or to do, and to permit believers to indulge the sensual pleasures. In the chapter Two Riccoldo writes that because Muslims cannot grasp the mystery of the Trinity, it is easier to prove to them that their law is false than to prove the truth of the Christian religion.[7]

Here in the second chapter, Riccoldo also says that the Saracens deny the miracles and words of the apostles, since they contradict the Qur'an. He insists that the Qur'an is not a divine law, but is in fact perfidious, and that the Saracens must accept the authority of the Gospel. To demonstrate these arguments, he analyzes the Qur'an, pointing out several

---

4. Rizzardi, "Introduzione," in *I saraceni*, Italian translation of the *Contra legem Sarracenorum* . Mérigoux publishes the critical edition of *Contra legem Sarracenorum*. See Emilio Panella, "Ricerche su Riccoldo da Montecroce."

5. *Contra legem*, Prologus, 62.

6. *Contra legem*, ch. 1, 64.

7. *Contra legem*, ch. 2, 2, 69.

times the theme of violence. The Qur'an does not fit with the divine law, he concludes, since God's law does not permit murder, robbery, or concupiscence, while the Qur'an, on the contrary, permits all these things. Riccoldo describes Muhammad as wicked, a thief, adulterous, incestuous, and a man who committed homicide.[8] Then, in chapter 10, Riccoldo repeats that the Qur'an is a violent law. By insisting on Muslims' violence and Muhammad's cruel nature, Riccoldo underlines the dangerous threat that Islam poses to Christianity.

Another tactic Riccoldo employs is to point out contradictions in the Qur'an.[9] Indeed, he argues that the Saracen law contains not only many contradictions, but also many lies and fabrications. Furthermore, he points to the lack of logic or order in the Qur'an. In chapter 11, he says, "I do not remember finding in all of that book [the Qur'an] an adequate argument. This law cannot derive from God, since it does not follow any order."[10]

Defensive arguments are found throughout the treatise. Riccoldo needs to defend Christianity against a powerful enemy, and he does this in three ways. Following the Dominican rhetorical tradition, he first presents some sentences from the Qur'an in order to prove their falsity. In contrast, he then exalts the coherence of the Christian texts and the rationality of Christian doctrine. Finally, he turns the Islamic denial of miracles against the "Muslim law" itself, since—unlike Christian faith—it cannot be verified by miracles.[11]

In sum, in the work of Riccoldo we note the following elements: fear of Islam as the enemy of Christianity and its persecutor; and rhetorical use of many defensive arguments, as well as the argument on the irrationality of the Qur'an. As we shall see, Riccoldo's later readers used and modified *Contra legem*'s elements in their own writings.

3. Fazio degli Uberti

We can see the influence of Riccoldo's *Contra Legem Sarracenorum* in vernacular literature in fourteenth-century Italy.[12] The poet Fazio degli

---

8. *Contra legem*, ch. 8, 91–93.
9. *Contra legem*, ch. 6, 83.
10. *Contra legem*, ch. 11, 113.
11. *Contra legem*, ch. 7, 90.
12. For example, Cod. 205, University of Bologna, cited in Fazio degli Uberti, *Il Dittamondo e le rime*.

Uberti (1301–67) makes extensive use of *Contra legem* in his *Dittamondo*,[13] composed around 1345. This work is an encyclopedic poem in six books, and its meter is chained triplets.[14] The poem's theme is a journey through Europe, North Africa, and Palestine. Many legends and much geographical and historical information are drawn from the works of Solino, Pliny the Elder, Martin Polonio, and Riccoldo. Of the latter, Fazio writes, "Here I came and I heard about Riccoldo / *Po di qua venni e di Ricoldo mè deto*,"[15] and *Dittamondo* contains many details about the Islamic tradition from *Contra legem*. Furthermore, Riccoldo travelled along the same route that Fazio intended to take, namely the route in the Eastern lands. However, Fazio died before completing his poem and travels.

In Book V, chapters 10–12 and 14 are dedicated to explaining Islamic religion and the figure of Muhammad. Among the claims about the Prophet that Fazio includes[16] is Riccoldo's assertion that Muhammad was lascivious and inclined to drink.[17] Fazio repeats this assertion in chapter 12,[18] where he describes Muhammad as attracted to the vices of gluttony and lust. Another theme likely drawn from the *Contra legem* is the absence of miracles in the Islamic tradition.[19] According to Fazio, Muhammad raised no one from the dead, nor did he heal the blind or disabled, but he often reiterated his support for strength through weapons. Fazio recalls the argument of the sword that is found in the *Contra legem*: Muhammad says that he was not sent to do miracles, but to fight with weapons, and the priests of the Qur'an wave the sword.[20] The themes of the sword and violence are also repeated to support the argument of the inconsistency of Qur'anic law: in the Qur'an,

---

13. About the work of Fazio degli Uberti, see Corsi's introduction to his edition of *Dittamondo*, and Whitmore, *The Lyrics of Fazio degli Uberti in their relation to Dante*. For a biography of Fazio, see Filippo Villani, *De civitatis Florentiae et eiusdem famosis civibus*. Also intriguing is the relationship between Fazio and Dante in order to trace the possible influence of Riccoldo in the work of Dante; see, for example, Olschki, "Mohammedan Eschatology and Dante's Other World"; Tolan, "Mendicants and Muslims in Dante's Florence."

14. Izzi, "Il vocabolario dantesco nel *Dittamondo* di Fazio degli Uberti."

15. I shall cite Corsi's edition of *Dittamondo* by page, Book, and chapter, as here: *Dittamondo*, 364, Bk. 5, c. 9.

16. *Dittamondo*, 365, Bk. 5, c. 10.

17. *Dittamondo*, 368, Bk. 5, c. 11.

18. *Dittamondo*, 373, Bk. 5, c. 13.

19. *Dittamondo*, 374, Bk. 5, c. 13.

20. *Dittamondo*, 371, Bk. 5, c. 12.

Fazio says, we read many indecent things, but it commands believers to obey Muhammad or to die.[21]

For all its reliance on *Contra legem*, *Dittamondo* is unclear in its use of sources about Islam.[22] For example, Fazio quotes the Qur'an to illustrate a legend that is found in the *Contra legem*, while Riccoldo correctly locates the legend's source not in the Qur'an, but in the *Doctrina Machumeti*. This misattribution reflects Fazio's broader confusion about his sources: although he also drew from the *Legenda Aurea* of Jacopo da Voragine, he attributes all information about Islam to Riccoldo.

In the work of Fazio we thus note the use of *Contra legem* as the unique source for information about Islam in a vernacular work, and the repetition of Riccoldo's stereotypes about the Islamic tradition and the figure of Muhammad. Yet Fazio takes a noticeably less aggressive tone towards Muhammad and the Islamic tradition than does Riccoldo.

4. Byzantine Authors: Demetrius Kydones and George of Trebizond

Contra legem was utilized even by Byzantine scholars. By analyzing works by two of these scholars, Demetrius Kydones and George of Trebizond, we can see how they use Riccoldo's work and repeat his stereotypes of Islam. Yet their rhetoric also displays a shift from perceiving Islam as "enemy" to viewing the Turk as "uncivilized."[23]

Demetrius Kydones

Demetrius Kydones (1324–98) was a Byzantine humanist at the Court of John Kantakouzenos, a *mesazon*, minister for government affairs. He was the teacher of George Gemisto Plethon, and travelled to Italy where he studied deeply Latin culture.[24] His work is important for two main reasons:

21. *Dittamondo*, 371, Bk. 5, c. 12.

22. Corsi, *Dittamondo*, appendix, vol. ii, 330–33.

23. The works of Kydones and Trebizond show also that "one last variable that encouraged classical treatment of the Turks was the influence of contemporary Byzantine attitudes. The result was not only an increase in classically inspired rhetoric on the Turks but also the development of a more unified discourse of European civility versus Asian barbarism," as Bisaha rightly states, *Creating East and West*, 44.

24. On Kydones, see Mercati, *Notizie di Procoro e Demetrio Cidone, Manuele Caleca e*

he translated many works from Latin into Greek, among them the *Summa contra gentiles* of Thomas Aquinas, and he was dedicated to fighting the Ottomans. Furthermore, his works provide valuable insight into the Byzantine scholar's attitude towards both Ottomans and Latins.

He also translated Riccoldo's *Contra legem Sarracenorum* from Latin into Greek,[25] and sent the work to Emperor Manuel II in 1358. Nor is this the end of the story. In the late fifteenth century, Bartolomeo Picerno di Montearduo retranslated *Contra legem* back into Latin from Kydones's Greek,[26] dedicating it to Ferdinand II, king of Aragon and Sicily. In the prologue, Bartolomeo asserts that Kydones' Greek translation admirably enriches Riccoldo's original text. Hence, rather than sending Riccoldo's Latin text, Bartolomeo himself was motivated to retranslate the *Contra legem* into more elegant Latin, as a gift to the king who was fighting the Muslims in Spain. These different versions of the *Contra legem* show how Riccoldo's treatise against Islam circulated from the Byzantine territories to Spain, and highlight the relation between Byzantine scholars and the Latin heritage. They also exemplify how a common image of Muslims was building between the Western and Eastern Empires.

Kydones's approach towards Turks can be seen in his works about relations with the Ottomans: the *Pro subsidio Latinorum* (1366) and the *De non reddenda Callipoli* (1369).[27] Both works concern the site of Gallipoli (Turkey), a strategic point in the Hellespont, and are important sources about the political strategies of Byzantines towards Ottomans and Latins. Kydones calls for Latin aid following the surrender of Gallipoli to the Turks. He considers the Latins as allies of Byzantium in the fight against Ottomans, and he treats the Turks as enemies of freedom.[28] The *De non reddenda* points to the fall of Gallipoli in 1354 as immediately "provoking

---

Teodoro Meleteniota. Cf. Frances Kianka, *Demetrius Cydones (c.1324–c.1397): Intellectual and Diplomatic Relations between Byzantium and the West in the Fourteenth Century*. Cf. Dennis, "Demetrios Cydones and Venice." See Ryder, *The Career and Writings of Demetrius Kydones*. See also Kianka, "Demetrios Kydones and Italy"; and Ševcenko, "The Decline of Byzantium Seen through the Eyes of its Intellectuals."

25. Ryder, *The Career and Writings of Demetrius Kydones*, 156. The translation, dated 1350, is found in PG 154. See Merigoux, "L'ouvrage d'un frère prêcheur florentin," 58; and works by Kianka, Ryder, and Mercati.

26. The Latin version of *Contra legem* translated by Picerno is in PG 154.

27. Demetrius Kydones, *Oratio pro subsidio Latinorum*, PG 154, cols. 961–1008; and *De non reddenda Callipoli*, PG 154, cols. 1012D–1013B.

28. See Ryder, *Career and Writings of Kydones*, 79.

great panic, while his work on the *Contra legem Sarracenorum* shows him already concerned with a theological confrontation with Islam."[29] Also, in the *Oratio pro subsidio Latinorum*, Kydones affirms that Western Europe and the papacy were not Byzantium's enemies, but its most natural political and military allies against the aggression of the Turks.[30]

How does Kydones describe the Ottomans? He uses term *"barbaroi"* to describe the Turks, and he uses it to refer to other social groups as well. As in the *Contra legem*, the Turks are represented as fundamentally uncivilized and cruel, "all characteristics directly in contrast with the Christians of the *oikumene*,"[31] where "Christianity" means the unity of Latin and Greek church. Here we see the process of building Western identity as a phenomenon in contrast with the Islamic tradition.[32]

Another description of Turks emphasizes the *"cupiditas Barbarorum,"*[33] a way to underline the evil nature of Ottomans; this seems to recall the argument of *Contra legem* about the depraved attitude of Muslims. But if in *Contra legem* the mistakes of Muslims are connected to the errors of Muhammad as a false prophet, in Kydones's works the negative attributes describe the entire community of Muslims, in contrast with the virtuous Christians. Kydones recalls also the violent character of the Islamic people, and affirms that they conquered the Greek territories though the use of enslavement and violence.[34] This theme of the violence again echoes Riccoldo's *Contra legem*.

In summary, we can see three distinguishing features in these Kydones's writings: his scorn towards Ottomans, called *"barbaroi"*; an attempt to reach unity between the Latin and Greek churches against the Ottomans; and the influence of the *Contra legem* on his approach to Islam.

29. Ryder, *Career and Writings of Kydones*, 156.

30. Kianka, "Kydones and Italy," 103

31. Ryder, *Career and Writings of Kydones*, 59. About the relationship between Byzantium and Islam, see Adel-Théodor Khoury, *Les théologiens byzantins et l'Islam*.

32. See Kianka, "Demetrios Kydones and Italy," 102: "Kydones attempted solutions [through] anti-Turkish, pro-Latin policy and an intellectual appreciation for and defence of the philosophy and theology of the Latin West, seen primarily in his attraction to the work of Thomas Aquinas."

33. Demetrius Kydones, *De non reddenda Callipoli*, PG 154, 1027.

34. See Kianka, "Demetrios Kydones and Italy," 103: "Faced with the continuing conquests and settlements of the Ottoman Turks in Byzantine territory, especially in Thrace, [Kydones] pursued the forging of alliances with the Catholic powers of the West—a new crusade, directed not at the recovery of the Holy Land but at rescuing what remained of Byzantine lands from the aggression of their Muslim enemy."

George of Trebizond

In his response to the Turks, George of Trebizond uses a very different rhetoric. He aims to convert the sultan Mehmed II, and thus his tone is more subdued and even laudatory.

George of Trebizond (1395–1472/73) was born in Crete, converted to Roman Catholicism, and began a new life in Italy, all the while remaining devoted to the Greek cause.[35] For most of his career he was attached to the papal court as a secretary and translator of Greek, but he also lectured and taught in Florence, Rome, and Venice on rhetoric, poetry, and the Greek language.

Here we shall focus on Trebizond's treatise *On the Eternal Glory of the Autocrat and His World Empire*, written to the Emir when he stormed Constantinople, as an attempt to convert Mehmed II to Christianity. We find this attempt also in other works of Trebizond, addressed to Mehmed.[36] As John Monfasani says about one of these treatises, *On the Truth of Faith of Christians to the Emir*, written in 1453:

> Nor was he alone in attempting to convert Muhammad II. We have the famous letter of Pope Pius II to the Conqueror. Scholars have never fathomed what George meant by this letter. He was not motivated by an extraordinary irenic spirit, as some have suggested, nor by eccentric political ideas, as others have supposed.[37]

According to Monfasani, the answer to what motivated Trebizond lies in his treatise *On the Eternal Glory of the Autocrat* and in another letter to Mehmed II, *On Divine Manuel, Shortly to be King of the Whole World*.[38] These writings are inspired by the apocalyptic text of Pseudo-Methodius, who predicted that the sons of Ishmael would conquer the Latin Empire.

---

35. The translation and comments on Trebizond works are in *Collectanea Trapezuntiana*. Trebizond, "Preface of His Translation of Plato's Laws." See Berns, "Construire un idéal vénitien de la constitution mixte à la Renaissance"; Gaeta, "Giorgio da Trebisonda, le *Leggi* di Platone e la costituzione di Venezia"; Monfasani, *George of Trebizond*; Ravegnani,"Nota sul pensiero politico di Giorgio da Trebisonda." See Bisaha, *Creating East and West*, 116: "George of Trebizond, by focusing on Greece's position in antiquity as defender of all Europe, and therefore as a crucial part of Europe, . . . firmly brings Byzantium within the Western cultural identity."

36. See Monfasani, *George of Trebizond*, 131–36.

37. Ibid., 131.

38. George of Trebizond, "On the Eternal Glory of the Autocrat," and "On the Divinity of Manuel," in *Collectanea Trapezuntiana*, 492–527, 564–74.

"By converting Mehmed II, Trebizond hoped to avert the dreadful reign of the Ishmaelites: he would remake the Moslem conqueror of Constantinople into the universal Christian Emperor. Trebizond considers Greece and Latin West as a unity."[39]

How does George of Trebizond try to convert Mehmed II? Which rhetorical strategies does he use? In *On the Eternal Glory of the Autocrat*, he calls Mehmed II "King of kings" and "Mightiness."[40] His words are extremely positive towards Mehmed II: "Now I do not think it escapes you, O wondrous autocrat, that God has selected you and yours to rule the whole world."[41]

At the beginning of *On the Eternal Glory of the Autocrat*, Trebizond proposes to use the Aristotelian rule "by which in the comparison of conflicting propositions, men would find the truth and cast falsity aside," since he heard that "every day you [Mehmed] philosophize as much as possible."[42] Although this exalts Mehmed, we note some topics drawn from the medieval tradition. Did Trebizond know the work of Riccoldo? Probably, since he quotes Demetrius Kydones, the translator of the *Contra legem*, in a letter of 1452 (Exhortation to Pope Nicholas V *Ad defendenda pro Europa Hellesponti claustra*[43]), and because in *On the Eternal Glory of the Autocrat* we find many topics about Islam from *Contra legem*: how it is difficult for Muslims to comprehend the Trinity (from chapter 6 to chapter 16), as well as the crucifixion and death of Christ (15–16) and his resurrection (chapter 17).[44] But unlike Riccoldo, George of Trebizond believes that for Mehmed,

---

39. Monfasani, *George of Trebizond*, 132: "According to the script of ps. Methodius, the all conquering Ishmaelites would usher in a reign of terror which would only end when the last true Christian emperor arose to disperse them and bring about the reign of peace which must precede the coming of Gog, Magog, and the Antichrist."

40. George of Trebizond, "On the Eternal Glory of the Autocrat," in *Collectanea Trapezuntiana*. See Bisaha, *Creating East and West*, 136: "By combining aspects of medieval conversion treatises with humanist rhetoric, they hoped to persuade the Turks to accept the enlightened path of Christianity."

41. George of Trebizond, "On the Eternal Glory of the Autocrat," in *Collectanea Trapezuntiana*, 524.

42. George of Trebizond, "On the Eternal Glory of the Autocrat," in *Collectanea Trapezuntiana*, 496.

43. George of Trebizond, "Exhortation to Pope Nicholas V ad defendenda pro Europa Hellesponti claustra," in *Collectanea Trapenzuntiana*, 434–44.

44. George of Trebizond, "On the Eternal Glory of the Autocrat," in *Collectanea Trapenzuntiana*. Although these themes are common in the medieval tradition on Islam, *Contra legem* was the most popular treatise on Qur'an. Furthermore, in Trebizond's elite

and indeed for all Muslim people, it is necessary to convert to Christianity, however difficult it may be. Furthermore, for Trebizond, the only real hope to save the Christian empire is by converting Mehmed II.

In this work, Trebizond perceives Westerners and Byzantines as a unity against the Turks.[45] But this perception changed after the warning of the capture of Constantinople,[46] as becomes clear in another work, the abovementioned Exhortation to Pope Nicholas V. Here the author requested the Pope's help in order to protect Constantinople from the Turks. Undoubtedly, after the fall of Constantinople, Trebizond's approach to Islam changed. Whereas he previously considered the Pope as the only one who could save the Empire, in his letter of 1466 to Mehmed, Trebizond invokes the help of the Autocrat himself. I suggest that this change was caused by multiple reasons. First, geopolitical strategy: after the fall of Constantinople, Christians inevitably acknowledged Mehmed to be both a great conqueror and a great political figure, as the famous letter of Pius II shows.[47] Second, traditional theological and eschatological beliefs (like the prediction of Pseudo-Methodius), as Monfasani stresses.[48] Third, a slow evolution of the perception of Muslims, no longer viewed so much as "enemies," but rather as Christians who do not know that they are Christians.

Although Trebizond uses many topics from medieval tradition—for example, the insistence on Muslims' incapacity to grasp the truth of the Trinity—he attempts to convert Mehmed by using an elaborate rhetoric of praise, rather than a fierce diatribe like Riccoldo's. In the works of Trebizond the perception of Islam seems to change: Mehmed is no longer considered an "enemy," but becomes a possible ally.

---

circle of humanists, Riccoldo's treatise was read and used. About the relations between Byzantine and Italian scholars, see Setton, "The Byzantine Background to the Italian Renaissance." Cf. Mérigoux: "George of Trebizond, humanist and theologian was affected by the influence of the work of Riccoldo" ("L'ouvrage d'un frère precheur florentin," 53).

45. See Bisaha, *Creating East and West*, 132: "Despite the hostility Europeans once felt toward Byzantines, and which some individuals continued to express, the year 1453 marked the beginning of a change in Western perceptions of the Greeks. Greeks had been settling in Italy before this date, and thousands more came to settle afterward."

46. About this point see Mazzucchi and Pertusi, *Bisanzio e i Turchi nella cultura del Rinascimento e del Barocco*; Weiss, *La scoperta dell'antichità classica nel Rinascimento*, Italian translation.

47. Enea Silvio Piccolomini, "Letter to Mehmed II"; see d'Ascia, *Il Corano e la tiara*.

48. Monfasani, *George of Trebizond*, in particular 131–35.

5. Use of *Preasuppositio*: Marsilio Ficino

This section will highlight the use of *Contra legem* in Marsilio Ficino's *De Christiana religione*. Specifically, I shall discuss Ficino's rhetorical strategy of *praesuppositio*. We shall also see how this strategy fits within the larger scheme of perceptions shifting from Islam as "enemy" to "other."

In the *De Christiana religione* of Marsilio Ficino (1433–99) we see clearly the influence of the *Contra legem*, as Angelo Michele Piemontese asserts: "The *Contra legem Sarracenorum* is the main source for Marsilio Ficino about Muhammad and the Qur'an in the *De Christiana religione* (1474), in particular chapters Twelve and Twenty-six. In chapter Two Ficino quotes his source."[49]

The *De Christiana religione* is not the only text where Ficino tackles the issue of Islamic culture. As Bisaha notes:

> In October 1480 Marsilio Ficino, the Florentine humanist and Neoplatonic scholar, wrote a letter to Matthias Corvinus of Hungary entitled "An exhortation to war against the barbarians." Ficino implores Matthias to help and save Italy and all of Christendom from the ravages of the inhuman Turks. He chose to emphasize the damage the Turks had done to learning.[50]

This theme (the Turks as "*barbaroi*," "uncivilized") is repeated also in *De Christiana religione*. The premises of Ficino's philosophy might seem open to an exchange, but this treatise clearly displays the opposite tendency.

According to Ficino, the soul is the fixed center of the world, and links all the things in a concrete unity.[51] He develops an original theory of natural religion, which is deeply rooted in man, and distinguishes men from animals.[52] The philosophical doctrine is meant to show the truths of religion with theoretical arguments.[53] Although Ficino bases these arguments on

---

49. *De Christiana religione*, in Marsili Ficini Florentini, *Opera quae hactenus extitere et que in lucem nunc primum prodiere omnia*. On Ficino and his work *De Christiana religione*, see Gentile and Toussaint, *Marsilio Ficino: fonti, testi, fortuna: atti del convegno internazionale (Firenze, 1–3 ottobre 1999)*. See also Saitta, *Marsilio Ficino e la filosofia dell'umanesimo*; Kristeller, *Marsilio Ficino and his work after five hundred years*; and Vasoli, "Per le fonti del *De christiana religione* di Marsilio Ficino."

50. Bisaha, *Creating East and West*, 74.

51. Kristeller, *Il pensiero filosofico di Marsilio Ficino*. See also Blum, *Philosophy of Religion in the Renaissance*.

52. Kristeller, *Il pensiero filosofico di Marsilio Ficino*, 344.

53. Ibid., 345. Bisaha, *Creating East and West*, 172.

the concept of natural religion, which would seem to make all religions equal, he firmly asserts the superiority of the Christian religion. Indeed, he tries to defend Christian theology, a project that he undertakes in his major apologetic work *De Christiana religione*. In the first part of the work, in addition to his famous remarks on the relationship between philosophy and religion, he explains how the authority of the Christian religion can be upheld with good reasons against the Jews and Muslims.[54]

In his library, Ficino had a Qur'an translated into Latin, other texts from the Islamic tradition (e.g., Avicenna's writings), and the *Contra legem* of Riccoldo. Indeed, Ficino uses several arguments found in Riccoldo's *Contra legem*: the disorder and fabrications of the Qur'an, the violence of Muhammad. This fiction of the Qur'an was credible among foolish people, as the Muslims are (as Ficino states), and spread through violence and deception (a theme from *Contra legem*), since this fiction seems ridiculous to intelligent and wise men. Here we can note a difference between Ficino and Riccoldo: although Riccoldo also describes Muslims as unlearned people, Ficino considers ignorance to be the primary fault of Muslims.

In the chapter 12 of the *De Christiana religione*, Ficino writes that Muslims seem Christian, but are in fact heretics or Arians or Manicheans: "We conclude that Jews, Muslims, and pagans recognize the Christian religion as the most excellent above all." He adds, "Although these people prefer their doctrine, however, they put the Christian religion before all the others."[55] Therefore, if a Muslim judges with sincerity, he will prefer the Christian religion without doubt. In this case Ficino uses the same rhetorical strategy of Cusanus, the *praesuppositio*: Muslims must recognize that the Truth is the Christian truth, since rational thinking necessarily leads to this conclusion. Unlike *Contra legem*, Ficino insists that Qur'anic statements confirm the truth of the Gospel, and he uses this argument to affirm that Muslims should believe Christianity. He underlines that Muhammad himself recognized the affinities between Islam and Christianity, and that this is a sign of the Gospel's superiority, since only ignorant people could not consider these similarities and would believe that Muhammad was the last Prophet and not Jesus.

By using the rhetorical figure of *praesuppositio*, Ficino aims to prove that there is only one truth, the truth of the Gospel, and that there is no possibility of making any other comparison without starting from this

54. Bisaha, *Creating East and West*, 265.
55. Marsilio Ficino, *De Christiana religione*, chapter 12.

presupposition. Like Cusanus, he uses the *praesuppositio* to claim that the Qur'an's author Muhammad perversely subverted the Gospel's order of truth. For this reason, some parts of the Qur'an deviate from the points where it agrees with the Christian text.

In Ficino's work we therefore note his insistence on the ignorance of Muslims and his description of them as "barbarians." Like Cusanus, Ficino uses the *praesuppositio* to insist on the affinities between Muslims and Christians, and to highlight how Muslims are really Christians but simply refuse to recognize this. Although Ficino drew many themes from *Contra legem*, he modifies these themes, and his perception of Islam is less focused on the dangers that it poses, and more on the ignorance of Muslims.

6. Enea Silvio Piccolomini

In 1464, some years after the composition of the *Cribratio*, Nicholas of Cusa was entrusted by Pius II with the task of gathering 5,000 crusaders[56] camped between Rome and Ancona, the city from which the Crusade wanted by Piccolomini would have departed.[57] In the *Cribratio*, however, we find an explicit reference to war, *bellum*, only once, and it is a quotation drawn from the Qur'an.[58]

Nicholas's thought about the need for war refers to the Western tradition,[59] especially to Augustine, who is generally considered the founder of the Christian conception of just war.[60] Augustine formulated the thesis according to which it is legitimate to respond to injustice with war.[61] In this case, war is inspired by God to punish peoples' corruption and educate them to peaceful life. The term *iustum* (just) refers therefore to divine

---

56. Orientalist scholars paid great attention to the Crusades and to the question of holy war, trying to understand whether Muslim developed a corresponding concept when they met with the western world of the Crusades.

The impact with the Western soldiers undoubtedly had some repercussions on Muslims' attitudes and concept of war. In the rise of a new literary genre which was called *pseudo-futuh* we can perceive the relevance attributed by the Islamic thought to the problem of war against non-believers. Lewis, *The Political Language of Islam*, 93–94.

57. Gaia, *Opere religiose*, 76.
58. *Cribratio Alkorani*, III.X.191.8–11.
59. Cf. Bamyeh, *The Social Origins of Islam*.
60. Calore, *"Guerra giusta"*?
61. Augustine, *Civ.* 19.7.

justice, the only source which can justify conflict.[62] In fact, most theoreticians of just war, like Nicholas, belong to the Augustinian tradition,[63] since in the *City of God* military service is justified for the purpose of protecting the political community represented by the empire.[64]

In the period immediately preceding the Crusade, Pius II wrote at Tivoli a compendium on the *Historiae Biondi Flavii* and completed his work *Asiae et Europae locorum descriptio*. But in Book XIII of his *Commentarii*[65] we can find the chronicle of the preparations made for the Crusade. During the last months of his life, the pope lived in Siena and in the thermal resort of Bagni di Petriolo, desperately hoping to recover his strength and health. He returned to Rome, but on 18 June he left again for Ancona, where he arrived on 18 July distressed and sad. He entrusted Cardinal Niccolò Forteguerri with the task of leading the army for the Crusade, which he expected would last at least three years.[66]

On 13 January 1460, Pius II had urged the Florentines to support his purposes. As a matter of fact, the Florentines were trying to gain time and were double-crossing: they had no interest in cutting their ties with the pope, but at the same time, their commercial interests and their need to compete with Venice motivated them to keep friendly relations with the sultan, who would allow them to exploit the former Byzantine markets. A letter dated 6 August 1460, sent by Pius II to the Turk prince, reveals that the pope had definitely changed his mind about the crusade considered as a "holy war." Commercial and economic reasons, which had strengthened over time, had become in the meantime far more important than theological and religious reasons. In the pope's epistle we read:

---

62. Cicero, *De off.* 1.36. Calore, "Guerra giusta"? *Le metamorfosi di un concetto antico*, 13: "For ancient Romans, it consisted in a procedure rigorously established by law, in particular during the long period in which the *civitas* began to form and develop (sixth-fourth century B.C.), which had to be strictly observed, for juridical and religious reasons, to ensure the successful outcome of a war. In that context, the adjective *iustum* did not refer to ethical values of justice, but rather to strict legal standards. The expression *bellum iustum* meant "war complying with the rules of law," a juridically legitimate war, we would say today, completely made within the sphere of law."

63. See Manganaro Favaretto, *La guerra*. Partner, *God of Battles*. Zerbi, "Medioevo: tolleranza o intolleranza religiosa."

64. Aquinas, *Summa theologica*, II/II, Question XL.

65. See Totaro, *Pio II nei suoi Commentarii*.

66. Baldi, *Pio II e le trasformazioni dell'Europa cristiana, 1457–1464*, 250.

To the Turk. Since our citizens, who in the past used to sail as far as Byzantium, your city, are well acquainted with Your clemency, honesty and justice in all things, as well as with Your special love for our city, we deem it almost useless to urge with many words Your Highness to address Your grace and benevolence to our fellow citizens. Therefore, we want to ask and beseech You, through this brief letter, to welcome and protect from any trouble or danger these men, who come to Byzantium once again on our ships, and allow them trading on the same conditions as those granted to the other merchants who used to trade in Your territories; each favour they will receive from Your Highness will be considered as a special grace we shall always bear in mind with gratitude.[67]

A number of strategic and military topics[68] and references to the historical and political situation of that time are included in the letter, but all that Pius II actually wants to ask Muhammad II is expressed in this epistle with few short phrases: why does the sultan not get baptized and convert to the evangelical creed?

From the very first lines, Piccolomini's long letter reveals a basically different approach from Nicholas's *Cribratio*. The way in which Pius II deals with the problem of Muslims' conversion is just the opposite of the method chosen by Nicholas of Cusa. While the latter is entangled in refined and learned theological and philosophical discussion, the pope limits himself to underlining the military and economic advantages Muhammad would achieve once he converted to the Christian religion. Pius II mentions the opportunity the sultan would have to rule over Eastern Europe, Greece, Macedonia, and Hungary. The reasons pointed out by Piccolomini are not merely religious but rather political, as Franco Cardini underlines:

> The Pope, whose greatest concerns in Europe consisted in his relations with France, on the one hand, the empire, some German princes and Bohemia, on the other, put the crusade at stake to delay the crucial steps he had to take in those areas, and impose in the meantime his merely arbitrary hegemony.[69]

---

67. The Latin text and the Italian translation can be found in D'Ascia, *Il Corano e la tiara*.

68. *Aeneae Sylvii Pii Pontificis, Epistola 386*, I, 234–35. Italian translation by D'Ascia: the letter was probably written in October or December 1461.

69. Cardini, *Studi sulla storia e sull'idea di crociata*, 149. Gaeta, *Sulla lettera a Maometto di Pio II*, 131: "the conflict between Christianity and Islam had taken for Pius II the characteristics of a real clash of civilizations."

Pius II also makes use of theological arguments, but unlike Nicholas, he does it concisely and without going into details and digressions. The pope makes reference to passages of the Bible and tries to introduce illuminating examples aimed at convincing the sultan to convert, wondering about the causes of the conflict between Christians and Turks.[70] The answer, according to the pope, is that the conflict was caused by misinterpretation of the dogma of the Trinity.

The pope continues his reasoning on the dogma of the Trinity, considered also by Nicholas a key issue for settling the religious conflict between Muslims and Christians. Another religious theme examined both by Piccolomini and Nicholas concerns the different conception of afterlife in the two religions.[71] The attention given to theological themes is evidence, in my opinion, of the pivotal role of theology and of its close links with the political matters of that age. In spite of the strong commercial intentions[72] of his letter, the pope resorts to arguments concerning dogmatic (Trinity) and eschatological (heaven) issues.

Some commentators have debated about the influence of Nicholas of Cusa's *Cribratio* on the epistle to Muhammad II composed by Enea Silvio Piccolomini.[73] The quotations from the Qur'an included in the epistle are indirect, as they were drawn from Juan de Torquemada's *Contra principales errores perfidi Mahumeti*, who in turn made extensive use of Riccoldo's work. D'Ascia argues that for this reason "it is difficult to precisely distinguish Riccoldo's contribution from Torquemada's, as ultimately, all that really matters is the Dominican tradition taken as a whole,"[74] a tradition which also considerably influenced Nicholas of Cusa, and the signs of which clearly emerge in the *Cribratio*. D'Ascia writes: "The arguments of Nicholas of Cusa focused on a sagacious and sometimes tendentious use of *auctoritates* shared also by his opponent, are subtle and softened; those of the pope are roughly effective, and filled with rationalistic sarcasm,

---

70. *Aeneae Sylvii Pii Pontificis, Epistola 386*, X, 251.
71. *Aeneae Sylvii Pii Pontificis, Epistola 386*, XVI, 263.
72. Cardini, *Studi sulla storia e sull'idea di crociata*, 149.
73. On this debate, see Gaeta, *Sulla lettera a Maometto di Pio II*, 141: "Pius II must have been fascinated by this prospect. But he was not Nicholas of Cusa and he did not let himself be carried away by an intellectual need for *concordantia*." Gaeta makes an in-depth analysis of both the letter of Pius II and the work of Torquemada, from which many congruences emerge.
74. D'ascia, *Il Corano e la tiara*, 104–5.

because in his opinion Islam does not deserve to be taken seriously at a religious level."[75]

The goal of Piccolomini is to convince the sultan to convert in order to gain territories and wealth once he has become a Christian prince. In the letter of Piccolomini, as in the work of George of Trebizond, the perception of Islam seems to change: Mehmed is no longer considered an "enemy," but becomes a possible ally. Furthermore Piccolomini, as Cusanus, considers Muslims "different" from Christians because of their ignorance, and he underlines the unawareness of Muslims, who must be converted to Christianity.

7. Conclusions

Here, by comparing the works of six authors, I have analyzed some themes in Christian apologetic treatises in order to show how the perception of Muslim culture changed over time. The different ways of writing on Islam are quite clear: if Riccoldo considers Muslims as enemies, Ficino describes Islamic people as "those who do not know." The main point is the ignorance of Muslims, and also the reason for being Muslim. This modification is also noticeable in the works of other authors, such as Piccolomini.

As the circulation of the Riccoldo's work demonstrates, humanists maintained medieval perceptions of Islam and carried them forward into modern Western thought.[76] If it is true that the *Contra legem* was the main source about Islam for Christian authors, it is essential to discover how this work was used, to identify translations of it, and to assess its influence on the course of history. Riccoldo wrote *Contra legem* according to his experience of an Arabic-speaking country: he appears scared, very angry, and shocked by Islamic culture, which seemed to continually grow, with no hope for accepting Christianity. In the space of one century, the perception begins to change, and Christian authors study Islam from a different perspective. Islam is no more the enemy but the "other," something that can be controlled and converted to Christianity.

---

75. The difference between the epistle and the *Cribratio* is described by D'Ascia, 106: "the intervention of Pius II is strictly rhetorical and public, and the pope completely exposes his charismatic person. Nicholas of Cusa's work is instead the reflection of a learned person who certainly does not lose sight of the political aspects of this problem, and begins to plead only when he feels sure enough at a doctrinal level."

76. Bisaha, *Creating East and West*, 41.

The work of George of Trebizond is extremely important for two reasons: it shows the change from a medieval to a humanist perception, as well as the development of a more unified discourse of European civility versus Asian barbarism.[77]

In regards to this last aspect, it is important to note that in the course of time fewer Italian scholars traveled to Byzantium, largely because Byzantine Greeks were coming to Italy in increasing numbers. "A combination of pressure from the Turks and growing opportunities in the West led many Greeks to leave their homelands in search of employment in Italy, while others relocated to different areas of Greece and Venetian Crete."[78] The work of Trebizond and others such as Bessarion, Plethon, and Kydones is an important sign of this tendency.

During the Renaissance, Islam was increasingly perceived to be the religion and culture of "ignorant" people, furthermore, the Turks were considered to be barbaric adversaries of learning.

---

77. Bisaha, *Creating East and West*, 44. See also Weiss, *La scoperta dell'antichità classica nel Rinascimento*.

78. Bisaha, *Creating East and West*, 140.

— 7 —
General Conclusions

In Book III of the *Cribratio*, where the blame on Muhammad is so virulent, we also find a chapter dedicated to the sultan Muhammad II. Nicholas of Cusa reverts to a theme he had already dealt with; he affirms that Muhammad's people must believe in the Virgin as *theotokos* and, consequently, embrace the truth of the Gospel. Among his arguments Nicholas includes the widespread belief in the Western world that the sultan was formerly a Christian and that he had converted to Islam for the purpose of climbing to power and ruling.

The sultan Muhammad, Nicholas advises, should rightly intend the Qur'an, which contains many passages dedicated to Mary. But these passages were unfortunately misinterpreted, this misinterpretation having been suggested by the Jews who accompanied the Prophet. "If Muhammad was deceived by the Jews who aided and convinced him that Mary, mother of Christ, was the sister of Aaron, then they could well have deceived him also in many other things."[1] Nicholas drew this information from Riccoldo's book.

In addressing the sultan in his appeal, Nicholas argues that Christianity chronologically precedes the coming of Islam. If peoples already believed in the Virgin Mary, Muhammad II should simply return to his original faith, to guarantee peace among different populations joined by a single creed.[2] According to Nicholas of Cusa, the Qur'an records that there shall be faith only in Christ, and thus he writes in the first book of the *Cribratio* "we learn from both the Gospel and the Qur'an that Muhammad cannot prevail, and Christ at the end shall be the winner,"[3] though no statement of this kind actually exists in the Qur'an.[4]

1. *Cribratio Alkorani*, III.XVII.223.1–7.
2. *Cribratio Alkorani*, III.XVII.223.7–13.
3. *Cribratio Alkorani*, tr. it.,737.
4. *Cribratio Alkorani*, I.III.nn.13–15, 29.

Nicholas writes about Muslims' violence against Christians, the violent nature of the Qur'anic law, and the "continuous persecutions" put into effect by the Muslims against the Christian populations. The issue of peace in the Qur'an is never dealt with by Nicholas, who instead insists over and over on Muhammad's dominating actions.

War and peace are semantically rich concepts in the Qur'an.[5] Majiid Khadduri[6] remarks that the ultimate objective of the Islamic world is peace and not war. War has the only purpose of defending the interests of the Muslim community, or *umma*, whose members fear God and follow the word of his prophet. The concept of *jihad*[7] includes in its meaning an attempt to define a variety of individual and collective efforts aimed at accomplishing the will of God, and it points out the behaviors that believers must follow in order to achieve such accomplishment. The moral obligation to follow the way of God (*jihad*) is essential and strictly connected to the precept to do good and fight against evil.

The Qur'an calls this process "the way to peace,"[8] and *reconciliation* represents the best way to pursue it,[9] since it is written that Allah abhors all that disturbs peace.[10] One of the names given to Allah in the Qur'an is *As-Salam*, which means "peace," and the ideal society is called *Dar as-Salam*, the abode of peace. The Qur'an presents the universe as a model characterized by harmony.[11] When Allah created heaven and earth, he made sure that every element was able to perform its function peacefully, without clashing with the other elements. "The sun is not allowed to surpass the moon, and the night cannot rise in the place of the day. Every thing follows its own way."[12] Peace subtends the whole Qur'anic cosmology: it is the eschatological objective religious history moves through and for which all the prophets, from Adam to Jesus, and finally to Muhammad, were sent.[13]

---

5. See Campanini, *Dizionario dell'Islam*, voce Jihad, 170–72.

6. See Khadduri, *War and Peace in the Law of Islam*; Khadduri, *Political Trends in the Arab World*.

7. Amoretti, *Tolleranza e guerra santa nell'Islam*, 1974.

8. Sura 5.16.

9. Sura 4.128.

10. Sura 2.205

11. Sura 36.40.

12. Sura 36.40.

13. Sura 48.4.

The Qur'anic doctrine warns mankind to live according to the Book and follow the message of the prophets, so as to build a community based on solidarity and mutual aid. The Islamic religious visions of political government were organized through this shared sense of "commitment to the path of God." Sura 2 makes explicit reference to the way in which the Prophet's *umma* shall behave: "we made of you a nation."[14]

Arguing on conversion, Nicholas of Cusa quotes Sura 16: "Those who deny God after having believed in him are lost, except those who were forced to do it but their heart is quiet in faith; but the wrath of God shall fall on those who have opened their heart to impiety, and they shall receive bitter punishment."[15] Nicholas affirms that Christians, too, might convert to Islam and nonetheless remain Christian in their heart; therefore, persecution on religious grounds is senseless for both religions.[16] The second Sura of the Qur'an opens with a long description of the difference between those who believe in God and in his revelation, and fear him, and those who, on the contrary, reject God and try to persuade believers to untruly profess a faith (2.1–29). In particular, hypocrites are described as followers of Satan. The struggle between truth, (*sidq*), and lie, and between acceptance, and rejection or ingratitude, represents a relevant thematic characterization in the verses of the second Sura dealing with the inborn conflict of the human condition.[17]

The opening passage of the second Sura is followed by the verses on the creation of Adam and Iblis' refusal, among the angels, to obey God's commandment of obedience to Adam. Then, it continues with the story of the first man and his companion in the Garden of Eden, Adam's instruction about the names of things and their obedience to him, and the role of Satan in the expulsion of Adam and Eve from paradise.[18] The struggle between lie and truth is an essential cosmologic problem[19] in Islamic symbolism. The second Sura continues with the account of the alliance between Israel and God, Israel's breach of the alliance and rejection of God's signs, and the consequent punishment of the people of Israel.[20] Subsequent passages

---

14. Cf. Sura 2.143.
15. Sura 16.106.
16. *Cribratio Alkorani*, III.VI.180.10–15.
17. Dammen McAuliffe, *The Cambridge Companion to the Qur'ran*, 83.
18. Sura 2.30–39.
19. Kelsay and Turner Johnson, *Cross, Crescent and Sword*, 94.
20. Sura 2.40–86.

describe the role played by the prophet sent by God to the different communities in urging them to fear and obey God.[21]

In Cusanus' opinion, Muhammad's purpose was solely to pursue power through the sword, to extend his property on the pretext of religion and God.[22] To prove Muhammad's longing for power, Nicholas points out further textual contradictions in the Qur'an, especially in the Sura describing Heraclius's defeat in Damascus, inflicted by the Persians in 614.[23] The acknowledgment of the Christians' later victory by the will of God is, in his opinion, evidence of the prophet Muhammad's misconduct, since in contradiction of the holy book, he persecuted the Christians and obliged them either to convert or to pay a tribute.

How can peace between Islam and Christianity be reached? Towards the end of Book III of the *Cribratio*, Nicholas introduces another topic, the affinity of the law of Abraham with the Qur'anic law. Sura 2.122 marks the beginning of a part devoted to Abraham, founder of the Ka'ba in Mecca, which states: "Two of your detachments wanted to lose their heart, but God was their guardian; in Him the believers shall trust. You are no part of it, whether God pardons or punish them, as certainly."[24]

Nicholas wants to prove that the law of the Qur'an is not the law of Abraham, and thus he tells the story of Abraham pointing out the Qur'anic contradictions in this regard.[25]

The *Cribratio Alkorani* is grounded on the basic idea:[26] if the Qur'an is correctly understood, it shall prove the truth of the Gospel, as Nicholas affirms in the prologue of the *Cribratio*. In *De pace fidei*, Nicholas aims to find a solution for achieving peace among religions, whereas the *Cribratio* is filled with polemical and apologetic intents. Both works share the common and essential theme concerning relations with "the other."[27] But

---

21. See Sura 2.87; 2.113.
22. *Cribratio Alkorani*, III.VIII.184.1–5.
23. *Cribratio Alkorani*, III.VIII.184.16–22.
24. Sura 2.128.
25. Nicholas devotes to this theme the last chapters of book III of the *Cribratio*.
26. Cf. Bonmariage, *Houris et autres jovenceaux*.
27. On the problem of alterity, or otherness, in the Islamic world, see Lewis, *Gli Ebrei nel mondo islamico*, 11: "Another perception of alterity was defined by the concept of *ahl al-kitab*, the people of the book, mentioned by the cosmology of the Qur'an, which identified it in particular in Jews and Christians.

As Qur'anic cosmology points out, the people of the book had previously received a book of divine revelations, and had sent their prophets, the Qur'an being the final

while in the work of 1453 the theme of alterity, or otherness, is addressed to several confessions, in the *Cribratio* this comparison concerns exclusively the Muslim religion and the Islamic people.

Nicholas of Cusa does not deal with the traditions and cults of Islam as he had done previously in *De pace fidei*: his glance is not introspective, and does not investigate whether historical reasons or common affinities exist. As Nicholas declares in the dedication to Pius II, his work aims to prove that the "Mohammedan sect is erroneous and has to be rejected." According to Hagemann, this approach makes certain that "any presupposition ensuring real dialogue is missing, as well as any presupposition for a correct understanding from within the Qur'an, that is to say, a correct interpretation of the meaning of the Suras, regardless, once for all, of the polemical passages included in the *Cribratio*."[28]

Cusanus resorts to the same concepts expounded in his previous works to defend his belonging to the Christian church, and he does not seem to change his theoretical approach in the *Cribratio*, since in this work, too, he analyzes the differences between the two religions based on their common Christian origin. He finds in the philosophical discourse developed in *De docta ignorantia* an instrument to identify the conceptual inconsistencies of the Qur'an and to reveal a truth that cannot be anything else but the truth of the Gospel. If anything beautiful can be found in the Qur'an, it necessarily originates from the Gospel.[29] In *De pace fidei*, mutual tolerance is made possible by pointing out identities and affinities existing among different religions, thus showing that there is no need to fight each other. In contrast, the *Cribratio Alkorani* is a work in which Nicholas' intention

---

revelation and Muhammad its official prophet. The ancient confessional communities had denied their prophets and twisted the scriptures. Some some historical versions of them still existed, which reflected the original archetype of the text, known as *umm-al-kitab*, Mother of the Book.

According to the Muslim point of view, these communities enjoyed a sacred legal status, the *dhimma*, a term which defines a protected confessional group entitled to follow its religion within the paradigms of its own rituals and authority structures, but not to make proselytes. The *dhimmis*, as members of the protected confessional community, were only obliged to pay the treasury a tax called *jiza*, Another important form of alterity for the early Muslim communities was the distinction between *dar al-Islam*—the abode of Islam—and *dar al-harb*—the abode of war. A later category was the *dar al sulh*—the abode of the treaty—which classified the non-Muslim neighbouring states with which it was temporarily allowed to avoid conflicts."

28. Hagemann, *Christentum contra Islam*, 133.
29. *Cribratio Alkorani*, I.VI.41.1–5.

to come to an analysis of the differences in favor of an identity synthesis is certainly less important. There are two different kinds of analysis of the Qur'anic text: first, Nicholas examines the Qur'an without criticizing its contents, since he wants to confront himself with his opponent on equal terms and prove that the Qur'an actually bears witness to Christian truths. But Nicholas also intends to prove that the Qur'anic text cannot be the fruit of a divine revelation.

The *Cribratio* shows a strong textual consistency[30]—consistency with the tradition of the Bible and consistency with Nicholas' thought. This consistency emerges in particular in the comparison between the holy books, especially in the chapter entitled "The Qur'an is not trustworthy in the points in which it contradicts the Holy Scriptures."[31] Nicholas of Cusa maintains that in a comparison between the two holy books, the term *variation* means not only the replacement of words, but also the different meaning of the Qur'an compared to the evangelical word. In that case, he adds, the Qur'an cannot be justified; we must only admit that it was not God who handed over the Qur'anic word.

Regardless of the differences emerging in Cusanus' works, and bearing in mind the different meaning of the concept of dialogue in our time, as well as the stylistic structure and the contents of his writings, can the *Cribratio* and *De pace fidei* be considered "interreligious dialogues"? According to Walter and Reiss,[32] the literary and philosophical production of the Middle Ages is strongly and constantly characterized by a polemical intention. As a matter of fact, disputes, apologetic treatises, polemical libels, and similar texts converged in the literary genre of "dialogue." Therefore, in reconstructing the red thread connecting Nicholas of Cusa's work with his age and context, it would be perhaps misleading thinking of the term *dialogue* from a contemporary point of view. In fifteenth-century political and social life, religious problems were hardly separable from the political context; they were particularly thorny everyday issues both for scholars and the mighty of that age. Dialogue between different confessions was therefore an urgent and topical matter on which authors debated, putting forward philosophical, theological, and political argu-

---

30. Assmann, *Das kulturelle Gedächtnis. Schrift, Erinnerung und politische Identität in frühen Hochkulturen,* Part I.

31. *Cribratio Alkorani,* III, VI.

32. Walther, "Das Streitgedicht in der lateinischen Literatur des Mittelalters," Reiss, "Conflict and Its Resolution in Medieval Dialogues."

ments. Furthermore, the medieval genre of "dialogue" was constructed through paraphrases, quotations that quite frequently were left implicit, and a range of textual "misinterpretations" which often depended on scarcely reliable sources and inaccurate translations of original texts. To the question of whether interreligious dialogue may have a relevant political dimension, a study of the work and life of Nicholas of Cusa from this point of view would perhaps help in giving some answers. In this question, two different categories—religion and policy—come into play, and their relationship, which in some respects is indissolubly intertwined, might be partly unraveled by an analysis of works, texts, and biographies of authors belonging to different periods. A question which paves the way for undertaking new and numberless research paths.

According to Thomas Burman, the translations of the Qur'an which circulated in Europe until the eighteenth century, though inaccurate, are nonetheless evidence of a deep interest among Western scholars in the Islamic and Muslim world.[33] Based on this textual comparison, it is possible to start weaving an intercultural and interreligious dialogue. Even a polemical and apologetic work can be considered a form of interreligious dialogue, since it is constructed through a continuous comparison of the essential texts and themes of two monotheistic religions, Christianity and Islam.

As mentioned in the sixth chapter, Bartolomeo Picerno re-translated *Contra legem Sarracenorum* from Greek back into Latin as a gift for Ferdinand II, who in 1492 conquered the kingdom of Granada; and Bartolomeo's letter invites the king also to liberate Jerusalem and the African countries from Muslim control. In the sixteenth century, anti-Islamic propaganda continued to use the *Contra legem* as the source of "inspiration" for fighting the Muslims. If it is true that dialogue is a sort of mutual knowledge, then it is also true that we see a change during the fourteenth and fifteenth centuries. If on one hand, the circulation of the texts on the interpretation of the Qur'an, like the work of Riccoldo, created a slow but growing knowledge about the affinities and the differences between Islam and Christianity, then on the other hand this textual and theoretical comparison supported the formation of a Christian and Western identity which saw itself as the center of Roman and Greek culture, in opposition to the "uncivilized" Turk. This theme must be considered as part of the birth of a particular image of the "West": the Turk is not only the "wild

---

33. This is the thesis on which Burman's *Reading the Qu'ran* is based.

beast" but also the barbarian. The West finds its own identity in contrast with a very distant East, totally strange and "other."

In the Middle Ages, as Christian sources on the Islamic world show, Muslim culture was perceived as extremely threatening: there were many defenses for Christianity, like the treatise on the "mistakes" of the followers of Allah. In the course of time, as analysis of works of the above authors has shown, this textual attitude was modified, and the authors aimed to point out the Christian truth in comparison with the "falsity" of Islamic theology, in order to reinforce Christian identity through the presupposition of its own absolute truth. The apologetic aim is gradually replaced by a systematic comparison based on partial translations of the Qur'an. The comparison with the "other" is the basis for reinforcing identity, in order to demonstrate the truth and consequently the supremacy of one's own theoretical position. The "other," the Muslim, is no longer the enemy; he becomes the non-Western, the non-European, that is, an "element" with neither identity nor legitimate existence. Alongside the forced conversion of Muslims and Jews conducted by the Spanish Inquisition, the works of Nicholas of Cusa and of authors analyzed above, show the passage from a position of open hostility and fear to a progressive position of supremacy of the Western world, and to the disappearance of the notion of "other" and its legitimate difference.

Bibliography

Primary sources

Abelard. *Dialogus inter philosophum, judaeum et christianum.* Edited by Maria Teresa Fumagalli Beonio. Milan: Rizzoli, 1992.
Al-Ghazali. *La bilancia dell'azione e altri scritti.* Edited by Massimo Campanini. Turin: Utet, 2008.
Bartolomeo da Picerno. *Contra legem Sarracenorum* (translation). PG 154. Paris: Migne, 1857–66.
Démétrius Cydonès. *Correspondance.* Edited by Raymond-Joseph Loenertz. Vatican City: Biblioteca apostolica vaticana, 1956.
———. *Oratio pro subsidio Latinorum,* PG 154, cols. 961–1008; *De non reddenda Callipoli,* PG 154, cols. 1012D–1013B. Paris: Migne, 1857–66.
Fazio degli Uberti. *Il Dittamondo e le rime.* Edited by Giuseppe Corsi. Rome: Laterza, 1952.
Ficino, Marsilio. *De Christiana religione.* In *Opera quae hactenus extitere et que in lucem nunc primum prodiere omnia,* Basileae, ex officina Henricpetrina, MDLXXVI, vol. II, edited by Mario Sancipriano. Turin: Bottega d'Erasmo, 1983.
George of Trebizond. *Collectanea Trapezuntiana: Texts, Documents and Bibliographies of George Trebizond.* Edited by John Monfasani. Binghamton, NY: Medieval & Renaissance Texts & Studies in conjunction with the Renaissance Society of America, 1984.
Llull, Ramón. "The Book of the Gentile and the Three Wise Men." In *Selected Works of Ramón Llull (1232–1316),* vol. 1, translated by Anthony Bonner. Princeton: Pricenton University Press, 1985.
Piccolomini, Enea. *Der Briefwechsel des Eneas Silvius Piccolomini.* Edited by R. Wolkan. Wien: n.p.,1918.
———. *Epistola 386.* In *Il Corano e la tiara. L'Epistola a Maometto II di Enea Silvio Piccolomini,* edited by Luca D'Ascia. Bologna: Pendragon, 2001.
Riccoldo da Montecroce. *Contra legem Sarracenorum.* Edited by Jean Marie Merigoux. Memorie Domenicane 17. Rome: Centro Riviste della Provincia Romana, 1986.
Segovia, Juan de. "Sumarios del opusculo 'De mittendo gladio.'" In *Juan de Segovia y el problema islamica,* edited by D. Rodriguez Cabanelas, 265–72. Madrid: Universidad de Madrid, 1952.
Villani, Filippo. *De civitatis Florentiae et eiusdem famosis civibus.* Edited by Giovanni Calò. Rocca San Casciano: Cappelli, 1904.

Wenck, Johannes. *De ignota litteratura*. Edited by Jaspers Hopkins. In *Nicholas of Cusa's Debate with John Wenck: A Translation and an Appraisal of De ignota litteratura and Apologia doctae ignorantiae*. Minneapolis; Banning Press, 1981.

Yehuda-ha Levi. *Il re dei Khazari*. Translated by Elio Piattelli. Turin: Bollati Boringhieri, 1961.

Works of Nicholas of Cusa

Nicolai de Cusa. *Opera omnia*. Iussu et Auctoritate Academiae Litterarum Heidelbergensis. Heidelberg: Meiner, 1927–.

———. *De concordantia catholica*. Edited by Gerhard Kallen. Hamburg: Meiner, 1959.

———. *Cribratio Alkorani*. Edited by Ludwig Hagermann and Reinhold Glei. 3 vols. Hamburg: Meiner, 1989, 1990, 1993.

———. *De coniecturis*. Edited by Josef Koch and Winfried Happ. Hamburg: Meiner, 2002

———. *De docta ignorantia*. Edited by Paul Wilpert and Hans G. Senger. Hamburg: Meiner, 1994

———. *De Pace Fidei. Cum epistola ad Iohannem de Segobia*. Edited by Raymund Klibansky and Hildebrand Bascour. Lipsiae: Meiner, 1970.

———. *De venatione sapientiae*. Edited by Raymund Klibansky and Hans G. Senger. Hamburg: Miener, 2003.

———. *Dialogus De Abscondito Deo*. Edited by Paul Wilpert. Hamburg: Meiner, 1969.

———. *Nicholas of Cusa on God as Not-Other. A Translation and an Appraisal of De Li Non Aliud*. Translated by Jasper Hopkins. Minneapolis: University of Minnesota Press, 1979.

———. *Nicholas of Cusa on Interreligious Harmony: Text, Concordance and Translation of De Pace Fidei*. Edited and translated by James E. Biechler and H. Lawrence Bond. Text and Studies in Religion. Lewinston, NY: Mellen, 1990.

———. *Nicholas of Cusa on Learned Ignorance*. Translated by Jasper Hopkins. Minneapolis: Banning, 1981.

———. *Nicholas of Cusa's Debate with John Wenck. A Translation and an Appraisal of De Ignota Litteratura and Apologia Doctae Ignorantiae*. Translated by Jasper Hopkins. Minneapolis: Banning, 1981.

———. *Nicholas of Cusa's De Pace Fidei and Cribratio Alkorani*. Translated by Jasper Hopkins. Minneapolis: Banning, 1990.

———. *The Catholic Concordance*. Edited and translated by Paul E. Sigmund. Cambridge: Cambridge University Press, 1991.

———. *Opere religiose*. Edited by Pio Gaia. Turin: Utet, 1971.

Secondary literature

Alberigo, Giuseppe. *Chiesa Conciliare, Identità e significato del conciliarismo*. Brescia: Paideia, 1981.

Aleksander, Jason, and F. Scott Aikin. "Nicholas of Cusa's *De pace fidei* and the Meta-exclusivism of Religious Pluralism." *International Journal for Philosophy of Religion* 74 (2013) 219–35.

BIBLIOGRAPHY

Althoff, Gerd, et al. *Medieval Concepts of the Past: Ritual, Memory, Historiography.* Cambridge: Cambridge University Press, 2002.

Amoretti, S. Biancamaria. *Tolleranza e guerra santa nell'Islam.* Florence: Sansoni, 1974.

Amos, L. Thomas. *Early Medieval Sermons and Their Audience, De l'homelie au sermon.* In *Historie de la predication medievale, Actes du colloque internationale de Louvain-La-Neuve 1992,* edited by Hamesse Jacqueline and Hermand Xavier, 1-14. Louvain-La-Neuve: Université Catholique de Louvain, 1993.

Anawati, C. Georges. *Islam e cristianesimo: l'incontro tra due culture nell'Occidente medievale.* Milano: Vita e Pensiero, 1995.

———. "Nicolas de Cues et le problème de l'Islam." In *Nicolò Cusano agli inizi del mondo moderno,* edited by Giovanni Santinello, 141-73. Firenze: Sansoni, 1970.

Andrè, Joâo Maria. "L'actualité de la pensée de Nicolas de Cues: La docte ignorance et sa signification herméneutique, éthique et esthétique". In *Nicholas of Cusa: A Medieval Thinker for the Modern Age,* edited by Kazuhiko Yamaki, 185-200. Richmond, UK: Curzon, 2002.

Angelov, G. Dimiter. *Church and Society in Late Byzantium.* Kalamazoo, MI: Medieval Institute Publications, 2009.

Apel, Karl-Otto. "Die Idee der Sprache bei Nikolaus von Kues." *Archiv für Begriffsgeschichte* 1 (1955) 200-211.

Arduini, Maria Lodovica. "Ad hanc supermirandam harmonicam pacem, Riforma della chiesa ed ecumenismo religioso nel pensiero di Nicolò Cusano: il De pace fidei." *Rivista di Filosofia Neo-scolastica* 72 (1980) 224-42.

Arfè, Pasquale. "Nicola Cusano interprete dell'Asclepius." In *Nikolaus zwischen Italien und Deutschland,* edited by Martin Thurner, 129-51. Berlino: Akademie Verlag, 2002.

Aris, Marc-Aeilko. "Zur Soziologie der Sermones-Rezipienten." *Mitteilungen und Forschungsbeiträge der Cusanus-Gesellschaft* 30 (2005) 93-115.

Assmann, Jan. *Erinnerungsräume: Formen und Wandlungen des kulturellen Gedächtnisses.* München: Beck, 1999 (Italian translation: *Ricordare, Forme e mutamenti della memoria culturale.* Bologna: Il Mulino 2002).

———. *Das kulturelle Gedächtnis: Schrift, Erinnerung und politische Identität in frühen Hochkulturen.* München: Beck, 1992 (Italian translation, *La memoria culturale: Scritti, ricordo e identità politica nelle grandi civiltà antiche.* Torino, Einaudi, 1997).

Ayoub, M. Mahmoud. *The Qur'an and Its Interpreters.* New York: SUNY Press,1984.

Azmeh, Al Aziz. *Arabic Thought and Islamic Societies.* London: Routledge, 1986.

Baldi, Barbara. *Pio II e le trasformazioni dell'Europa cristiana, 1457-1464.* Milano: Unicopli, 2006.

Bakos, T. Gergely. *On Faith, Rationality, and the Other in the Late Middle Ages: A Study of Nicholas of Cusa's Manuductive Approach to Islam.* Eugene, OR: Pickwick, 2011.

Bamyeh, A. Mohammed. *The Social Origins of Islam: Mind, Economy, Discourse.* Minneapolis: University of Minnesota Press, 1999.

Bashir, Hassan. "Visions of Alterity: The Impact of Cross-Cultural Contacts on European Self-Understanding in the Pre-Enlightenment Period." PhD diss., Texas A&M University, 2008.

Beierwaltes, Werner. *Identität und Differenz.* Frankfurt am Main: Klostermann, 1980.

———. *Pensare l'uno, Studi sulla filosofia neoplatonica e sulla storia dei suoi influssi.* Translated by M. L. Gatti. Milan: Vita e Pensiero, 1991.

Bellitto, M. Christopher, et al. *Introducing Nicholas of Cusa: A Guide to a Renaissance Man.* New York: Paulist, 2004.

BIBLIOGRAPHY

Benveniste, Émilè. *Le Vocabulaire des institutions indo-européennes*. Paris: Minuit, 1969.

Berns, Thomas. "Construire un idéal vénitien de la constitution mixte à la Renaissance. L'enseignement de Platon par Trébizonde". In *Le Gouvernement mixte: de l'idéale politique au monstre constitutionnel en Europe*, edited by Marie Gaille-Nikodimov, 25–38. Saint-Etienne, France: Université de Saint-Etienne, 2005.

Bertelloni, Francisco. "Observaciones sobre la argumentación cusana en el *Proemium* al Libro III del *De Concordantia Catholica*." In *El problema del conocimiento en Nicolás de Cusa: genealogía y proyección*, edited by Claudia D'Amico and Jorge Machetta, 253–67. Buenos Aires: Biblos, 2005.

Biechler, E. James. "Christian Humanism Confronts Islam: Sifting the Qur'an with Nicholas of Cusa." *Journal of Ecumenical Studies* 13 (1976) 1–14.

———. "A New Face towards Islam: Nicholas of Cusa and John of Segovia." In *Nicholas of Cusa in Search of God and Wisdom*, edited by Gerald Christianson and Thomas M. Izbicki, 185–202. Leiden: Brill, 1991.

Bisaha, Nancy. *Creating East and West: Renaissance Humanists and the Ottoman Turks*. Philadelphia: University of Pennsylvania Press, 2004.

Black, Anthony. *Council and Commune. The Conciliar Movement and the Fifteenth-Century Heritage*. London: Burns and Oates, 1979.

Blum, Paul Richard. *Philosophy of Religion in the Renaissance*. Farnham, UK: Ashgate, 2010.

Blumenberg, Hans. *Die Lesbarkeit der Welt*. Frankfurt am Main: Suhrkamp, 1981.

Bocken, Inigo. *Conflict and Reconciliation: Perspectives on Nicholas of Cusa*. Leiden; Brill, 2004.

———. "Les dimensions morales de l'art des conjectures." In *Nicolas de Cues, Les méthodes d'une pensée*, edited by Jean-Michel Counet et Stéphane Mercier, 175–205. Louvain: Université Catholique, 2005.

Bond, H. Lawrence. "Nicholas of Cusa and the Reconstruction of Theology: The Centrality of Christology in the Coincidence of Opposites." In *Contemporary Reflection on the Medieval Christian Tradition: Essays on Honor of Ray. C. Petry*, edited by George H. Shriver, 81–94. Durham, NC: Duke University Press, 1974.

Bond, H. Lawrence and Gerald Christianson. *Reform, Representation and Theology in Nicholas of Cusa and His Age*. Burlington, VT: Ashgate, 2011.

Bonmariage, Cécile. "Houris et autres jouvenceaux: les promesses du paradis comme lieu d'analyse de la lecture du Coran par Nicolas de Cues." In *Nicolas de Cues: les méthodes d'une pensée*, edited by Jean-Michel Counet and Stéphane Mercier, 22–32. Louvain: Université Catholique, 2005.

Bonner, Anthony. "Introduction." In *Selected Works of Ramón Llull (1232–1316)*, translated by Anthony Bonner, 91–103. Princeton: Princeton University Press, 1985.

———. "Der neue Weg Ramon Lulls." In *Ramon Lull: Buch vom Heiden und den drei Weisen*, edited by Raimundo Panikkar et al., 26–31. Freiburg: Herder, 1986.

Bosl, Karl. *Die Sozialstruktur der mittelalterlichen Residenz-und Fernhandelsstadt Regensburg: Die Entwicklung ihres Bürgertums vom 9. bis zum 14. Jahrhundert*. Munchen: Verlag der Bayerischen Akademie der Wissenschaften, 1966.

Bosl, Karl, et al. *Statuti città territori in Italia e Germania tra medioevo ed età moderna*. Translated by Giorgio Chittolini and Dieter Willoweit. Bologna: Il Mulino, 1991.

Boumrane, Cheick. *Le Problème de la liberté humaine dans le pensée musulman*. Paris: Vrin, 1978.

BIBLIOGRAPHY

Burman, E. Thomas. "How an Italian Friar Read His Arabic Qur'an." *Dante Studies* 125 (2007) 93–109.

———. *Reading the Qur'an in Latin Christendom*. Philadelphia: University of Pennsylvania Press, 2007.

Butterworth, E. Charles, et al. *The Introduction of Arabic Philosophy into Europe*. Leiden: Brill, 1994.

Campanini, Massimo. *Islam e politica*. Bologna: Il Mulino, 1999.

Canfora, Davide. *Prima di Machiavelli*. Rome-Bari: Laterza, 2005.

Canning, Joseph. *A History of Medieval Political Thought, 300–1450*. London: Routledge, 1996.

Cardini, Franco. *Studi sulla storia e sull'idea di crociata*. Rome: Jouvence, 1993.

Casarella, J. Peter. *Cusanus: The Legacy of Learned Ignorance*. Washington, DC: Catholic University of America Press, 2006.

Caspar, Robert. *Traité de Théologie musulmane. Histoire de la Pensée religieuse musulmane*. Rome: PISAI, 1987.

Chenu, Marie-Dominique. *La Teologia nel dodicesimo secolo*. Translated by Paolo Vian. Milan: Jaca, 1986.

Christianson, Gerald, et al. *The Church, The Councils, and Reform: The Legacy of the Fifteenth Century*. Washington, DC: Catholic University of America, 2008.

Christianson, Gerald. *Cesarini: e Conciliar Cardinal: The Basel Years, 1431–1438*. Erzabtei Sankt Ottilien, Germany: EOS, 1979.

Christianson, Gerald, and Thomas Izbicki. *Nicholas of Cusa in Search of God and Wisdom: Essays in Honor of Morimichi Watanabe*. Leiden: Brill, 1991.

Classen, Carl Joachim. "The Rhetorical Works of George of Trebizond and Their Debt to Cicero." *Journal of the Warburg and Courtauld Institutes* 56 (1993) 75–84.

Constable, Olivia Remie. *Medieval Iberia: Readings from Christian, Muslim, and Jewish Sources*. Philadelphia: University of Pennsylvania Press, 1997.

Costigliolo, Marica. "The Interreligious Dialogue in De docta ignorantia of Nicholas of Cusa." *Medieval Encounters* 20 (2014) 217–37.

———. "The Interreligious Dialogue before and after Nicholas of Cusa: An Exegetical Approach." *Mirabilia Journal* 2 (2014) 62–78.

———. *Islam e Cristianesimo. Mondi di differenze nel Medioevo, Il dialogo con l'Islam di Nicola da Cusa*. Genoa: Genova University Press, 2012.

———. "Organic Metaphors in 'De concordantia catholica' of Nicholas of Cusa." *Viator* 44 (2013) 311–21.

———. "Predicazione e Metafora; il sermone XXI di Nicola da Cusa." In *Miti e metafore nella storia del pensiero politico*, edited by Anna Maria Lazzarino, 37–66. Florence: CET, 2009.

———. "Perspectives on Islam in Italy and Byzantium in the Middle Ages and Renaissance". In *Nicholas of Cusa and Islam: Polemic and Dialogue in the Late Middle Ages*, edited by Ian C. Levy, Rita George-Tvrtkovic ⊠, and Donald F. Duclow, 123–44. Boston: Brill, 2014.

Counet, Jean-Michel. "Essai de lecture non-duale du *de coniecturis* (1440–45)." In *Identité et différence dans l'oeuvre de Nicolas de Cues*, edited by Hervé Pasqua, 15–34. Louvain: Éditions Peeters, 2011.

———. "La pensée de Nicolas de Cues: une philosophie de l'événement?" In *Nicolas de Cues: les méthodes d'une pensée*, edited by Jean Marie Counet and Stéphane Mercier, 175–205. Louvain: Université Catholique, 2005.

BIBLIOGRAPHY

Cuozzo, Gianluca. "Mystice videre." In *Nicolaus Cusanus: Perspektiven seiner Geistphilosophie*, edited by Harald Schwaetzer, Klaus Reinhardt, 163–76. Regensburg: Roderer-Verlag, 2003.

———. "Il tema del peccato originale nella teoria della conoscenza di Cusano." In *El problema del conocimiento en Nicolás de Cusa: genealogía y proyección*, 121–39. Buenos Aires: Biblos, 2005.

D'Amico, Claudia, and Jorge Machetta, eds. *El problema del conoscimento en Nicolàs de Cusa:genealogía y proyección*. Buenos Aires: Biblos, 2005.

D'Ancona Costa, Cristina. *Storia della filosofia nell'Islam medievale*. Turin: Einaudi, 2005.

D'Ascia, Luca. *Il Corano e la tiara*. Bologna: Pendragon, 2001.

D'Ascia, Luca, and Enzo Mecacci. *Conferenze su Pio II nel sesto centenario della nascita di Enea Silvio Piccolomini (1405–2005)*. Siena: Accademia senese degli intronati, 2006.

Dallmayr, Fred. *Border Crossings: Toward a Comparative Political Theory*. Lanham, MD: Lexington, 1999.

———. *Civilizational Dialogue and Political Thought: Teheran Papers*. Lanham, MD: Lexington, 2007.

———. "Nicola Cusano: l'infinito e la pace." *Reset* 97 (2006) 64–66.

Dammen McAuliffe, Jane. *The Cambridge Companion to the Qur'ān*. Cambridge: Cambridge University Press, 2006.

Daniel, Norman. *Islam and the West: The Making of an Image*. Edinburgh: Edinburgh University Press, 1960.

Decaluwé, Michiel. "Three Ways to Read the Constance Decree *Haec sancta* (1415): Francis Zabarella, Jean Gerson and the Traditional Papal View of General Councils". In *The Church, The Councils, and Reform: The Legacy of the Fifteenth Century*, edited by Gerald Christianson, Thomas M. Izbicki, Chistopher M. Bellitto, 122–39. Washington, DC: Catholic University of America Press, 2008.

Decorte, Jos. "Tolerance and Trinity." In *Conflict and Reconciliation: Perspectives on Nicholas of Cusa*, edited by Inigo Bocken, 107–17. Leiden: Brill, 2004.

De Libera, Alain. *La philosophie médiévale*. Paris: Press Universitaire de France, 1994.

De Lubac, Henri. *Corpus Mysticum. L'Eucaristia e la Chiesa nel medioevo*. Translated by Luigi Rosadoni. Milan: Jaca, 1968.

Dennis, T. George. "Demetrios Cydones and Venice." In *Bisanzio, Venezia e il mondo franco-greco (XIII–XV secolo): Atti del Convegno Internazionale Organizzato nel Centenario della nascita di Raimond-Joseph Loenertz, Venezia, 1-2 dicembre 2000*, 495–502. Venice: Istituto ellenico di Studi Bizantini e Postbizantini di Venezia, 2002.

Douglas, Mary. *Purity and Danger*. London: Routledge, 1966.

Duclow, Don F. "Life and Work." In *Introducing Nicholas of Cusa: A Guide to a Renaissance Man*, edited by Christopher M. Bellito et al., 5–56. New York: Paulist, 2004.

———. *Masters of Learned Ignorance: Eriugena, Eckhart, Cusanus*. Aldershot, UK: Ashgate, 2006.

Duprè, Wilhelm. "Spirit, Mind and Freedom." In *Conflict and Reconciliation: Perspectives on Nicholas of Cusa*, edited by Inigo Bocken, 207–21, Leiden: Brill, 2004.

Euler, Walther Andreas. "An Italian Painting from the Late Fifteenth Century and the *Cribratio alkorani* of Nicholas of Cusa." In *Cusanus: The Legacy of Learned Ignorance*, edited by Peter Casarella, 127–42. Washington, DC: Catholic University of America Press, 2006.

BIBLIOGRAPHY

———. "*Una religio in rituum varietate*—Der Beitrag des Nikolaus von Kues zur Theologie der Religionen." In *Jahrbuch für Religionswissenschaft und Theologie der Religionen* 3 (1995) 67–82.

Euler, Walther Andreas, et al. *Nicholas of Cusa on the Self and Self-Consciousness*. Turku, Finland: Åbo Akademi University Press, 2010.

Fidora, Alexander, et al. *Ramon Llull und Nikolaus von Kues: Eine Begegnung im Zeichen der Toleranz*. Turnhout: Brepols, 2005.

Fine, Lawrence. *Judaism in Practice: From the Middle Ages through the Early Modern Period*. Princeton: Princeton University Press, 2001.

Flasch, Kurt. *Nicolaus Cusanus*. Munich: Beck, 2001.

Friedlein, Roger. *Der Dialog bei Ramon Lull, in Literarische Gestaltung als apologetische Strategie*. Tübingen: Max Niemeyer, 2004.

Gaeta, Franco. "Giorgio da Trebisonda, le *Leggi* di Platone e la costituzione di Venezia." *Bullettino dell'Istituto storico italiano per il medio evo e Archivio Muratoriano* 82 (1970) 479–501.

———. "Sulla lettera a Maometto di Pio II." *Bollettino dell'Istituto Storico Italiano per il Medio Evo e Archivio Muratoriano* LXXVII (1965) 128–227.

Gardet, Louis. *Les hommes de l'Islam. Approche des mentalités*. Paris: Hachette, 1977 (Italian edition, *Gli uomini dell'Islam*, Como, Jaca Book, 2002).

Gardet, Louis, and Georges Anawati. *Introduction a la Théologie Musulmane*. Paris: Vrin, 1948.

Gentile, Sebastiano, and Stéphane Toussaint. *Marsilio Ficino: fonti, testi, fortuna: atti del convegno internazionale (Firenze, 1–3 ottobre 1999)*. Rome: Edizioni di storia e letteratura, 2006.

Gómez, Mariano Álvarez, and João Maria André. *Coincidencia de opuestos y concordia: Los caminos del pensamiento en Nicolás de Cusa*. Salamanca, Spain: Sociedad Castellano-Leonesa de Filosofía, 2002.

Hagemann, Ludwig. *Christentum contra Islam: Eine Geschichte gescheiterter Beziehungen*. Darmstadt: Primus, 1999.

Hankins, James. *Plato in the Italian Renaissance*. Leiden: Brill, 1991.

———. "Renaissance Crusaders: Humanist Crusade Literature in the Age of Muhammad II." *Dumbarton Oaks Papers* 49, *Symposium on Byzantium and the Italians, 13th–15th Centuries* (1995) 111–207.

Harries, Karsten. "The Infinite Sphere; Comments on The History of a Metaphor." *History of Philosophy* 13 (1975) 5–15.

Haubst, Rudolf. *Die Christologie des Nikolaus von Kues*. Freiburg im Breisgau: Herder, 1956.

———. "Die Wege der christologische manuductio." In *Der Friede unter den Religionen nach Nikolaus von Kues*, edited by Rudolf Haubst, 164–82. Mainz: Matthias Grünewald, 1984.

———. "Studien zu Nikolaus von Kues und Johannes Wenck." *Beiträge zur Geschichte der Philosophie des Mittelalters* 38 (1955) 1–143.

Hourani, F. George. *Divine Justice and Human Reason in Mu'tazilite Ethical Theology*. Malibu: Undena, 1985.

Huntington, Samuel. *The Clash of Civilizations and the Remaking of World Order*. New York: Simon & Schuster, 1996.

———. *The Soldier and the State*. Cambridge: Harvard University Press, 1981.

Izbicki, Thomas. "The Possibility of Dialogue with Islam in the Fifteenth Century." In *Nicholas of Cusa: In Search of Wisdom*, edited by Thomas Izbicki and Gerald Christianson, 175–85. Leiden: Brill, 1991.

Izbicki, Thomas, and Christopher Bellitto. *Nicholas of Cusa and His Age: Intellect and Spirituality*. Leiden: Brill, 2002.

Izzi, Pierangela. "Il vocabolario dantesco nel Dittamondo di Fazio degli Uberti." www.italinisti.it.

Jedin, Hubert, and John Dolan. *A History of the Council of Trent*. London: Nelson, 1961.

Johnston, Mark. *The Evangelical Rhetoric of Ramon Lull: Lay Learning and Piety in the Christian West around 1300*. Oxford: Oxford University Press, 1996.

Jones, William R. "The Image of the Barbarian in Medieval Europe." *Comparative Studies in Society and History* 13 (1971) 376–407.

Jourdian, E. F., "Holyday's 'Survey of the World' and the *Dittamondo*." *Modern Language Review* 2.1 (1906) 44–55.

Kantorowicz, Ernst. *The King's Two Bodies: A Study in Mediaeval Political Theology*. Princeton: Princeton University Press, 1957.

Kapr, Albert. "Gab es Beziehungen zwischen Johannes Gutenberg und Nikolaus von Kues?" *Gutenberg-Jahrbuch* 47 (1972) 32–40.

Kelsay, John. *Arguing the Just War in Islam*. London: Harvard University Press, 2007.

———. *Islam and War: A Study in Comparative Ethics*. Louisville: John Knox, 1993.

Kelsay, John, and James Turner. *Just War and Jihad: Historical and Theoretical Perspectives on War and Peace in Western and Islamic Traditions*. Santa Barbara: Greenwood, 1991.

Khadduri, Majid. *War and Peace in the Law of Islam*. Baltimore: Johns Hopkins University Press, 1955.

———. *Political Trends in the Arab World: The Role of Ideas and Ideals*. Baltimore: Johns Hopkins University Press, 1970.

Khoury, Adel-Théodor. *Les théologiens byzantins et l'Islam: textes et auteurs (VIII–XIII s.)*. Paris: Béatrice-Nauwelaerts, 1969.

Kianka, Frances. "Byzantine-Papal Diplomacy: The Role of Demetrius Cydones." In *The International History Review* 7.2 (1985) 175–213.

———. "Demetrius Cydones (c.1324–c.1397): Intellectual and Diplomatic Relations between Byzantium and the West in the Fourteenth Century." Ph.D. diss., Fordham University, 1981.

———. "Demetrios Kydones and Italy." *Dumbarton Oaks Papers* 49 (1995) 99–110.

Kristeller, Paul Oskar. *Marsilio Ficino and His Work after Five Hundred Years*. Florence: Olschki, 1987.

———. *Studies in Renaissance: Thought and Letters*. Rome: Edizioni Storia e Letteratura, 1956.

Levy, Ian C., et al. *Nicholas of Cusa and Islam: Polemic and Dialogue in the Late Middle Ages*. Leiden: Brill, 2014.

Lewis, Bernard. *Islam: From the Prophet Muhammad to the Capture of Constantinople*. New York: Harper-Row, 1974.

Lücking-Michel, Claudia. *Konkordanz und Konsens, Zur Gesellschaftstheorie in der Schrift De concordantia catholica des Nikolaus von Cues*. Würzburg: Bonner dogmatische Studien, Bd. 16, 1994.

Lutz-Bachmann, Matthias, and Alexander Fidora. *Juden, Christen und Muslime: Religionsdialoge in Mittelalter*. Darmstadt: Wissenschaftliche Buchgesellschaft, 2004.

BIBLIOGRAPHY

Mallette, Karla. "Muhammad in Hell Author(s)." *Dante Studies* 125 (2007) 207–24.

Mandonnet, Pierre Felix. "Pierre le Vénérable et son activité littéraire contre l'Islam." *Revue Tomiste* (1893) 328–42.

Manganaro Favaretto, Gilda. *La guerra. Una riflessione interdisciplinare.* Trieste: Edizioni Università di Trieste, 2003.

Martinez Gasquez Josè. "Las traducciones latinas medievales del Coran: Pedro el Venerable-Robert Ketton, Marcos de Toledo y Juan de Segovia." *Euphrosyne* 31 (2003) 491–503.

Martínez Gázquez, José, and Andrew Gray. "Translations of the Qur'an and Other Islamic Texts before Dante." *Dante Studies* 125 (2007) 79–92.

Matheus, Michael, and Massimo Miglio. *Stato della ricerca e prospettive della medievistica tedesca.* Rome: Istituto Storico Italiano per il Medioevo, 2007.

Mazzucchi, Carlo Maria, and Agostino Pertusi. *Bisanzio e i Turchi nella cultura del Rinascimento e del Barocco.* Milan: Vita e Pensiero, 2004.

McGinnis, John, and David C. Reisman. *Classical Arabic Philosophy: An Anthology of Sources.* Indianapolis: Hackett, 2007.

McLuhan, Marshall. *The Gutenberg Galaxy: The Making of Typographic Man.* Toronto: Toronto University Press, 1962.

Meier-Oeser, Stephan. "Die Prasenz des Vergessenen. Zur Rezeption der Philosophie des Nikolaus von Kues vom 15-18 Jahrhundert." *Buchreihe des Cusanus-Gesellschaft* 10. Münster: Aschendorff, 1989.

Mercati, Giovanni. *Notizie di Procoro e Demetrio Cidone, Manuele Caleca e Teodoro Meliteniota.* Vatican City: Biblioteca Apostolica Vaticana, 1931.

Merigoux, Jean Marie. *L'ouvrage d'un frère Precheur, Va a Ninive: un dialogue avec l'Irak, Mossoul et les villages chrétiens : pages d'histoire dominicaine.* Paris: Les editions du cerf, 2000.

———. "L'ouvrage d'un frère prêcheur florentin en Orient à la fin du XIIIe siècle: *Le Contra legem Sarracenorum* de Riccoldo da Monte di Croce." In *Memorie Domenicane* 17. Rome: Centro Riviste della Provincia Romana, 1986.

Mervin, Sabrina. *Histoire de l'islam: fondements et doctrines.* Paris: Flammarion, 2000 (*Fondamenti e dottrine*, Italian translation by L. Cortese, Milano, Mondatori, 2001).

Meserve, Margaret. *Empires of Islam in Renaissance Thought.* Cambridge: Harvard University Press, 2008.

Merlo, Maurizio. *Vinculum concordiae. Il problema della rappresentanza nel pensiero di Nicolò Cusano.* Milan: Franco Angeli, 1997.

Meuthen, Eric. *Nicholas of Cusa: A Sketch for a Biography.* Translated by David Crowder and Gerald Christianson. Washington, DC: Catholic University of America Press, 2010.

Miroy, Jovino. "From Unity to Union: The Relationship between the *De concordantia catholica* and the *De docta ignorantia.*" In *Nicolas de Cues: les méthodes d'une pensée*, edited by Jean-Michel Counet and Stéphane Mercier, 135–54. Louvain-la-Neuve: Université Catholique, 2005.

———. *Tracing Nicholas of Cusa's Early Development: The Relationship between* De concordantia catholica *and* De docta ignorantia. Louvain: Éditions Peeters, 2009.

Monfasani, John. *George of Trebizond: A Biography and a Study of His Rhetoric and Logic.* Leiden: Brill, 1976. Berlin: Akademie Verlag, 2002.

———. "Nicholas of Cusa, the Byzantines, and the Greek Language." In *Nikolaus zwischen*, edited by Martin Thurner, 215–52.

BIBLIOGRAPHY

Motzki, Harald. "Alternative Accounts of the Qur'an's Formation." In *The Cambridge Companion to the Qur' ān*, edited by Dammen McAuliffe, 59–78. Cambridge: Cambridge University Press, 2006.

Murphy, James. *Three Medieval Rhetorical Arts*. Berkeley: University of California Press, 1985.

Nederman, Cary J. "Nature, Sin, and the Origins of Society: The Ciceronian Tradition in Medieval Political Thought." *Journal of the History of Ideas* 49 (1988) 3–26.

———. *Worlds of Difference: European Discourses of Toleration c. 1100–1550*. Philadelphia: University of Pennsylvania Press, 2000.

Nederman, Cary J., and Kate L. Forhan. *Medieval Political Theory: A Reader*. London: Routledge, 1993.

Nevola, Fabrizio. *Pio II Piccolomini: il papa del Rinascimento a Siena: atti del convegno internazionale di studi, 5–7 maggio 2005*. Colle Val d'Elsa, Italy: Protagon, 2009.

Nicolle, Jean Marie. "Quelques sources philosophico-mathématiques de Nicolas de Cues." In *Nicolas de Cues: les méthodes d'une pensée*, edited by Jean-Michel Counet and Stéphane Mercier, 47–59. Louvain-la-Neuve: Université Catholique, 2005.

Olschki, Leonardo. "Mohammedan Eschatology and Dante's Other World." *Comparative Literature* 3.1 (1951) 1–17.

Orlandi, Giovanni. "Per una nuova edizione del Dialogus di Abelardo." *Rivista critica di storia della filosofia* 24 (1979) 474–94.

Palma de la Cruz, Óscar. "Alcuni argomenti della polemica antiislamica in Raimondo Lullo e Niccolò Cusano." In *Ramon Llull und Nikolaus von Kues. Eine Begegnung im Zeichen der Toleranz*, edited by Ermenegildo Bidese et al., 25–40. Turnhout: Brepols, 2005.

Panella, Emilio. "Ricerche su Riccoldo da Montecroce." *Archivum Fratrum Praedicatorum* 58 (1988) 5–85.

Paravicini Bagliani, Agostino. *Il corpo del Papa*. Turin: Einaudi, 1994.

Parel, Anthony, and Ronald C. Keith. *Comparative Political Philosophy: Studies under the Upas Tree*. Thousand Oaks, CA: Sage, 1992.

Partner, Peter. *God of Battles: Holy Wars of Christianity and Islam*. Princeton: Princeton University Press, 1997.

Peters, Rudolf. *Jihad in Classical and Modern Islam*. Princeton: Wiener, 1996.

Piazzoni, Ambrogio M. "Un falso problema storiografico. Note a proposito dell'amicizia tra Pietro Il Venerabile di Cluny e Bernardo di Clariveaux." *Bollettino dell'Istituto storico per il medioevo e Archivio Muratoriano* 89 (1980–81) 443–87.

Piemontese, Michele Angelo. "Il Corano latino di Ficino e i Corani arabi di Pico e Monchates." *Rinascimento* 36 (1996) 227–73.

Pinzani, Roberto. *The Logical Grammar of Abelard*. Dordrecht: Kluwer, 2003.

Platvoet, Jan, and Kaerl van der Toorn, eds. *Pluralism & Identity, Studies in Ritual Behaviour*. Leiden: Brill, 1995.

Quillet, Jeannine. "La paix de la foi: identité et différence selon Nicolas de Cues." In *Studi su Niccolò Cusano e l'umanesimo europeo offerti a Giovanni Santinello*, edited by Gregorio Piaia, 237–50. Padova: Editrice Antenore, 1993.

Ravegnani, Giorgio. "Nota sul pensiero politico di Giorgio da Trebisonda." *Aevum* 49 (1975) 310–29.

Reinhardt, Klaus, and Harald Schwaetzer. *Nikolaus von Kues als Prediger*. Regensburg: Roderer-Verlag, 2004.

BIBLIOGRAPHY

———. *Cusanus-Rezeption in der Philosophie des 20. Jahrhunderts.* Regensburg: Roderer-Verlag, 2005.
Reinhardt, Klaus. "Identité et différence: la question de l'église chez Nicolas de Cues." In *Identité et différence dans l'oeuvre de Nicolas de Cues*, edited by Hervé Pasqua, 177–88. Louvain: Éditions Peeters, 2011.
Reiss, Edmund. "Conflict and its Resolution in Medieval Dialogues." In *Arts libéraux et philosophie au Moyen Age, Actes du quatrième Congrès international de philosophie médiévale*, 863–72. Paris: Vrin, 1969.
Riedenauer, Markus. "Pluralità di prospettive finite nell'orizzonte dell'infinito, Conseguenze dell'epistemologia nuova di Cusano." In *El problema del conoscimento en Nicolàs de Cusa: genealogia y proyeccion*, edited by Jorge Machetta and Claudia D'Amico, 282–89. Buenos Aires: Biblios, 2005.
———. *Pluralität und Rationalität. Die Herausforderung der Vernunft durch religiöse und kulturelle Vielfalt nach Nikolaus Cusanus.* Stuttgart: Kohlhammer, 2007.
Rizzardi, Giuseppe. "Introduzione." In *I saraceni* (Italian translation of the *Contra legem Sarracenorum*). Firenze: Nardini, 1992.
Ryder, Judith R. *The Career and Writings of Demetrius Kydones: A Study of Fourteenth-Byzantine Politics, Religion and Society.* Leiden: Brill, 2010.
Rotta, Paolo. *Il cardinale Niccolò da Cusa.* Milano: Vita e pensiero, 1928.
Rozemond, Keetje. *La christologie de saint Jean Damascène.* Ettal: Buch-Kunstverlag, 1959.
Ruocco, Ilario. *Il Platone Latino: Il Parmenide: Giorgio di Trebisonda e il cardinale Cusano.* Florence: Olschki, 2003.
Saitta, Giuseppe. *Marsilio Ficino e la filosofia dell'umanesimo.* Bologna: Fiammenghi & Nanni, 1954.
Schwaetzer, Harald, and Georg Steer. *Meister Eckhart und Nikolaus von Kues.* Stuttgart: Kohlhammer, 2011.
Schwaetzer, Harald, "Der Anspruch der Wahrheit bei Nicolaus Cusanus." In *Cusanus: Ästhetik und Theologie*, edited by Michael Eckert and Harald Schwaetzer, 43–55. Münster: Aschendorff, 2013.
Scipioni, Luigi. *Nestorio e il concilio di Efeso: Storia, dogma, critica.* Milano: Vita e pensiero, 1974.
Sen, Amartya. *Identity and Violence.* New Delhi: Penguin, 2007.
Setton, Kenneth M. "The Byzantine Background to the Italian Renaissance." *Proceedings of the American Philosophical Society* 1 (1956) 1–76.
Shōgimen, Takashi, and Cary J. Nederman. *Western Political Thought in Dialogue with Asia.* Lanham, MD: Lexington, 2008.
Sigmund, Paul E. *Nicholas of Cusa and Medieval Political Thought.* Cambridge: Harvard University Press, 1963.
Southern, Richard W. *Western Views of Islam in the Middle Ages.* Cambridge: Harvard University Press, 1962.
Stadelmann, Rudolf. *Vom Geist des ausgehenden Mittelalters.* Halle-Saale: Niemeyer, 1929.
Stammkötter, Franz Bernd. "*Hic homo parum curat de dictis Aristotelis.* Der Streit zwischen Johannes Wenck von Herrenberg und Nikolaus von Kues um die Gültigkeit des Satzes vom zu vermeiden Widerspruch." In *Herbst des Mittelalters? Fragen zur Bewertung des 14. und 15. Jahrhundert*, edited by Jan A. Aertsen, Martin Pickavé, 233–44. Berlin: de Gruyter, 2004.
Tabacco, Giovanni. *Profilo di storia del medioevo latino germanico.* Turin: Scriptorium, 1996.

BIBLIOGRAPHY

Santinello, Giovanni. *Il pensiero di Nicolò Cusano nella sua prospettiva estetica*. Padova: Antenore, 1958.
Ševcenko, Ihor. "The Decline of Byzantium Seen through the Eyes of its Intellectuals." *Dumbarton Oaks Papers* 15 (1961) 167–86.
Syros, Vasileios. *Die Rezeption der aristotelischen politischen Philosophie bei Marsilius von Padua: Eine Untersuchung zur ersten Diktion des Defensor pacis*. Leiden: Brill, 2008.
Stump, Philip H. *The Reforms of the Council of Constance 1414–1418*. Leiden: Brill, 1994.
Tedeschi, Mario. *Cristiani, ebrei e musulmani nel basso medioevo spagnolo*. Turin: Giappichelli, 1996.
Thomas, David, Barbara Roggema, et al. *Christian-Muslim Relations: A Bibliographical History*. 11 vols. Leiden: Brill, 2009–12.
Thurner, Martin. *Nicolaus Cusanus zwischen Deutschland und Italien. Beiträge eines deutsch-italienischen Symposiums in der Villa Vigoni*. Berlin: Akademie Verlag, 2002.
Tierney, Brian. *Crisis of Church and State 1050–1300*. Englewood Cliffs, NJ: Prentice-Hall, 1964.
Toffanin, Giuseppe. *Ultimi saggi*. Milano: Zanichelli, 1960.
Tolan, John. "Mendicants and Muslims in Dante's Florence." *Dante Studies* 125 (2007) 227–48.
———. *Minorités et régulations sociales en Méditerranée médievale*. Rennes: Presses Universitaires de Rennes, 2010.
Totaro, Luigi. *Pio II nei suoi Commentarii: un contributo alla lettura della autobiografia di Enea Silvio de Piccolomini*. Bologna: Pàtron, 1978.
Trupia, Piero. *Logica e linguaggio della politica*. Milano: Franco-Angeli, 1986.
Tucci, Giuseppe. *Le civiltà dell'oriente: storia, letteratura, religioni, filosofia, scienze e arte*. Roma: Edizioni Casini, 1962.
Turner Johnson, and James Kelsay. *Cross, Crescent and Sword: The Justification and Limitation of War in Western and Islamic Tradition*. New York: Greenwood, 1990.
Tvrtković-George Rita. *A Christian Pilgrim in Medieval Iraq: Riccoldo da Montecroce's Encounter with Islam*. Turnhout: Brepols, 2012.
Ullmann, Walter. *Medieval Papalism: The Political Theories of the Medieval Canonists*. London: Methuen, 1949.
Valkenberg, Pim. "Sifting the Qur'an: Two Forms of Interreligious Hermeneutics in Nicholas of Cusa." In *Interreligious Hermeneutics in Pluralistic Europe: Between Texts and People*, edited by David Cheetham et al., 27–48. New York: Rodopi, 2011.
———. "*Una Religio in Rituum Varietate*: Religious Pluralism, the Qur'an, and Nicholas of Cusa." In *Nicholas of Cusa and Islam: Polemic and Dialogue in the Late Middle Ages*, edited by Ian C. Levy, Rita George-Tvrtković, Donald F. Duclow, 30–48. Boston: Brill, 2014.
Vansteenberghe, Edmond. "Le *De ignota litteratura* de Jean Wenck de Herrenberg contre Nicolas de Cuse." *Beiträge zur Geschichte der Philosophie des Mittelalters*. Munster: Aschendorff, 1912.
Vasoli, Cesare. "Per le fonti del *De christiana religione* di Marsilio Ficino." *Rinascimento* 38 (1988) 135–234.
Vine, Aubrey R. *The Nestorian Churches*. London: Independent, 1937.
Walther, Hans. "Das Streitgedicht in der lateinischen Literatur des Mittelalters." In *Quellen und Untersuchungen zur lateinische Philologie des Mittelalters*, 1–272. Munich: Beck, 1920.

BIBLIOGRAPHY

Watts, M. Pauline. *Nicolaus Cusanus: A Fifteenth-Century Vision of Man*. Leiden: Brill, 1982.

———. "Renaissance Humanism." In *Introducing Nicholas of Cusa: A Guide to a Renaissance Man*, edited by Christopher M. Bellitto, et al., 169–204. New York: Paulist, 2004.

Weiss, Roberto. *La scoperta dell'antichità classica nel Rinascimento*. Padua, Italy: Antenore, 1989.

Weiss Bernard G. *Studies in Islamic Legal Theory*. Leiden: Brill, 2002.

Whitmore, Charles Edward. *The Lyrics of Fazio degli Uberti in Their Relation to Dante*. Boston: Ginn, 1917.

Winter, Tim. *The Cambridge Companion to Classical Islamic Theology*. Cambridge: Cambridge University Press, 2008.

Watanabe, Morimichi. "Concord and Discord: Nicholas of Cusa as a Legal and Political Thinker." In *Nicholas of Cusa: A Medieval Thinker for the Modern Age*, edited by Kazuhiko Yamaki, 47–59. Richmond, UK: Curzon, 2002.

———. "Cusanus, Islam, and Religious Tolerance." In *Nicholas of Cusa and Islam: Polemic and Dialogue in the Late Middle Ages*, edited by Ian C. Levy, Rita George-Tvrtkovic ⊠, and Donald F. Duclow, 9–19. Leiden: Brill, 2014.

———. *Nicholas of Cusa: A Companion to His Life and His Times*. Edited by Gerald Christianson and Thomas M. Izbicki. Burlington, VT: Ashgate, 2011.

———. "Nicholas of Cusa and the Idea of Tolerance." In *Concord and Reform. Nicholas of Cusa and Legal and Political Ought in the Fifteenth Century*, 217–26. Aldershot, UK: Ashgate, 2001.

———. *The Political Thought of Nicholas of Cusa*. Geneva: Droz, 1963.

Yusuf Ali Abdullah. *The Meaning of the Holy Qur'an*. Beltsville, MD: Amana, 2004.

Zerbi, Pietro. *Medioevo: tolleranza o intolleranza religiosa?* In *La tolleranza religiosa: Indagini storiche e riflessioni filosofiche*, edited by Mario Sina, 13–26. Milan: Vita e Pensiero, 1991.

Zepp-La Rouche, Helga. "Für einen Dialog der Kulturen." www.solidaritaet.com/neuesol/2002abo/zepp-lar.htm.

Ziebart, K. Meredith. *Nicolaus Cusanus on Faith and the Intellect: A Case Study in 15th-Century Fides-Ratio Controversy*. Boston: Brill, 2014.

Zonta, Mauro. *La filosofia antica nel Medioevo ebraico: le traduzioni ebraiche medievali dei testi filosofici antichi*. Brescia: Paideia, 1996.

www.ingramcontent.com/pod-product-compliance
Lightning Source LLC
Chambersburg PA
CBHW071458150426
43191CB00008B/1388